THE BASICS

————— of —————

WORLD RELIGION

THE BASICS
of
WORLD RELIGION

Christopher D. Martinez

Saint Petersburg College

FIRST EDITION

 cognella®
SAN DIEGO

Bassim Hamadeh, CEO and Publisher
Jennifer McCarthy, Acquisitions Editor
Emely Villavicencio, Senior Graphic Designer
Trey Soto, Licensing Coordinator
Natalie Piccotti, Director of Marketing
Kassie Graves, Vice President of Editorial
Jamie Giganti, Director of Academic Publishing

Printed in the United States of America.

3970 Sorrento Valley Blvd., Ste. 500, San Diego, CA 92121

Brief Contents

Contents

Preface

This textbook is an outgrowth of more than a decade of teaching religion at the college level as this author watched students struggle with the subject matter in religion textbooks. Compared to other textbooks, this one emphasizes the basics of religion and is designed for first- and second-year college students. The foundations of religion that students need to build on in more advanced courses is clearly stated in the chapters in an orderly fashion.

Students also appreciate illustrations, and this text has photographic examples of religious rituals, figures, and houses of worship in the United States to localize the content.

The author has traveled the world studying religions and collecting artifacts and holds a master's degree in religious studies. With a PhD in adult education, he has applied learning strategies and developed curricula for several colleges and universities. Through a combination of academic research and classroom experience, the text is presented in a lively and humorous way to engage students. The term is known as "edutainment."

The author would like to thank his wife, Ellen, for the extensive proofreading she has done on this manuscript.

Timeline of Religions

1500 B.C.
Writing of Rig Veda
begins (Hinduism)

500s B.C.
Dao de Jing is written
(Daoism)

500 B.C.
Shinto rituals
begin

1210 B.C.
Israel mentioned on Merenptah
Stele (Judaism)

Late 500s B.C.
Confucius implements his
philosophy in government (Confucianism)

36 A.D.
Pentecost
(Christianity)

1487 A.D.
Nanak is married, Soon
starts preaching (Sikhism)

612 A.D.
Muhammad receives
his first revelation (Islam)

CREDITS

- Figure 0.1a: Source: https://commons.wikimedia.org/wiki/File:Rigveda_MS2097.jpg.

- Figure 0.1b: Source: https://commons.wikimedia.org/wiki/File:DaoDeJingWangBi.jpg.

- Figure 0.1c: Source: https://commons.wikimedia.org/wiki/File:Amaterasu_cave_crop.jpg.

- Figure 0.1d: Copyright © Webscribe (CC BY-SA 3.0) at https://commons.wikimedia.org/wiki/File:Merenptah_Israel_Stele_Cairo.jpg.

- Figure 0.1e: Source: https://commons.wikimedia.org/wiki/File:Confucius_and_His_Disciples_Yanzi_and_Huizi_at_the_Apricot_Altar_(Confucius).jpg.

- Figure 0.1f: Source: https://commons.wikimedia.org/wiki/File:CelaStMiquel_Pentecosta_3585.jpg.

- Figure 0.1g: Source: https://commons.wikimedia.org/wiki/File:Guru_Nanak_Dev_by_Raja_Ravi_Varma.jpg.

- Figure 0.1h: Source: https://commons.wikimedia.org/wiki/File:Mohammed_receiving_revelation_from_the_angel_Gabriel.jpg.

WHAT IS RELIGION?

LEARNING OBJECTIVES

1. Learn that religion is universal and historical

2. Realize that religious studies is a branch of cultural anthropology

3. Know how philosophers and anthropologists contributed to the study of religion

4. Know the four types of religion and how to apply them to different religions

> He who would valiant be
> 'Gainst all disaster
> Let him in constancy
> Follow the Master.
> There's no discouragement
> Shall make him once relent,
> His first avowed intent
> To be a pilgrim.
> —John Bunyan, Pilgrim's Progress[1]

Introduction

Religion: one little word that seems to move nations or cause them to stagnate, spark wars or bring almost unheard-of pacifism, and change society for good and bad. Religion is the one topic on which everyone has an opinion. If you want to start a fight, talk about religion. If you don't, talk about the weather—nobody can do anything about the latter. Religion is the only topic that activates the major centers of our brain[2]—not puppies, chocolate, or sex. We are hardwired for religion, and we will find out why later in this chapter. As we also shall see later in this book, society is eminently social: society and religion have been linked together like white on rice. Have you ever noticed how close white is to rice? It is on there tight. The same is true with society and religion. There has never been a time when humans did not have religion. Religion goes back to the Neanderthal era and possibly even further back in human history.

A good place to start talking about religion is to define it. What is religion? Is bowling religiously a religion? "Religion" comes from a thirteenth-century Latin word meaning "one is bound to a monastery as a monk." The meaning of the word evolved into referring to a particular system of faith by the fourteenth century, which it mostly still means today. But this is not a definition of religion. It just means people have different beliefs.[3]

As mentioned, religion is eminently social. Societies have always had religion. For instance, the oldest European city in the United States is San Juan, Puerto Rico, named after St. John, the gospel writer. Florida's original name was Pascua Florida, or La Florida—"flowery Easter" or "the flowers," named by Ponce de León. Los Angeles ("the angels") was named after Mary, Our Lady Queen of the Angels. San Francisco was named after St. Francis of Assisi, and Corpus Christi, Texas, means the "Body of Christ."

Although religion has been around since humanity has, religious studies is a relatively new discipline. It is so new that colleges disagree on how to categorize it. The author of this textbook teaches at four different colleges and universities, and religious studies is a philosophy course in one, a humanities course in two, and an interdisciplinary course in the last one.

Religion was taught with other disciplines in the Middle Ages. If one was a scientist, one was also a theologian. For instance, Gregor Mendel, the father of modern genetics, discovered dominant and recessive genes using pea plants. Mendel's daytime job was serving as a monk and an abbot, and his famous pea plants grew in his monastery's garden. So he was a scientist and a theologian. It wasn't until the Age of Enlightenment that these disciplines were divorced from each other: a scientist no longer needed to believe in God; a mathematician could be a physicist, engineer, or teacher; and a philosophy major would be unemployed (just kidding). In the 1800s and 1900s, religious studies was placed in the field of philosophy. But today some colleges still do not know in which department to place it. Some colleges have it labeled as "humanities." Others call religious studies "philosophy." One college calls it "history and language." Perhaps college administrators place religious studies in the department that needs more students because they know students will register for it. Maybe one day it will be a math course because colleges need more students to take math.[4]

What religious studies actually is, is cultural anthropology.[5] Cultural anthropologists observe the behavior of living cultures and their members. If you are walking along a sidewalk to class and someone is following you with a notepad, have no worries: the person following you is probably a cultural anthropologist. When you go home and find someone hiding in the bushes, relax: he probably has a research grant. When you are taking a shower ... okay, maybe not that. Many religious studies scholars, like cultural anthropologists, follow people around to their churches, synagogues, mosques, gurdwaras, temples, and so on and study how they do religion. The idea is that because everyone does everyday activities the same—eating, breathing, and so on—that they would do religion the same way, too. We will see that later when we examine Immanuel Kant's beliefs.

FIGURE 1.1 René Descartes

Founders of Religion as a Discipline

Religious studies as a discipline grew out of the field of philosophy. Modern philosophers have debated how best to study religion to be able to define what religion is. The end result has been the creation of the field of religious studies. The following are some of their opinions. From these, you will be encouraged to create your own class definition of religion in our next exercise.

Rene Descartes (1596–1650)

Rene Descartes was the first modern philosopher. This Frenchman, who was a scientist as well as a metaphysicist, is probably best known for his comment, "*Cogito, ergo sum*" ("I am thinking, therefore I am"). Descartes spent a good part of his scholarly life pursuing a common method that could be used for math, science, and religion. He believed there were common arrangements in these disciplines (Sorell, 2000).[6] With religion, he ran into the problem that many people do. Religions are so different. How is one able to create a common definition for all of them? He suggested discounting all elements of religion until a common bedrock held in common by all religions was discovered—the same theory he used for science and math.

The way to get to this common bedrock—think of it as a basement—was through intellectual analysis that followed "decompositional" pathways. This approach involves discarding the contradictory elements of religions. Once a common elemental base, something all religions have in common, was discovered, then an elaborate structure (a good definition of religion) could be built from it.[7]

Immanuel Kant (1724–1804)

Immanuel Kant, born in East Prussia, a bastion of German culture that was Russian occupied at the time, was one of the Enlightenment thinkers who were suspicious of religious beliefs and hostile to religious leaders.[8] Kant maintained that the definition of religion should be sought in natural or "received" religion (how people do religion), not in revealed religion such as doctrine and "dogmatic tyranny" (what followers or their religious leaders say their religion is about).

To do this, one approached "meaningful religion" by certifying its individual human accessibility by getting down to basics. Kant sought the certifiable (things one can see, and not simply abstract or theoretical) "first principles."

To discover how people did or practiced religion, he asked questions such as the following:

FIGURE 1.2 Immanuel Kant

- What effect does religion have on human habit, capacity, temperament, or quality? Does religion make you happy in the morning like a cup of Starbucks® coffee: it's a sunny day, you are singing on the way to school or work, and the squirrels are waving to you from the park? Or does religion make you grouchy: it's raining, and the squirrels are flipping you off in the park?

- Is religion associated with the world of thought or ideas? Is it an intellectual or personal thing, and is it nobody's business what religion is? Or does it pertain to the human capacity to sense and appreciate order, harmony, balance, and proportion? People know what religion you are because you wear it on your sleeve.

Kant's objective was to define religion by identifying "that without which it would not be what it is."[9] What this means is that after collecting all your information, the data that matches is the essence of religion. Without that, there would be no religion.

Karl Marx (1819–1883)

Born in the Palatinate, southwestern Germany, Karl Marx is considered to be the father of communism. He coauthored *The Communist Manifesto,* and he hated religion. Originally Jewish, his family converted to the Prussian Evangelical Church to avoid anti-Semitic laws. In Berlin, he joined the Young Hegelians, whose one common denominator was their passionate opposition to all established religions, political institutions, and social systems.[10]

Marx called religion "the opiate of the people." Opium is a highly addictive drug in use at the time. If it were modern times, Marx might have said religion was "the crack or spice of the people." He said religion represented a protest against whatever dehumanizing conditions kept human beings in social and political bondage. Marx

FIGURE 1.3 Karl Marx

wanted to create the perfect workers' paradise, a utopia. He believed that if the dehumanizing conditions were removed, as in a utopia, religion would not be necessary.[11]

Emile Durkheim (1858–1917)

Emile Durkheim was called the "father of sociology." Although this Frenchman came from a long line of rabbis, he became an agnostic. He believed that problems with society are moral ones and that "the collective spirit has been weakened in us."[12]

Durkheim believed that there are exact evolutionary correlations between elementary and contemporary forms of religious life. Society evolved, and religion evolved right along with it. So religion has been tied to society like white on rice. It's that close. There never has been a time in human history when religion did not exist. Therefore, religion is defined as "something eminently social." Religion is basic to human intelligence, so basic and primary that it carries a host of formative influences.

Reality is constituted by social order, and the "collective conscience" is the source and sustainer of moral values, cultural ideas, and religious aspirations.[13] So, we all think alike because of religion. At birth, we believe in fair play. We believe everyone is equal. We respect other people's property. For instance, if you have a car, do you expect it to be where you left it before reading this paragraph or upside down on fire? The former, because you believe your neighbors think the way you do.

Those who don't think the way we do are often placed in insane asylums or prisons because we cannot trust them.

FIGURE 1.4 Emile Durkheim

Sigmund Freud (1856–1939)

Sigmund Freud, a Moravian nonpracticing Jew, was a psychologist who believed religion is mere illusion. Human beings fabricate religion because they cannot handle themselves. They have a choice: they can use "restrictive" society to protect them from unruly impulses—rape, theft—or they can use religion to do so.[14] So they put on religion, like Superman's suit and cape, masking their baser impulses. Religion is produced out of a desire to fulfill a wish. The wishes are products of human weakness and recognition of helplessness.[15] So Freud believed that if he could cure us of our other mental illnesses, we would no longer need the mental crutch of religion.

Carl Jung (1875–1961)

Carl Jung, the withdrawn son of a Swiss minister and at one time a friend of Freud, created his own imaginary world as a child. This world was what he drew upon as he studied medicine, science, and psychiatry. Jung believed that archetypes in the "collective unconscious," a predisposition toward creating specific symbols, are passed along from each generation.[16] Mythical symbols provide a visible disclosure of the rudiments of human consciousness. Because

FIGURE 1.5 Sigmund Freud, by Max Halberstadt

human consciousness is the same all over the world, the same myths or mythological themes will occur in folk literatures of different cultures. Greek gods will be reborn as other mythical figures. For instance, the Greek god Zeus became the Roman god Apollo. The Greek Hermes became the Roman Mercury, the messenger god, and now in modern times delivers flowers for FTD. We use these same symbols because they are hardwired in our brains.

The elements of religion can be found in this self-consciousness,[17] which is why we use the same symbols over and over again. For instance, ancient Mexicans used the cross as a symbol before Christianity came to Mexico.

FIGURE 1.6A Carl Jung

Claude Levi-Strauss (1908–2009)

Claude Levi-Strauss, born in Belgium, was a philosopher turned ethnologist. He said myths (religious stories) reflect everyday life because myths have contradictory elements in them, as life does, more so than does scientific theory. Having walked through the jungles of Brazil[18] studying the native tribes, he concluded, "although experience contradicts theory, social life validates cosmology (mythology) by its similarity of structure. Hence cosmology is true."[19] So an indication that we all have a collective conscience, that we all think alike, can be found in the same myths—religious stories—that we use.

For example, examine the similarities between the following flood stories:

> So God said to Noah, "I am going to put an end to all people, for the earth is filled with violence because of them. I am surely going to destroy both them and the earth. So make yourself an ark of cypress wood; make rooms in it and coat it with pitch inside and out. This is how you are to build it: The ark is to be three hundred cubits long, fifty cubits wide and thirty cubits high. Make a roof for it, leaving below the roof an opening one cubit high all around. Put a door in the side of the ark and make lower, middle and upper decks."
>
> —Gen. 5:13–16 (New Revised Standard)[20]

FIGURE 1.6B Ancient Mexican medallions with crosses. Ancient Mexicans were using crosses before Christianity came to Mexico.

> Take up an axe, Gilgamesh, to your side, go down to the forest, cut three hundred poles each thirty meters long. Trim them and put "knobs" on them; then bring them to me at the boat. ... In the evening a rain of wheat/"heaviness" I shall shower down: enter the boat and shut your door!
>
> —Sumerian Epic of Gilgamesh, 10:3, 11:2[21]

Mayans, Lakota Sioux, and Buddhists all have flood stories. This is a myth used over and over again by different religions and cultures.

FIGURE 1.7 Claude Levi-Strauss

Class Exercise: Creating a Definition of Religion

Religion has been defined many different ways. Based on the aforementioned opinions of religious scholars, create a class definition of religion that you will use the whole semester. It will have to be a universal definition of religion that covers all religions in the textbook. Some items you may want to take into consideration:

- Christianity, Islam, Judaism, Hinduism, and Jainism believe in a heaven; Theravada Buddhism does not—one's ultimate goal is Parinirvana, ceasing to exist.

- Christianity, Islam, and some Jews believe failing to achieve heaven results in a soul going to hell, although Catholics believe in a third temporary state of existence, purgatory; Hinduism, Jainism, and Buddhism believe failure results in reincarnation.

- Buddhism does not believe in an immortal soul.

- Buddhism and Jainism do not believe in God or gods, so there is no worship.

Four Types of Religion

Scholars have been debating how to classify or categorize religion. There are different opinions. The four types listed below are the preference of the author.

Church: This religion is an official religion of a country. For instance, a church would be Catholicism in Vatican City, the Church of England in England, and Islam in Saudi Arabia.

Denomination: This religion is a major societal religion in a country. It is large and open to the society around it, meaning one can be a good American and belong to this religion. In the United States, this includes Baptists, Presbyterians, Methodists, Catholics, and so on.

Sect: This religion is a small, antisocial religion with a closed membership. This religion is closed off from the society around it, views other people as potential threats, and screens members before they can join. Scientology can be seen as one of these.

Cult: This religion is like a sect, a small, antisocial religion with a closed membership and a living, charismatic founder. The religion is the alter ego of the founder and most often dies with the founder. Peoples Temple and Branch Davidians can be considered cults.

Religions of the World

If you consider Durkheim's "religion is eminently social" comment, then you would suppose religion would be everywhere around the globe. And you would be right, except for Antarctica. There is no scholarly evidence that penguins have religion. But the scientists visiting the different research stations on this continent may have religion.

Religion textbooks shy away from stating the number of religions in the world, because apparently no one knows the exact number. Estimates range from 4,300[22] to more than 34,000.[23] The counting of religions varies depending on how the counters classify religion. For instance, is Christianity one religion, or is it thousands of denominations, sects, and cults? Islam, Buddhism, and Jainism have divisions. To further complicate the count, members of religions differ as to which category they belong in. Sunnis and Shi'a generally do not believe the other group's members are true Muslims. Theravada and Mahayana Buddhism differ on what is Buddhism. The religions of Native American tribes differ. Daoism is usually practiced with another religion. And there are the individualistic practices of neopagans and witches that differ from each other.

Most texts and articles sidestep this by listing the general groupings of the world religions—Christianity, Islam, Judaism, and so on—from largest to smallest that can be reliably counted (Figure 1.8). Christianity is the

The Religions of the World

FIGURE 1.8 Major Religions Distribution[25]

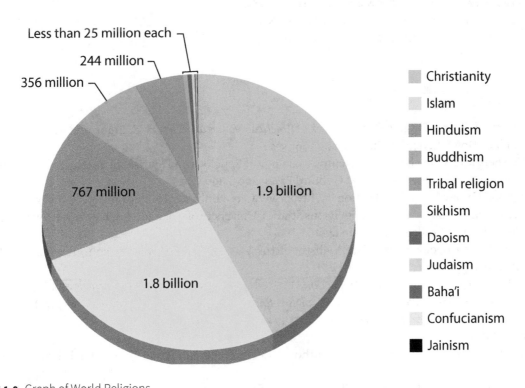

FIGURE 1.9 Graph of World Religions

largest religion in the world, with its different denominations totaling about 1.9 billion members. Islam is a close second, with 1.2 billion followers, and Hinduism is third, with about 777 million.[24]

In more ancient times, religions tended to be close to their places of origin, but then they spread to other places. Buddhism was centered in northeast India but has since moved to Tibet, China, Nepal, South Korea, Japan,

Cambodia, Laos, Malaysia, and Vietnam. Islam began in a small town in Arabia and, at its height, conquered a good part of the known world.

The largest individual branch of any religion is Catholicism, with 1.2 billion members. Large numbers are in Mexico and South America, with Africa having the fastest-growing Catholic population.[26] North America is made up of mainly Protestant denominations, whereas Europe is shared by both Catholics and Protestants. North Africa has a plurality of different types of Muslims, along with the Middle East, whereas central and southern Africa has a mix of Islam, Christianity, and indigenous religions. Russia and its government lean heavily toward the Russian Orthodox Church. China is mainly a mix of Daoism, Confucianism, and Buddhism.[27] India, the birthplace of Hinduism, is still mainly Hindu. Australia, settled by the British, is 27 percent Anglican and 41 percent Catholic (Christian denominations).[28]

So I hope this textbook will be an educational and interesting guide for your journey through the beliefs of the people of the world. You will meet cultures that are familiar and ones that you may not have known existed. But you will be more knowledgeable about the rest of the people who inhabited the same planet as you.

FOR FURTHER READING

1000 Faces of God, Rebecca Hind, Carlton Books, 2004

Atlas of World Religions, Ailsa Heritage, cartographic ed., Pearson/Prentice Hall, 2005

Man and His Symbols, Carl Jung, ed., Dell Publishing, 1968

Myth and Meaning: Cracking the Code of Culture, Claude Levi-Strauss, Schocken, 1995

Religious Studies: The Making of a Discipline, William Capps, Fortress Press, 1995

Sacred Architecture, Caroline Humphrey & Piers Vitebsky, Barnes & Noble, 1997

The Swastika: Symbol Beyond Redemption?, Steven Heller, Allsworth Press, 2000

ENDNOTES

1   J. Bunyan, "Pilgrim's Progress," in *The Book of American Values and Virtues,* E. Braun and R. Getzen, R. (New York: Black Dog & Leventhal Publishers, 1996), 577.

2   A. Newberg and S. Newberg, "The Neuropsychology of Religious and Spiritual Experience," in *Handbook of the Psychology of Religion* (New York: Guilford Press, 2005), 199–215.

3   "Religion," Online Etymology Dictionary, http://www.etymonline.com/index.php?term=religion.

4   "The Academic Study of Religion," Religious Studies, University of Colorado Boulder, https://www.colorado.edu/rlst/about-us/academic-study-religion.

5   "Cultural Anthropology," Merriam Webster, https://www.merriam-webster.com/dictionary/cultural%20anthropology.

6   T. Sorell, *Descartes: A Very Short Introduction* (Oxford, UK: Oxford University Press, 2000).

7   W. Capps, *Religious Studies: The Making of a Discipline* (Minneapolis, MN: Fortress Press, 1995).

8   A. Wood, *Kant* (Malden, MA: Blackwell, 2005), 179.

9   Capps, *Religious Studies.*

10   J. Smulkstys, *Karl Marx* (Twayne's world authors series, Vol. 296, New York: Twayne Publishers, 2008), 15–29).

11   Capps, *Religious Studies.*

12   M. Emirbayer, "Introduction—Emile Durkheim: Sociologist of Modernity," in *Emile Durkheim: Sociologist of Modernity,* eds. M. Emirbayer and I. J. Cohen (Malden MA: Blackwell Publishing, 2004), https://doi: 10.1002/9780470756133.ch1.

13   Capps, *Religious Studies.*

14   A. Storr, *Freud: A Very Short Introduction* (Oxford, UK: Oxford University Press, 2001).

15   Capps, *Religious Studies.*

16   A. Stevens, *Jung: A Very Short Introduction* (Oxford, UK: Oxford University Press, 2001).

17   Capps, *Religious Studies.*

18 R. Champaign, *Claude Lévi-Strauss* (Twayne's world authors series, Vol. 792, Boston: Twayne Publishers, 1987), xiii–xv.

19 C. Levi-Strauss, "Structural Anthropology," in M. del Rocío Martinez Lucas, "Structuralism" (2000), http://mural.uv.es/madelro/myth.html.

20 *New Revised Standard Bible* (Glassport, PA: Biblica, International Bible Society, HarperCollins Christian Publishing, 2011), http://biblehub.com/niv/genesis/6.htm.

21 S. Dalley, *Myths from Mesopotamia* (Oxford, UK: Oxford University Press, 2000).

22 Reference* Online Encyclopedia (IAC Publishing Labs Co., 2016), https://www.reference.com/world-view/total-number-religions-world-ff89ae17c6068514.

23 B. A. Robinson, "Ontario Consultants on Religious Tolerance" (2015), http://www.religioustolerance.org/worldrel.htm.

24 A. Heritage, ed., *Atlas of World Religions* (Boston: Pearson Education, 2005).

25 A. Heritage, *Atlas.*

26 "How Many Catholics Are There in the World?" BBC News (2013), http://www.bbc.com/news/world-21443313.

27 L. Hopfe, et al., *Religions of the World,* 13th ed. (Boston: Pearson Education, 2016).

28 "Christian denominations in Australia 2011," Department of Education, NSW Government (2015), [unable to insert comment with this style applied: citation needs url]

CREDITS

- Figure 1.1: Source: https://commons.wikimedia.org/wiki/File:Frans_Hals_-_Portret_van_Ren%C3%A9_Descartes.jpg.

- Figure 1.2: Source: https://commons.wikimedia.org/wiki/File:Kant_foto.jpg.

- Figure 1.3: Source: https://commons.wikimedia.org/wiki/File:Karl_Marx.jpg.

- Figure 1.4: Source: https://commons.wikimedia.org/wiki/File:Emile_Durkheim.jpg.

- Figure 1.5: Source: https://commons.wikimedia.org/wiki/File:Sigmund_Freud,_by_Max_Halberstadt_(cropped).jpg.

- Figure 1.6a: Source: https://commons.wikimedia.org/wiki/File:CGJung.jpg.

- Figure 1.7: Copyright © UNESCO/Michel Ravassard (CC by 3.0) at https://commons.wikimedia.org/wiki/File:Levi-strauss_260.jpg.

- Figure 1.8: Source: https://commons.wikimedia.org/wiki/File:Religion_distribution.png.

- Figure 1.9: Adapted from A. Heritage, Atlas of World Religions. Pearson Education, Inc., 2005.

2

ANCIENT AND INDIGENOUS RELIGIONS

NEW VOCABULARY AND CONCEPTS

- Ancient symbols
- Divine fertility
- Totems
- Shamanism
- Harmony and disharmony
- Rituals
- Magic
- Creation stories
- Pantheon of gods
- Divination and astrology
- Tocobaga's three souls

LEARNING OBJECTIVES

1. Understand how ancient people practiced religion like modern people
2. Know what shamans do and why as well as their connection to totems
3. Know the link between divine fertility and totems
4. Understand how ancient people created common rules by organizing their gods
5. See how ancient creation stories, divination, and astrology have modern counterparts
6. Understand how the Tocobaga's concept of three souls works
7. Understand how rituals maintain harmony, fix disharmony, and pass on myths

FIGURE 2.1 Lakota author, Black Elk.

Hey-a-a-hey! Hey-a-a-hey! Hey-a-a-hey! Hey-a-a-hey!

Grandfather, Great Spirit, once more behold me on earth and learn to hear my feeble voice. You lived first, and you are older than all needed, older than all prayer. All things belong to you—the two-leggeds, the four-leggeds, the wings of the air and all green things that live. You have set the powers of the four quarters to cross each other. The good road and the road of difficulties you have made to cross; and when they cross, the place is holy. Day in and day out, forever, you are the life of things.

—Black Elk[1]

If you remember from the last chapter, Rene Descartes believed we all have a collective conscience and we all think alike at a basic level. Consequently, as we have seen, we do practice religion alike on a basic level. So, assuming that is the case, we must have inherited our religious practices from our ancestors. No religion comes out of a vacuum. So, because we are related to our ancestors, we must share a collective conscience with them.

So let us look at our ancestors and see how their religious practices are similar to our more modern ones.

Neanderthal

The Neanderthals lived between 40,000 and 400,000 years ago in Europe and southwestern and central Asia.[2] They were probably a separate species from *Homo sapiens* (us), but they are related to us. Scientists have discovered we have slices of the Neanderthal genome.[3] The Neanderthal burial practice demonstrated clear evidence that the Neanderthal had religion. They buried their dead with food, tools, and weapons. So apparently the Neanderthal thought that Og, who got splattered by a woolly mammoth, was going to need his food, tools, and weapons in the afterlife. The Neanderthal apparently did not have much of an imagination: the afterlife was a lot like their current life. Still, the Neanderthal believed that death was not the end of Og: he was going to need his possessions. There is really no other reason to bury perfectly good food, tools, and weapons. Burying food with a dead Neanderthal was significant because they went through periods of starvation that led them to cannibalism.[4] So it is significant that, when facing possible starvation, Neanderthals buried their dead with food. The afterlife may have been more important than this life.

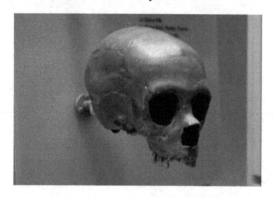

FIGURE 2.2 La Quina 18. Homo neanderthalensis child

In modern times, we also bury our dead with their possessions. Sometimes it is a toy, like a teddy bear, or something dear to the deceased, like a rosary. I attended a funeral where a pianist was buried with her sheet music. Apparently, there are pianos in the afterlife but no sheet music, so BYOSM: bring your own sheet music. In Holiday, Florida, a man was buried with his motorcycle. It is a big grave site, because there is a lot of machinery in it.

Neanderthal also had a "bear cult": they collected bear skulls. The skulls were some type of sacred symbol, but its original meanings are unknown, because the Neanderthal did not leave written accounts. The skulls were set apart for possible reverence, a custom that continues today.[5] Although modern people may not collect bear skulls, though some may, we have other sacred symbols: crosses, crescent moon, Star of David, and so on.

Cro-Magnons

Cro-Magnons may have eventually replaced the Neanderthal, because their fossil record is more recent. An indication that they believed in an afterlife is shown in their practice of burying their dead with ornaments, such as shell bracelets and hair circlets. Apparently, the afterlife has a dress code, and only well-dressed deceased get past the bouncer. Cro-Magnon dead can be well bedecked with shell bracelets, necklaces, and even anklets.

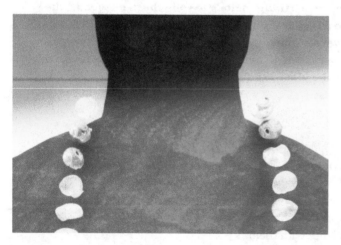

FIGURE 2.3 Shell bead necklace (reconstruction) with ten shell beads

Well-dressed dead are phenomena today. I have never gone to a wake where the deceased is wearing a torn T-shirt and shorts. The body always looks good, sometimes better dressed than when the person was alive. He or she may be wearing his or her best suit or dress, and everything matches. Muslims are buried in their Hajj robes (if they made the pilgrimage to Mecca) so they will be greeted by God in paradise wearing the symbol of their accomplishment of one of the Five Pillars: making the pilgrimage to Mecca.

Cro-Magnons also painted their dead with red ochre to represent life blood. They probably figured out early on

FIGURE 2.4 Cro-Magnon burials with jewelry. Cro-Magnons were known to be buried with shell jewelry.

that a person with blood was alive and one without blood was dead.[6] So Og, the victim of that woolly mammoth, was going to need blood in the next life so he would be born alive again, not dead, like opossums on the side of the road. It is common knowledge that opossums are actually born dead alongside the road. At least it seems to be.

Modern societies also do similar things with their dead. Nobody actually is painted red, but the embalming process makes a person look alive and viable. Some people look more healthy dead than when they were alive. I had a student who was enrolled in the college's mortuary science program, and she painted deceased people to make them look alive and healthy. She also painted her eyebrows in a different shape each day: sometimes she painted an ocean, sometimes a forest.

Cro-Magnons also returned to graves of the dead and had a meal with them. Not many people in North America have lunch at the local cemetery, but in Mexico, people celebrate with their dead during the Dia de Muertos (Day of the Dead). Graves are decorated with food, liquor, and jewelry. One would suppose if the living and dead drank enough tequila, they could see each other and carry on a conversation. On the Indonesian island of Sulawesi, families keep the bodies of dead relatives around for days to years, praying with them and dressing them in new clothes.[7] In North America, people pay to talk to dead people. This is not so much going to a séance but buying an advertisement in the local newspaper. Have you ever seen a paid ad in the obituaries section that read: "In memory of (name of deceased), it has been three years, your loving family." To whom is that addressed? It can only be one person. Apparently, some believe the deceased has a subscription to the newspaper. Maybe they get it off the (pause) cloud (ahem). And they read the ad and say, "Oh, look, my family remembers me. Why did they have to include my driver's license photo? Yech. But they still remember me." Or have you ever seen a car driving down the road with "RIP, (person's name), (date of birth and death)" painted or stickered on the back window? To whom is that addressed? Only one person. Apparently, the afterlife is hovering above the interstate. The deceased looks down, sees the car on the road, and exclaims, "Look, my family remembers me! A 1975 AMC Matador? Seriously? Trade it in, guys. Still, they remember me."

Shamanism

Cro-Magnons and *Homo sapiens* developed a sense of kinship and interaction between human and animal spirits. Shamans, who may have first appeared in what is now Siberia, are people who are attuned to the spirit world of animals and people and deal with that world on behalf of others.[8] For example, a one-inch likeness of a lion man was found in Hohle Fels Cave, Germany, dating to about 35,000 years ago.[9] It seems the ancient people living in the area were having problems with lions coming into town for a quick snack. So the people asked the shaman to go out and talk to the lion. How would you like that job? So the people of the time believed that the shaman would be able to turn himself into a lion so the lion thought it was talking to another lion. And the shaman would be able to tell the lion to go eat somewhere else, such as a walk-through at a fast-food restaurant. Apparently, this worked. Otherwise, there would be a likeness called the idiot man.

Shamans used masks disguised as birds, jaguars, crows, ravens, and even cats to talk to the appropriate animal. An ancient Inuit shaman rattle from Alaska had a raccoon skull, deer fur and antlers, and raven and eagle feathers, enabling the shaman to converse with all these animals. The reason this worked was that indigenous people believed that humans and animals were equal: all animals had human souls. Lakota apologized to the buffalo spirit for killing the buffalo. In another instance, a totem, stacked on others in a totem pole, had a raven with a human face where the belly button of a raven would be, if the bird had one. Another example was a human face on the flukes and dorsal fin of a painted orca totem: the parts of the killer whale that can be seen by a shaman above the water. These human faces are the human souls to whom the shamans talk.

The Eskimo, Inuit, and Tlingit also had two types of shamans. Shamans were traditionally known as "witch doctors" in that they were the tribes' physicians and used herbs, spells, and other ingredients to cure or heal an ailing person. Indigenous peoples who lived in the northwest of North America also had this type of shaman: they were called practitioners. A second type of shaman was called the Wild Man of the Woods. These were certifiably insane individuals who lived out in the snowy woods by themselves and talked to animals. No one would let them near a sick family member, but they had a purpose: they passed on survival rules to their tribe from the animals sent by Mother Earth. This will be discussed in more depth in the section on totems.

In comparison, priests, ministers, imams, rabbis, and so on intercede for the faithful in modern religions.

Divine Fertility

I always thought it was a man's world, but it turns out that earth is a woman: she gives birth. The fecund goddess mother, depicted with exaggerated female attributes, was used in hunting and—later on—as agricultural magic to make fields fertile.[10] In Mexico, an ancient cave painting shows Father Sky and Mother Earth linked. The implication is clear: Father Sky fertilizes Mother Earth, and she gives birth to animals, plants, and humans. The concept of earth as a "mother" is seen in modern liberation theology, Native American religions, and Hinduism. In the latter religion, rivers are also goddesses. The holiest, the Ganges River, removes adverse effects of karma.

Totems

Totems rose out of the concept of a goddess mother, establishing survival rules for the tribe in matters of food gathering, relationships, and so on in the realm of the supernatural (see Figures 2.5–2.16). Totems told the tribe where to hunt, when to plant, and who should marry whom. For example, do not marry your sibling, because the children will look funny. Totems were two things: they were the rules and regulations Mother Earth sent to her people, and they were the animals that brought those rules and regulations to Mother Earth's people.[11] The shamans, of course, acted as the mediators and delivered the messages to the rest of the tribe. They could talk to the animals because, as mentioned above, animals are also people.

Totems are seen in many cultures. In Hawaii, they are also stacked on each other as totem poles, though the spirits are called tikis. Hawaiian war clubs have an evil-looking totem on them. Totems also become the protective spirits of a tribe and play prominent positions in oral and written traditions. In North America, totem poles tell the history of a tribe as far as when they interacted with a particular totem. A bear may be included because a tribe relocating by boat saw one on the riverbank, thought it was a sign, and pulled in

FIGURE 2.5 Shaman bird mask

FIGURE 2.6 Cat mask

FIGURE 2.7 Stop sign with totem also signifying stop

FIGURE 2.8 Raven with human face totem pole

FIGURE 2.9 Shaman rattle with raccoon skull

FIGURE 2.10 Three totem poles in Vancouver, Canada. Poles are read top to bottom.

FIGURE 2.13 Mayan glyphs on a temple in Chichen, Itza, Mexico can be read as letters or concepts.

FIGURE 2.11 Two-tiki (spirits) pole from Hawaii

FIGURE 2.12 Hawaiian war club with god of war on it

and set up camp. Another totem pole can have an orca on it because an orca had interacted with the tribe in some way.

Modern religions have totems, such as dietary laws in Islam and Judaism—neither allows its followers to eat pork—and these religions attribute those rules to God.

Pantheon of Gods

The concept that there is a hierarchy of gods came out of the Sumero-Akkadian pantheon in ancient Mesopotamia (3100–1600 BCE).[12] Gods of different rural areas and cities eventually united into a pantheon. When people settled down and became farmers, they no longer followed herds of animals as hunters. Not only did they bring their luggage into town when they moved in, they also brought their gods. This made it difficult to have an orderly society when everyone had his or her own gods and morals. So the gods were arranged like a pyramid: top god or gods at the peak, mediocre gods in the middle, and the really wussy gods at the bottom. And the whole town agreed to the arrangement: order restored. Ishtar, a virginal love goddess, came closest to being a universal deity in that she was the head goddess of several of these towns. Apparently, people liked virginal love goddesses. Randy, the pimp god, did not make the cut.

The Romans and Greeks made their own pantheons of gods. Mount Olympus is just the Greek pantheon of gods. Pantheons of gods exist in modern Hinduism—there are more than 300 million gods but only three top gods—and Tibetan Buddhism, which adopted gods from the Chinese Bon tribe.

Creation Stories

All religions have creation stories: Where do we come from, why are we here, what is our purpose? The Sumerians believed that a primordial sea first existed and then land and air were created. The Sumerian epic of Gilgamesh tells about a man who built a boat to save his family while the world was flooded.[13] Creation stories tend to be xenophobic. For instance, the Lakota Sioux believed they were created first and are people (along with the buffalo) but no one else was, including the White man.[14] Followers of Shinto, one of the religions of Japan, believe that Japan was created first and everything else was leftovers.[15] The aborigines of New Zealand believed New Zealand was created first and Australia was just where dead people and spirits went: no one actually lived in Australia. But still, creation stories—particularly the great flood—have parallel accounts in the Christian Bible, the Jewish Tanak, and the Muslim Qur'an.

Divination and Astrology

Divination was used to foretell the future, or at least to prepare someone for a future event. This includes whether you are going to graduate or not. Omens were read in ancient times, and still are, through divination of objects such as a sheep's liver (which is why I always carry one to plan my day), the arrangement of sticks on the ground, tea leaves in the bottom of a cup, and so on. Some restaurants have specially trained waiters who will read your coffee grounds (for an extra tip). In one particular instance, I dumped the coffee grounds out of my cup onto a saucer, and I wrote the word "Hi" in it. "Look," I exclaimed to my underwhelmed dining partners, "It's talking to me!" The one time I went to a palm reader, she told me, "You idiot, that is a ficus. I can't read that." So modern society also has diviners.

Astrology was the reading of the gods in the disposition of the heavenly bodies: stars, planets, and comets. The Maya used astrology to develop intricate calendars. Astronomy benefited from this research. Astrology is a major part of mystical Judaism (Kabbalah) and Hinduism (one does not get married until an astrologer picks an auspicious wedding date),[16] and it was a feature of Christianity in the Middle Ages. One can see the signs of the zodiac on Christian basilica floors.[17]

Another example of modern astrology is horoscopes. These are popular parts of the newspaper, though they do have a legal disclaimer that reads: "For entertainment purposes only," meaning, "Don't sue us if your day does not turn out like we said it would." My problem with horoscopes is that they are vague. They can mean almost anything. My horoscope once read: "You will be hit by a northbound bus at 8:17 p.m." What does that mean? It is too vague. Is the bus a county bus, city bus, Greyhound bus, or school bus? There is not enough detail. One cannot plan one's life around that. "Signs" are very important to horoscope followers. "What sign were you born under?" is a common question, particularly in the dating scene. The sign I was born under was "Maternity Hospital, Next Exit." It was a rush job.

Tocobaga

The Tocobaga were an indigenous people who lived around the shores of Tampa Bay in Florida. They would eventually die out after European settlements took over the area. Tocobaga subsisted on shells. They ate shellfish, they made tools out of shells, they slept on shells, and they were buried in shells. They were very "shell-fish." There are two types of Tocobaga mounds around the bay: garbage mounds made of shells and burial mounds made of shells. Sometimes it is hard to distinguish between the two. In Safety Harbor, on the northwest side of Tampa Bay, is the largest mound, called the Temple Mound, although it is not known if a temple was ever built on it. There are sidewalks and stairs leading up to the

FIGURE 2.14 The largest Tocobaga mound in the Tampa Bay, FL area is near Safety Harbor and is overgrown with vegetation.

FIGURE 2.15 The mound has a clear view of Tampa Bay where the Tocobaga gathered shellfish.

top for a nice view of the bay. The European settlers also built a settlement on top of this mound after the Tocobaga were gone.

The Tocobaga had the concept of three souls. There was a shadow, which followed a person around most of his or her life (except at night). The reflection in the pond was the second soul. Tocobaga did not have mirrors, so personal reflection was done in the local body of water. The third soul was the pupil of the eye. This latter was the immortal soul. Upon death, the other two souls would go into the bodies of lesser beings, such as fish, while the pupil hung around the burial mound. Shamans could talk to this pupil and would consult with it when the tribe needed advice.[19] Suppose hypothetically—and I know this can never happen—but suppose there were an oil spill in the Gulf of Mexico. And this oil came ashore and all the birds, plants, and shellfish were covered with what looked like chocolate. What would the Tocobaga do? Their primary staple was now fouled with oil. So the shaman would go to the mound and talk to the pupil of the eye and get advice. He would ask something like "What did your people do when Hurricane Hermine dumped sewage into the bay?" And the eye would give advice, like "Go eat at Red Lobster for a while. They have a special on shellfish."

One other thing before we close this chapter: what are good and bad in ancient and indigenous religions are harmony and disharmony. Harmony is when everything goes your way: you graduate, you get a Ferrari, and you move into a beautiful home. Disharmony is when things go south: you flunk out of school, you get a shopping cart, and you move into a cardboard box underneath an overpass. In the case of ancient religions, it had to do with eating or starving.

FIGURE 2.16 The road to the top of the mound is now paved.

Rituals maintain harmony and fix disharmony. You want to maintain something good, like your running car. You don't want to wait to schedule maintenance until the wheels fall off: then it becomes more expensive. The same is true with ancient religions: rituals helped maintain harmony. If things went bad, rituals were also good at restoring harmony. The reason rituals work is because of magic. Magic is not pulling a banana out of one's ear. It is the concept that the gods/spirits are subject to the same laws as humans. So if it rains, the gods get wet. If it is hot, they get thirsty. So if one does the right ritual, invoking the laws of Earth—laws the gods obey—the gods have to fulfill the request. If a shaman does a rain dance correctly, the rain god has to make it rain. The god has no free will, unlike modern times, when God can tell you where to get off. If it did not rain, then that meant the shaman missed a word or a step in the dance and had to do it over. The shaman may want to check the Weather Channel beforehand for credibility issues.

Rituals also pass on myths. As mentioned in the previous chapter, myths are religious stories, the stories of the tribe. Many ancient religions did not have writing, so they did not have scripture, which by definition are sacred writings. So the stories or myths of the tribe were passed on to younger members through the oral tradition of rituals. While the shaman was doing the rain dance, he would also speak about other shamans who did similar rituals in the past. During a hunting dance, stories of great hunters of old would be recited. So youth learned about the past also through these rituals.

SUMMARY

As we have read, different philosophers have addressed what religion is—some factual, some derogatory—and created a definition of it. Consequently, we learned some religions, such as Buddhism and Jainism, do not have common beliefs with other religions about divine entities or God. Religion is also universal and has always been part of human history. We saw how our ancestors practiced religion similarly to modern humans.

FOR FURTHER READING

Atlas of the North American Indian, Carl Waldman, Checkmark Books, 2000

Myths from Mesopotamia, Stephanie Dalley, trans., Oxford, 2000

Popol Vuh: The Sacred Book of the Maya, Allen Christenson, O Books, 2003

Sacred Images: A Vision of Native American Rock Art, Leslie Kelen and David Sucec, Gibbs-Smith, 1996

Scribes, Warriors and Kings, William Fash, Thames and Hudson, 1991

Tribal Art, Judith Miller, DK, 2006

ENDNOTES

1   J. Neihardt and N. Black Elk, *Black Elk Speaks* (Lincoln: University of Nebraska Press, 2000).

2   "Homo neanderthalensis," Smithsonian Institute, 2016, http://humanorigins.si.edu/evidence/human-fossils/species/homo-neanderthalensis.

3   E. Callaway, "Modern Human Genomes Reveal Our Inner Neanderthal," *Nature: International Weekly Journal of Science* (2014), http://www.nature.com/news/modern-human-genomes-reveal-our-inner-neanderthal-1.14615.

4   A. Thompson, "Neanderthals Were Cannibals, Study Confirms," *Live Science* (2016), http://www.livescience.com/1187-neanderthals-cannibals-study-confirms.html.

5   Philip G. Chase, "The Cult of the Cave Bear," *Expedition Magazine* 29.2 (1987), Penn Museum, http://www.penn.museum/sites/expedition/?p=14616.

6   P. Puech and B. Puech, "Can We Still Hear the Cro-Magnon Man?" *Academia* (1987), https://www.academia.edu/266798/CAN_WE_STILL_HEAR_THE_CRO-MAGNON_MAN.

7   K. Everly and B. Lehmann, videographers. "Here, Living with Dead Bodies for Weeks—or Years—Is Tradition," *National Geographic* (2016), https://www.youtube.com/watch?v=hCKDsjLt_qU.

8   C. Smith, "Shamanism," Cabrillo College, http://www.cabrillo.edu/~crsmith/shaman.html.

9   J. Lobell, "New Life for the Lion Man," *Archeology* 65, no. 2 (2012), https://archive.archaeology.org/1203/features/stadelhole_hohlenstein_paleolithic_lowenmensch.html.

10   J. Westenholz, "Goddess Worship: Goddess Worship In The Ancient Near East," Encyclopedia.com, 2005, https://www.encyclopedia.com/environment/encyclopedias-almanacs-transcripts-and-maps/goddess-worship-goddess-worship-ancient-near-east.

11   J. Esposito, D. Fasching, and T. Lewis, *World Religions Today,* 3rd ed. (Oxford, UK: Oxford University Press, 2009).

12   Joshua J. Mark, "The Mesopotamian Pantheon," *Ancient History Encyclopedia*, last modified February 25, 2011, https://www.ancient.eu/article/221/.

13   Stephanie Dalley, trans., *Myths from Mesopotamia* (Oxford: Oxford University Press, 2000).

14   Cheyenne River Sioux Tribe, "Lakota Creation Story," http://www.sioux.org/lakota-creation-story.html.

15   "Core Stories of Shinto," BBC, 2009, http://www.bbc.co.uk/religion/religions/shinto/texts/stories_1.shtml.

16   Joyce Flueckiger, *Everyday Hinduism* (West Sussex: John Wiley & Sons, 2015), https://books.google.com/books?hl=en&lr=&id=0inWBgAAQBAJ&oi=fnd&pg=PA145&dq=astrology+marriage+Hinduism&ots=b-5bCxAhiip&sig=FJh0_Rb5pyumyIKe-CJOvQODYzs#v=onepage&q=astrology%20marriage%20Hinduism&f=false.

17   Simon Bartolini and M. Pierozzi, (2016). "Astrology and Solar Symbology in the Basillica of San Giovanni in Florence," *Mediterranean Archeology and Archaeometry* 16, no. 4, http://maajournal.com/Issues/2016/Vol16-4/Full63.pdf.

18   M. Perry, "Tocobaga Indians," Sacred Lands Preservation and Education, http://www.sacredlandspreservationandeducation.org/mp_bizarre_tocobaga.aspx.

19   Perry, "Tocobaga Indians."

CREDITS

3

ISLAM

LEARNING OBJECTIVES

1. Understand the historical context of the origins of Islam
2. Learn about the life of Muhammad and teachings of Islam
3. Understand the theology and philosophy of the Qur'an and its origins
4. Understand the myth of Islam and how Muslims see the world
5. Understand the viewpoint of the Islamic resurgence

> In the name of Allah, the Beneficent, the Merciful.
> All praise is due to Allah, the Lord of the Worlds.
> The Beneficent, the Merciful, Master of the Day of Judgment.
> You do we serve and you do we beseech for help.
> Keep us on the right path.
> The path of those upon whom you have bestowed favors, not the
> path of those upon whom your wrath is brought down,
> nor of those who go astray.
>
> —Qur'an, Sura 1

Usually textbooks on religion start with the oldest religions: ancient and indigenous religions, and then Hinduism. Many texts usually present the religions in chronological order. This textbook could also, but Islam is much more interesting. When is the last time you read about Hinduism in the newspaper or saw anything about it on television or the Internet? When is the last time you heard or read anything about Islam? Point proven. Although Hinduism is also interesting, and we will get to it soon enough, Islam is in the news. So this text will cover the three great monotheistic religions first—Islam, Judaism, and Christianity—before addressing other religions.

Islamic Statistics

In the early 21st century, there were 1.6 billion Muslims in the world—roughly 23% of the global population, according to a Pew Research Center estimate. But although Islam is currently the world's second-largest religion (after Christianity), it is the fastest-growing major religion. Indeed, if current demographic trends continue, the number of Muslims is expected to exceed the number of Christians by the end of this century.[1]

The largest Muslim population is not in the Middle East but in the Pacific Ocean—specifically, on the hundreds of islands that make up the nation of Indonesia. About 80 percent of the 235 million of the country's population are Muslims. Only 18 percent of Muslims live in the Middle East.[2] Of that 18 percent,

FIGURE 3.1 Islamic Center of Dearborn

a small percentage are the troublemakers and rabble-rousers you read or hear about in the news: ISIS, al-Qaeda, Hezbollah, and Hamas. So these troublemakers tend to paint all Muslims with the same brush, compelling non-Muslims to view all Muslims with suspicion.

Significant numbers of Muslims are found in the nations of the former Soviet Union, North and South America, Africa, China, and Europe. The Pew Research Center predicts by 2050, 10 percent of Europeans will be Muslim.[3]

Muslims may soon be the second-largest religious group in the United States: 3.3 million Muslims live in that country, though they only make up about 1 percent of the adult population).[4] But that average may be up to 2.1 percent by 2050. Most Muslims in the United States are immigrants.[5] Islam still has a ways to go to catch up with Christianity, which is about 70 percent of the population.

By and large, Muslims have lived peacefully in the United States. There have been a few issues: Muslims have been implicated in mass shootings, such as when 14 people were killed at a holiday party in San Bernardino, California, in 2015 and when 50 people killed at an Orlando, Florida, nightclub in 2016. But most Muslims do not do anything that merits news coverage. For instance, one of the largest Muslim populations in the United States is in Dearborn, Michigan. When is the last time you heard about an airplane being hijacked out of Dearborn? When was the last time a bomb went off in Dearborn? Muslims are generally boring people who do not do anything to merit news coverage: they eat, go to school, go to work, and shop at the supermarket (yawn).

The largest mosque in the country is also in Dearborn: the Islamic Center of America, which is located on the same road where the carmaker Ford has its headquarters. The mosque shares Ford Road with its neighbors: Warren Community Church, St. Clement Orthodox Church, St. Sarkis Armenian Apostolic Church, and the Mother of the Savior Lutheran Church, which has its marquee partly written in Arabic. On the sunny day when the author visited the mosque, children were running around the building as parents tried to herd them toward religious instruction classes as well as Girl and Boy Scout meetings.

Muslim Myth

The Muslim myth (religious story) of the creation of the world is similar to that of the Jewish and Christian chronology, with some differences. Muslims believe Allah has revealed his truth to prophets throughout history. The first was Adam, who had a wife named Eve (*Hawa* in the Qur'an). Sound familiar? Also, there was Noah (*Nûh*), who saved his family and animals from a flood. Then along came the patriarch of Islam, Judaism, and Christianity: Abraham (*Ibraham),* who almost sacrificed his son, Ishmael (Isaac in the Jewish and Christian Bibles). Moses (*Mûsa*) led Allah's people out of captivity in Egypt and received the Ten Commandments. Jesus (*Isal*) is also considered to be a Muslim prophet, but Muslims do not believe he was the son of God because he was not divine, as Christians believe. In fact, Jesus says he is Muslim in the Qur'an and condemns self-professed Christians to hell during Judgment Day (because he will be the judge). Muhammad is the last prophet, receiving the perfect revelation (the Qur'an). All these prophets are human, and none are divine. But Muhammad is the perfect human—as perfect as a human can be—and Muslims are encouraged to emulate him.

History of Islam

Pre-Islam Arabia. The history of Islam, meaning the written contemporary record of the times, is at odds with the myth. Historically, there is no evidence that Islam existed prior to Muhammad. Arabia in the seventh century was animistic. Nature was worshipped as gods or goddesses: every sandstorm, shamal (north wind), or oasis had a god or spirit in it. The Bedouin tribes of the desert were polytheistic and had a pantheon of deities and spirits, including evil *jinn* (or genies), with the head god named Allah. So the name of Allah predates Islam.[6]

In Mecca, one stop on a major north-south caravan route, was a black meteor venerated as a spirit inside an enclosure called the Kaaba (the cube). Arabs called the black rock a spirit that fell out of the sky. Muslims believe it dates back to the time of Adam and Eve. Arabs were also worshipping different stones with varying colors around the Arabian Peninsula at the time. The rock is still in the Kaaba, although it has been broken and pieced back together from time to time, and the Kaaba, destroyed and rebuilt several times, is the center of worship for Islam.

FIGURE 3.2 This Qur'an from Baghdad shows Muhammad's family tree back to Adam.

FIGURE 3.3 Kaaba. The Kaaba, since ancient times, has been the center point of Arabic worship.

Tribes would vie for control over the annual pilgrimage to the Kaaba because it was also a moneymaker. Tribes would visit their god idols in the Kaaba and while there would engage in trade. It was difficult to separate religious activities from trade in Mecca: they were tied together. When tribe members went to visit their god or gods, they would also trade in camels, spices, linens, and blankets from the Silk Road, which ran from China and India to Europe through the Middle East and Asia. The tribe in control of the pilgrimage in the beginning of the seventh century was the Quraysh tribe of Mecca, a very rich tribe.[7]

One had to belong to a tribe in the desert to survive. No lone individual had a chance because Arabian tribes had been engaging in constant warfare for centuries, battling over oases, possessions, and perceived grudges. Figuratively, grudges had big handles on them: people carried them for generations, so what your grandfather did to a particular family may come back at you in the form of a sword or an arrow. So belonging to a powerful tribe such as the Quraysh was advantageous.

Muhammad's early life. The Prophet Muhammad was not born into the Quraysh tribe. He was born to a poor family in 570 or 571 CE. (A word about the use of "CE." It means "Common Era" and is a less Christian designation for the same period of time as AD—"anno Domini," which means "in the year of our Lord." Similarly, instead of BC—"before Christ"—historians now use BCE—"before the Common Era.") Muhammad's father died when he was young, and so did his mother, but not before she gave him to a woman in the Quraysh tribe to raise. Muhammad was raised by his grandfather, then adopted by his uncle, Abu Talib, a leader of the Quraysh tribe.[8]

Besides running the annual pilgrimage, the Quraysh tribe's business was trade with the coastal cities of Arabia along that particular route of the Silk Road. So Muhammad would accompany Quraysh caravans and earned the reputation as being a fair negotiator and a settler of disputes. He also talked to Jewish rabbis and Christian priests and learned the stories of the prophets Abraham, Noah, Moses, and also of Jesus and Mary. Some of these Christians were Nestorians, who were particularly adept at the sciences but were branded as heretics by mainstream Christianity because they were Gnostics. Gnosticism means "secret knowledge," and Gnostics claimed they had information that no one else knew, such as: Yahweh was the evil god of the Old Testament; Jesus was the good god of the New Testament, and he married Sophia, the earth goddess, and they vanquished Yahweh. Another Nestorian secret concerned a blind, insane, jealous angel who came down to earth and had sex with women, who then gave birth to giants. The secret Muhammad came away with was part of Gnostic belief about Jesus's divinity: Jesus was God but not human; he only appeared to be human and did not die on the cross because he left the human suit he was wearing nailed to the cross. To this day, Islamic belief includes the myth that Jesus escaped crucifixion.[9]

Muhammad's relationship with the rest of his adoptive tribe was tenuous.[10] They considered him an outsider and treated him as such. For instance, he was illiterate: he never learned to read or write. Scholars speculate he was kept that way so he would not be able to advance in the tribe into a position of power. Muhammad had this relationship thrown in his face when he asked to marry Abu Talib's daughter. Abu Talib said no: it was clear he did not want his adoptive son to have a claim on the leadership of the tribe. So Muhammad left Abu Talib's trading business and went out on his own. Years later, when his uncle eventually converted to Islam on his deathbed and witnesses told Muhammad that he did profess Allah, Muhammad's response was "I did not hear him."

On one of his own caravan trips to Syria, he caught the eye of the woman who owned the shipment he was carrying across the sand on his camels. Khadija, age 40, was an anomaly among Arabian women: she was a rich, independent widow. At the time, women were treated as property: they were often swapped as wives or concubines. Khadija stood out, having inherited her late husband's business and wealth. She was so taken with Muhammad, who was 25 years old at the time, that she proposed marriage to him. He accepted. So Muhammad not only inherited a fortune and a business, he also acquired a seasoned and experienced mentor who probably assisted him in his business deals.[11]

At some time in his life, Muhammad stopped working. Islamic tradition says he had an interest in religion.[12] A retroactive story said angels came and warmed his heart when he was an infant. So Muhammad spent a lot of time in caves in the hills around Mecca meditating. Two issues apparently occupied his mind. One was the constant warfare of the Bedouin tribes in the desert. Muhammad had a dream that he could unite them and stop the bloodshed. The second was the role of women in Arabia. As mentioned before, their status was lower than the belly of a camel. His future efforts to elevate the status of women, although not to the same level as that of men, may have been influenced by Khadija.

Muhammad's revelation. During one of these meditation sessions in front of a campfire in a cave, a disturbing event would completely change Muhammad's life at age 40. While meditating on Mount Hira during the time of year now marked by the Islamic month of Ramadan, the angel Gabriel appeared and spoke to him. Now this was the same angel Gabriel that Christians may know from the Bible who appeared to Mary and asked her if she would bear a child. However, this angel who accosted Muhammad was no namby-pamby angel from a Hallmark card. No, this was a fiery angel with an attitude. One account in the Hadith, which includes the sayings and actions of Muhammad, has Gabriel stepping right out of the campfire. Now if you were roasting s'mores and someone stepped out of your campfire, what would you do? That is the last place from which you would expect someone to emerge. The Qur'an said Gabriel embraced Muhammad twice (think "fiery bear hug") and with a flaming nose inches from Muhammad's face, Gabriel roared: "Read in the name of the Lord!" Then the angel let Muhammad go, slightly singed. Muhammad's illiteracy must have quickly manifested itself, so Gabriel said: "Recite in the name of the Lord!" This meant Muhammad should memorize every word Gabriel burned into his brain.

Now if this happened to you, what would you do? Psychologists say there are two responses among humans when they encounter perceived danger: fight or flight. Muhammad apparently did not want to take on a fiery angel, so he bolted out of that cave like a bat out of you-know-what. Screaming, he ran down the side of the mountain, skated on rock slides, and jumped over boulders while looking over his shoulder for that fiery apparition. He saw Khadija's tent in the valley below. She had left the light on for him, like in the Motel 6 commercials.

He ran into the tent yelling, "Wrap me up! Wrap me up!" He was so scared he was cold. Khadija wrapped him up in blankets and gave him a cup of hot chocolate. . . camel milk. "I think I'm one of those people who talk to animals," he exclaimed. Now in Western culture, talking to animals is considered to be a gift. There have been successful TV series called "The Dog Whisperer," "The Horse Whisperer," and even "The Ghost Whisperer." There was even a series called "The Cat Whisperer," but it was cancelled during the first season when people realized the cats weren't listening. But in Arabia in the Middle Ages, if someone talked to an animal, he or she was considered one sandwich short of a picnic, one card short a full deck, bonkers, crazy, or a lunatic. Muhammad thought he had gone off the deep end. Khadija, being the good wife she was, assured him he was not and told him to sit down and describe everything that had happened to him.[13]

She apparently believed him, because Muhammad's first convert was his wife, then his cousin 'Ali, and Zayd, a freed slave in the family. And they were the only converts for many years. A reason for this is that Muhammad began preaching monotheism (that there was only one God), and he said the Kaaba was contaminated by false gods. The upper castes, particularly members of the Quraysh tribe who ran the pilgrimage to Kaaba, were threatened by this kind of talk. It would be like Muhammad standing in front of Disney World and telling children that Mickey Mouse had died. The Quraysh tribe thought Muhammad was lunatic, dangerous, or a dangerous lunatic, but no one could touch him because he was still under the protection of Abu Talib.

So Muhammad took his message to the lower castes of Mecca. They didn't have a share in the pilgrimage money-making machine, so they joined his movement. So Islam began as a grassroots movement. Wait, there is no grass in Arabia. Well, Islam began as a rock-gravel movement. And it spread.

Muhammad continued preaching, as the angel Gabriel had prompted him. The Prophet would receive revelations from the angel for 23 years. Sometimes Gabriel would drop thoughts in his head; other times, Gabriel showed up as that fiery you-know-who-in-your-face angel. One time, according to an account in the Hadith, Gabriel showed up in camp with slicked-back hair, wearing a very clean white suit. Everybody else had the sand of the desert all over them, but Gabriel looked like he had just stepped out of an air-conditioned limousine. In this particular instance, Gabriel questioned Muhammad about God and then left, with Muhammad telling everyone afterward that the stranger in the camp was the angel. Because he was illiterate, Muhammad memorized everything Gabriel told him, and scholars wrote down the accounts on bones, stones, and other ready material because paper was scarce. Muslims believe the contents then became their holy book, the Qur'an.

Hirjah. In 622 CE, Muhammad lost his protection: his uncle died. Members of the Quraysh tribe came gunning for him. Muhammad had known his uncle would not live forever, so he created a Plan A and even a Plan B for when things went sour. So when the Meccans broke into his house, he was gone. He had sent one group of his followers across the Red Sea in boats to Ethiopia: they were the first Muslims to land in Africa. Then he and the rest of his group headed north in the middle of the night on their camels to a little oasis, a mud hut of a town called Yathrib. Muhammad had been in secret negotiations with Yathrib. They needed a strong leader because

Christians, Jews, and animists were fighting for control of the town. He needed a place to go when his uncle died. So he headed toward Yathrib and took control. This journey to Yathrib would be called the Hirjah (migration) and marks the beginning of the Islamic calendar. Muslims start counting time from the Hirjah.[14]

Muhammad took control of the city, which would eventually be renamed Medina (City of the Prophet), built the first mosque there, and became both the spiritual and temporal leader of the town. If one had a spiritual problem, one went to Muhammad. If one had a garbage collection problem, one went to Muhammad. Muhammad was also the head judge, so he settled disputes, and the accounts of these decisions are recorded in the Hadith. Muslims use these accounts in settling disputes in the way the Prophet would have. One problem Muhammad had concerned the Jews in town. Muhammad approached them after his arrival and told them he had it on good authority that the Jewish prophets and patriarchs—Noah, Abraham, Moses—were all Muslims. So he invited the Jews to join Islam. You can imagine the cold reception he received. So Muhammad, who had been praying toward Jerusalem to the north—where the Qur'an said the final judgment would occur—turned his rug south toward Mecca, and Muslims have been praying toward Mecca ever since. Jews continued to make their opinion of Muhammad known. One account in the Hadith said a Jewish woman threw her garbage out her window and hit Muhammad every time he walked by. But one day Muhammad was spared the shower of trash. He grew concerned and sent women up to the lady's apartment, and they discovered she was very ill. So she received medical care.

War with Mecca. Muhammad began attacking Meccan caravans as they traveled around Arabia, taking their goods. Now he had a good reason to attack them: the Meccans had tried to kill him. But he was also after their economic strength, hitting them where it hurt. He also received a revelation from Gabriel to do so, as recorded in the Qur'an:

> Permission to fight has been given to those who are being fought, because they were wronged. Verily, Allah is able to give them victory. They are those who have been evicted from their homes without right and only because they say: Our Lord is Allah.

> —Qur'an, Surah 22:39

FIGURE 3.4 Hand of Fatima with a blessing inscribed on it

There is a debate about whether Muhammad was just redressing a grievance—the Muslims had lost their caravans and possessions when they fled—or whether he was provoking a war. But he did provoke a war. The Meccans gathered Bedouins (promising them part of the loot in the sack of Medina), assembled an army of 10,000, and headed north. But Muhammad learned from his spies that they were coming. So the prophet did something no one had attempted before: he had his troops dig ditches around most of the city. Then he placed archers in the ditches. So when the Meccans arrived with their ladders to scale the city walls, they were stopped by soldiers in the ditches. The Meccans and their allies did not know how to fight someone in a hole. So they pulled back, facing defeat by default because they were running out of food and water in the desert. But Muhammad was not some armchair commander content to sit behind the walls of Medina and stick his tongue out at the Meccans. Instead, he got on his horse and rode out to single-handedly attack 10,000 enemies. Have you ever seen the movie *300*, in which a small group of Spartans stopped the much larger Persian army? Well, they were a bunch of wimps. This was *1*. Fortunately for Muhammad, his tomboy of a daughter, Fatima, took after him on her horse. It was a good thing, too, because the Meccans had a weapon of mass destruction (WMD). Their WMD was a giant who threw boulders, and he never missed. The giant saw Muhammad and his young whelp coming. So he looked around, found a Muhammad-sized boulder, picked it up and—when Muhammad was in range—threw it. And, splat. The boulder knocked the prophet off his horse. The Meccan army charged, finally getting to carve Muhammad up. Fatima, though, swept in on her horse, grabbed her dad, and rode him back into Medina, saving his life. That is why, to this day, Bedouin women wear the "Hand of Fatima" to protect their families, like Fatima had protected dear old dad.

When Muhammad recovered, his followers told them that some Jews had conspired to turn the town over to the Meccans and get rid of Muhammad. Historians do not know if this ever happened, but it was the excuse Muhammad needed to get rid of the quarrelsome Jews. All the Jews were branded as traitors, the men were executed and buried in a long ditch in Medina, and the women and children were sold as slaves.

After two battles with the Meccans, Muhammad's army surrounded Mecca with 10,000 soldiers. The Bedouins joined Muhammad because he was on the winning side. In the Middle Ages, conquering armies had what was considered standard operating procedure: rape, pillage, and burn. Muhammad broke from that tradition, issuing new orders for Muslim armies from that point on. Sieged peoples had two choices: surrender or die. If they surrendered, they had two other choices: convert to Islam or pay a tax. The latter is called zakat, a poor tax. Muslims had to pay it, so Muhammad decreed everyone should. Muhammad did not want forced conversions. He said a forced convert is a poor convert, one you could not trust, particularly in battle. So, Mecca surrendered. Other than executing a few of the leaders he did not like, Muhammad harmed no one in the city or anyone's property. He and his cousin 'Ali walked to the Kaaba, and—with one getting on the other's shoulders—they destroyed the 360 idols in the Kaaba. Then Muhammad emerged from the structure and announced that the Kaaba had been built by Abraham for Allah. The Meccans were relieved: the pilgrimages could continue. Okay, everyone became monotheistic, but money was money.

Death of Muhammad and succession. Muhammad died in 632 at age 63. He had been in poor health and never fully recovered from being poisoned by two of his wives. They were slaves who did not want to be married to him. So with Muhammad's death, a crisis loomed. Was the religion going to die with its founder? After Muhammad's death, one of his companions emerged from the prophet's tent outside Medina to tell the crowd sitting vigil that "the man you know as Muhammad has died. But for those of you who worship Allah, know he lives!" So at that point, the Muslim focus went from Muhammad to Allah, and Islam transformed from a cult to a sect that within 10 years would become a church that would conquer most of the Middle East. After a raucous debate, the Muslims elected a new leader, called a caliph, or successor, to Muhammad. It was Muhammad's friend Abu Bakr.

Dynasty period. But Abu Bakr died within a year, and the second caliph, Umar, ruled from 634–644, conquering Damascus and most of Syria, large parts of Persia (Iran), Jerusalem, and all of Palestine and Egypt before he was assassinated by a Persian slave.

I don't know about you, but dating slaves seems to be a bad idea.

'Uthman, Muhammad's father-in-law, succeeded him and conquered the rest of Persia after a nine-year war. Then 'Ali, Muhammad's cousin and son-in-law (he married Fatima), was the next caliph in 656. But in a power struggle, he was forced to flee to Iraq and was killed in 661. That was the beginning of the split between the Sunni and Shi'a Muslims. We will talk more about that later.

That was also the beginning of the dynasty period that began with the Ummayad dynasty, members of Muhammad's tribe. They conquered most of the known world. The Ummayads expanded their empire to southern France and China. They crossed the Mediterranean and invaded Spain in 711, initiating the dominant Moorish culture for the next eight hundred years. The Muslims' ultimate goal was to conquer Rome.

The Battle of Tours in 732, with Charles Martel leading the Frank army, finally stopped the Muslim advance. So the armies of Islam came to a halt in their European advance. It would not be until centuries later, with the Spanish Reconquista and the Crusades, that Islam would be driven out of Europe.

FIGURE 3.5 Silver platter illustrating the luxury of the dynasty period

Coincidentally, this is where Shiraz wine comes from.[15] A group of homesick soldiers from Shiraz, Persia (now Iran), renamed the conquered lands in southern France after their hometown. The grapes in that region became known as Shiraz grapes, and the wine from those grapes, of course, became known as Shiraz. So at your next cocktail party or beer bash, depending on your social venue, you can impress your family and friends with this tidbit of knowledge. And strangers will be asking for your phone number on a cocktail napkin.

In an inside job, the 'Abbasids took over the Ummayad dynasty. 'Abbasid soldiers were stationed throughout the Ummayad dynasty. At an agreed-upon signal, the 'Abbasids attacked the Ummayad throughout the kingdom. They took over the entire dynasty except for Spain, where the culture of the Cordova Empire grew. In that empire, Muslims and Jews worked together. From this period we have a Jewish Torah written in Arabic so Muslims could read it.

During the Middle Ages, the Muslims brought the works of Greek scientists and philosophers from Europe to the House of Wisdom in Baghdad, Iraq. The House of Wisdom had scholars from all over the known world contributing to many disciplines.

Then a split occurred. The 'Abbasid Muslims did not believe the Spanish were true Muslims, so they invaded Spain, resulting in a Muslim-versus-Muslim conflict. Then a Shi'ite branch occupied Egypt, Syria, and Palestine, creating a third empire that waded into the war. This resulted in Muslims fighting Muslims fighting Muslims.

When Europeans launched the Crusades to retake Jerusalem and other formerly Christian lands, they encountered an unprepared and disorganized Muslim front. Thus, the Crusaders took sides in the Muslim conflict, as did the Muslims, to forward their goals. The Crusades were a combination of Crusader and Muslim armies fighting other Muslim armies. Ultimately, the Fourth Crusade was able to retake Jerusalem and establish a Latin patriarch there for a century.

Then the Sejuk Turks gained power in the Middle East. Sultan Salah-al-Din recaptured Jerusalem from the Crusaders after luring them from their castle stronghold on top of the Mount of Transfiguration and burning them in the fields below. Islam would then spread across north and east Africa and to Indonesia by the 14th century.

Then a catastrophe happened. The Mongols, led by the sons of Genghis Khan, came storming into the Islamic lands. The Mongols were horse-riding barbarians: they lived on their horses, they slept on their horses, they ate on their horses, they ate their horses while riding their horses, and they defecated and procreated on their horses.

The Mongols, who had already conquered China and most of Asia, carved through Islam. The Turks disappeared. Arabia fell to their conquest. They sacked Baghdad, and then they moved on to Syria. When they got to Jerusalem, the Muslim Mamluks of Egypt, former slave soldiers, attacked them and defeated them for the first time in Mongol history. Thus, the Mamluks saved Islam. When they could no longer advance, the Mongols got off their horses for the first time and settled down to rule the Middle East. After a century or two, they converted to Islam.

With the resurgence of Islam, the Mughal Empire established itself in northern India and would eventually conquer most of the subcontinent, bringing Muslim rule to the continent of Hindus. During this time the Mughal emperor Shah Jahan built the Taj Mahal, a tomb, for his favorite wife. The British Empire would eventually end the empire when it took over India in the 19th century.

In the Middle East, the Ottoman Empire in Asia Minor (Turkey) reached the height of its power and influence in the 16th and 17th centuries. The Ottomans conquered most of the area that had been previously controlled by the Muslims, except for Spain. The Spanish King Ferdinand and Queen Isabella reconquered Spain in 1492, the same year they funded Christopher Columbus's journey west. Columbus was convinced the world was round, and the Spanish monarchy hoped he would find a way around the Muslim blockade of the Silk Road in the Middle East and get to India. So Columbus's exploration was the economic part of their war on Islam.

The Ottomans had better luck advancing in Eastern Europe far from Spain. Mehmed II planned to head for Rome through Constantinople, the capital of the Byzantine Empire. Unfortunately, Constantinople was a hard nut to crack. Standing in the way on a peninsula leading to Europe, the city had high walls, a chain across the harbor to keep Muslim ships at bay, and a secret weapon: Greek fire. Historians have speculated what this weapon was. Apparently fired out of a cannon, it stuck to whatever it hit and started a fire. Pouring water on this fire made it burn more. So Mehmed decided to attack the city a different way: by having his troops cut trees down for 30 miles across the Kocaeli Peninsula east of Constantinople. The troops placed the trees as giant rollers on the ground and rolled his navy from the Mediterranean Sea to the Black Sea, where there was not a chain across the harbor. When his navy attacked the city, Mehmed launched an artillery barrage from land using siege cannons, blowing down the walls of Constantinople. Mehmed's army swarmed in and took the city. The Ottomans then converted the second-largest church in the world into the world's largest mosque, Hagia Sophia, and renamed the city "The City" (Istanbul).[16]

After taking Istanbul, Mehmed marched his armies north, conquering Eastern Europe as they headed to Rome. There was no apparent force that could stop them—except for Dracula. Dracula was the title of Vlad Tepes, the ruler of Wallachia in what is now Romania. Using a scorched-earth policy, surprise attacks, and psychological warfare, Vlad Tepes kept the Muslims at bay, slowing their advance into Eastern Europe. The Ottomans never made it to Rome. Vlad Tepes inherited the title Dracula from his father, who had it bestowed on him when the Holy Roman Emperor, Sigismund of Luxembourg, initiated him into the Order of the Dragon, or Drac. Romanians did not have such titles, so they called Vlad Dracula, little Drac, or Drac Jr. Vlad's bloodthirstiness, which included impaling captives on spikes, worked on dissuading the Ottomans from further invasion and caught the imagination of Irish writer Bram Stoker, who transformed Vlad into a bloodthirsty vampire in *Dracula* in 1897. Vlad was also known as Vlad the Impaler.[17] So at your next cocktail party or beer bash, you can say—never mind, nobody likes a know-it-all.

As mentioned earlier, the Ottoman Empire reached its height under Suleiman the Magnificent and Mehemed II, conquering most of North Africa and Hungary. But European colonization began to reduce Islamic holdings in Africa, Asia, and India. As the last Islamic empire, the Ottomans eventually fell after allying with Germany in World War I, and both suffered defeat at the hands of the allies. From its remains come the modern nations of Egypt, Palestine (Israel), Transjordan (Jordan), Syria, Lebanon, and Turkey; the latter was created by the political party of the Young Turks.[18]

Many Muslims blame not only European domination for its political decline but also the weakening of faith among Muslims. Allah only remembers those who remember him (paraphrase of Qur'an 2:152). Only renewal of Islam and its rules, shari'a, would bring about change. This would set up the revival of Islam in modern times, which we will discuss later in this chapter.

Islamic Contributions. Islamic civilizations brought about advances in medicine, math, physics, astronomy, geography, architecture, art, and literature. Many of these advances occurred in the House of Wisdom in Baghdad. During the ninth century, Musa and his sons were major scholars in Baghdad, contributing such developments as Arabic numerals, algebra, trigonometry, and the concept of zero. Zero came out of Indian astronomy, but Muslims applied it to algebra and trigonometry. Before that time, no one who did not own any camels or goats would say they had "zero" animals. You either have one or more or none. One certainly does not have negative two camels. But zero was needed for higher math to make the equations work.[19]

Muslims also developed navigation instruments from translations of the ancient Greeks' astronomical observations. So Islam kept these discoveries and innovations safe during the plague in Europe before they were reintroduced to Europe during the Renaissance.

Modern and Militant Groups

In the late 20th and early 21st centuries, several new Islamic groups have grown, hoping to recapture the glory of the Islamic empires that once ruled the known world. Some of these are peaceful movements welcoming of world change, and some are not. Some gave birth to others.

Wahabbi Movement. This movement sprang from a branch of Sunni Islam founded by Ibn al-Wahabbi (1703–1791) to purify Islam. Al-Wahabbi allied with the House of Sa'ud, and Wahabbism became the official version of Islam in Saudi Arabia when the Sa'uds expanded their kingdom. Saudi Arabia demands a strict, simple lifestyle among its population. Adultery is punished by beheading or stoning. But more modern initiatives, such as allowing women to drive, have been implemented in the kingdom.

Taliban. Led by students of Wahabbism, the Taliban seized power in Afghanistan in 1996 after the expulsion of the Soviets. The Taliban implemented strict rules in the areas under its control, such as requiring women to wear burkas, banning music and TV, and not allowing girls to attend school. The group lost power in Afghanistan after U.S. forces attacked and invaded the country in 2001 following the 9/11 terrorists attacks, when the Taliban government refused to give up al-Qaeda members. By 2018, the Taliban was still fighting coalition forces.

Al-Qaeda. Al-Qaeda was founded by Saudi and Wahabbi Osama bin Laden after he fought with the Taliban against the Soviets in Afghanistan in the 1980s. Al-Qaeda means "base"— literally, "database" of names of potential allies bin Laden had collected on his computer. It wages war in Wahabbi tradition against un-Islamic influences. It views the United States, as well as the U.S.-backed Saudi Arabian leadership, as the principal evil threatening Islam. It took responsibility for the 9/11 attacks as well as other terrorist activities. Since bin Laden was killed by American forces in 2011, al-Qaeda has grown weaker, though one of his sons, Hamza bin Laden, has reportedly taken over a large part of the group.

ISIS, the Islamic State in Iraq and Syria. Also known as the Islamic State in Iraq and the Levant, or Islamic State, ISIS began when a group broke off from al-Qaeda, led by former al-Qaeda member Abu Bakr al-Baghdadi (changing his name to Al-Khalifah Ibrahim). He established a caliphate in Syria and Iraq. ISIS has killed dozens of people at a time and has carried out public executions, crucifixions, and other brutal acts when it has moved into new areas. In addition to regions in Syria, it originally took over large swaths of northern and western Iraq before coalition forces, including those with U.S. military support, reclaimed all of the regions under its control. It now instigates terrorist attacks using underground groups. ISIS has seen itself as an apocalyptic movement bringing down the enemies of Islam by summoning Jesus as a prophet of Islam.

Muslim Brotherhood. Founded in Egypt by Hasan al-Banna in 1928, it was a movement created to purge Islamic societies of negative secular and Western influences. The Muslim Brotherhood was not violent until the assassination of al-Banna by Egyptian secret police. It has been banned several times by the Egyptian government. It has also been a social services agency, supplying food, medical care, and housing for the poor who were neglected by the Egyptian government; hence its local popularity. The group won the presidency with Mohammed Morsi in 2012, but its government was overthrown by a military coup. Members are now being persecuted by the Egyptian government. Muslim Brotherhood members have responded with terrorist attacks.

Hamas. Hamas, an acronym for Harakat Al-Muquawama Al-Islamiya fi Filistin (Islamic Resistance Movement in Palestine), was founded by Muslim Brotherhood members in the 1980s during the first Palestinian intifada ("uprising") in Israel. Hamas's goal is to free Palestine from the Jews through military action. One of its basic goals is the destruction of Israel. Centered in the Gaza Strip, Hamas won a majority of seats in the Palestinian government in early 2006. But civil war broke out between Hamas and other Palestinians affiliated with Fatah, the party of the Palestinian presidency.

Islamic Republic of Iran. The current government in Iran was founded in 1979 by Shi'ites overthrowing the pro-Western government of the Baath Party, led by Mohammad Reza Shah. The Shah went into exile, and the victorious Shi'ites, led by Ayatollah Khomeini, began an attempt to purify Iran of secular and Western influences. Iran also has called for the destruction of Israel. In recent years, Iran has had to face an international trade embargo due to its nuclear ambitions. However, in 2016, the UN trade embargo was lifted when Iran agreed to suspend its weapons program. That agreement, though, is still being debated.

Hezbollah. Hezbollah, or the "Army of Allah," was formed in Lebanon by Shi'ites swearing loyalty to Iranian leader Ayatollah Khomeini in the war against American, European, and especially Israeli interests. It is a state within a state, providing social services to residents, and it has taken over most of the Lebanese government. It has been fighting a border war with Israel that flares up and dies down from time to time. Hezbollah has also received support from the Syrian government in its fight against al-Qaeda, which is Sunni, in Syria.

JUI. The Jamaiyat-i-Ulama-i-Islam (JUI) has its source in the Muslim-driven division of Pakistan from India after the latter's independence from England. The JUI is a group of militant Sunnis in Pakistan who have been dedicated to creating a puritanical Muslim government. It is violently, as well as legislatively, at odds with the secular-leaning Pakistani government.[20]

Islamic Scripture

Qur'an

"Qur'an" literally means "reciting, recitation" because that was how Gabriel delivered it to Muhammad. Muslims believe the Qur'an is the direct and literal word of Allah: every word, punctuation mark, and so on. It is eternal and irrevocable. The original text sits in the lap of Allah. The Qur'an is a guide to individual and collective life. It has rules for individual behavior and rules for trade and government. The Qur'an does not envision a separation of religion and state. It conceives of the state as run by religious rulers. The Qur'an cannot be translated: Arabic is the language of Allah's revelation. A Qur'an in any other language is just a translation and someone's opinion about what the Qur'an means.

The Qur'an has 114 surahs (chapters) and runs about as long as the Christian New Testament. The surahs are organized (after the opening) roughly in terms of length. So the second surah is the largest, and the last is one of the smallest. Each surah has a name based on some word unique to the surah ("The Cow," "The Ant"). The Qur'an includes hymns of praise to Allah, warnings of the Day of Judgment, and guidelines. With the Hadith (sayings and actions of Muhammad), the Qur'an is the basis of the principles of law in Muslim societies.

The way the Qur'an was written down made it difficult to assemble all of its parts after Muhammad's death. As mentioned before, it was written down on stones and bones along with the prophet's followers memorizing parts of it. Tradition says that the second caliph, 'Umar, feared that some of it would be lost as followers died, so he directed Muhammad's scribe, Zayd, to copy it down onto sheets of equal size, gathering it from its many sources. The sheets were passed down to one of Muhammad's widows, Hafsa. But during Caliph 'Uthman's military campaign, arguments broke out among his soldiers about Muhammad's sayings, because only Hafsa had a copy. So 'Uthman commissioned Zayd and several others to again create copies of the Qur'an and send it to the troops.[21] This became the Qur'an that Muslims use today.[22] However, civil war would break out among Muslims who remembered Hafsa's version differently, leading to divisions in Islam.

FIGURE 3.6 Tubes such as these held passages from the Qur'an that were carried with the Bedouins of the Arabian desert.

Hadith

Although there is only one Qur'an, there are hundreds of Hadith. The Hadith are the sayings and actions of Muhammad written down by his companions or other people to whom the companions related the stories. The reliability and historical accuracy of a hadith is determined by the *isnad*, which are the names of whom told whom about the story that is at the beginning of each hadith. The closer to a companion of the Prophet the *isnad* gets, the more reliable it is considered for interpretation of Shari'a ("way"), Islamic law. There are six collections known as the most reliable, called the Sihah Sittah, or Six Reliable Works. The Hadith range from mundane to monumental. One account has a man inviting people to a wedding and a description of what was served—"bread and meat"[23]—whereas another explains how Muhammad received his revelation from Gabriel: "Read in the name of thy Lord Who created—He created man from a clot—Read and thy Lord is most Honorable."[24]

Beliefs of Islam

The very first chapter of the Qur'an, the holy book of Islam, is called the "Opening." It pretty much sums up the theology and worldview of Islam, which is why it is the first chapter of the Qur'an. All the other chapters, which are called suras or surhas, are arranged by length: longest to some of the shortest.

The first verse of the Opening (see the quote at the beginning of the chapter) describes God's relationship with his people. Allah, which in Arabic means "the God," is "beneficial" to believers. God gives you what you need, not what you want. The reason you may not have a red Ferrari is that God knows you cannot afford the insurance or the payments, much less the repair bills. The conveyance you now use to get around is enough. God is also merciful: he is not an ogre god who plays Whac-a-Mole at Chuck E. Cheese's: "There's a sinner—whack! There's another one—whack!"

The second verse states that Islam is true monotheism, which is the belief in one god: "All praise is due to Allah, the Lord of the Worlds." Notice the "s" on the end of "Worlds." Allah is the lord of the whole universe. This is true monotheism. Muslims say Christians and Jews also worship Allah; they just do not realize it, but Allah is the only god around.

The third verse states that Allah is the "master of the Day of Judgment." This is very similar to Christians' Judgment Day. The good will go to paradise (heaven), and the evil will go to hell. And the judge will be the same as in Christianity: Jesus. For those scratching their heads about Jesus being the judge, this will be explained later. And judgment will occur in Jerusalem, which is why Muslims initially prayed toward Jerusalem.

The next verse states, "keep us on the right path." This has been a point of contention for Muslims for centuries. Muslims believe Allah micromanages everything a person does. There is an expression: "If Allah wills it." In the Middle East, the author discovered this usually means "no." For example, if someone were to say, "May we go over there?", the answer is usually "If Allah wills it," which means "no." But among Muslims, nothing happens unless Allah wills it. This is called predestation. For instance, some of you are going to paradise, and some of you are not going to graduate. Allah has already decided the outcome: there is nothing you can do about it. But Muslims also believe in free will. One can reject Allah: the Qur'an clearly states that. So how is it possible that predestation—the idea that God has decided one's every move—and free will—the idea that one can do what one wants to—coexist in Islam? As mentioned, this has led to arguments among Muslims for years. There is an answer, and again, we will come to that later, though obviously it is not a commonly accepted answer, in that Muslims are still arguing.

The last verse—"The path of those upon whom you have bestowed favors, not the path of those upon whom your wrath is brought down, nor of those who go astray"—is a no-brainer. Because God is directing your life, would you rather have a great life and go to paradise or a miserable life and go to hell? Not many people would be saying, "Well, that hell sounds pretty good."

According to Islam, humanity was created from a single soul, Allah's breath. This is why Sufis want to return to that one soul. God creates humans with no original sin, so they do not need to be baptized, as in Christianity, and people are created with a disposition toward virtue, knowledge, and beauty.

Muslims believe in predestination. Allah controls the daily life of humans. There is the expression "If Allah wills ..." ("inshallah"), it will happen. But Muslims also believe in the concept of free will. The Qur'an clearly states a person can reject Allah. That is why predestination and free will have been in conflict in Islam over centuries. Sin happens when humans are distracted from Allah's will by jinn (evil spirits appealing to earthly nature) or by Iblis, the equivalent of Satan.

There are two goals in Islam. One goal is paradise or heaven. No Muslim wants to go to hell. The Qur'an says that 72 perpetual virgins will serve faithful males who go to paradise. One scholar more recently interpreted the Qur'an as stating that 72 white grapes (not virgins) are awaiting faithful males, because grapes were a delicacy at the time. The newspaper that ran the story, *The Tampa Tribune*, had the headline: "Martyrs in for Letdown." There are also heavenly delights for women, but they are not as explicit as those for men. The dead will sleep until resurrection day. Muslim tradition has the good dead lying faceup so they can contemplate paradise, while the evil dead are lying facedown to contemplate hell.

The other goal for Muslims is the "House of Islam," a mandate to convert the world to Islam. Remember, Islam indirectly means "peace." So if people stay outside the House of Islam, they live in the House or Abode of War, where they will get what they deserve.

Umma means "people." It means all faithful Muslims are members of an international Muslim community. It is an attempt to overcome nationalism. Muhammad used it to unite the Bedouins of the desert. So a person is a Muslim first and the nationality of their country second. This ties in with the House of Islam because Muslims are not allowed to fight brother Muslims. Islam's sects are able to fight other sects by declaring their enemies are not true Muslims. This has been the case between the Sunni and Shi'a.

The House of Islam is focused on submission to the will of Allah, which is what the word Islam means. This is also known as "remembering" Allah: true joy in life will come from acting on the basis of a relationship of submission to Allah and living a righteous life.

The foundation of the Muslim faith is summarized by the Five Pillars. These can be compared to the 10 commandments for Christians and Jews.

Five Pillars

- *Shahadah*, creed: "There is no God but Allah, and Muhammad is his messenger (or prophet)"

- *Salat*: daily prayer (five times a day)

- *Zakat* ("purity, integrity"): almsgiving to the poor, which can be between 2½ and 10 percent of disposable wealth

- *Sawm*: fasting during the daylight hours of the month of Ramadan

- *Hajj*: pilgrimage to Mecca once in lifetime if physically or financially able

There is a sixth unofficial pillar, and that is *jihad*. When non-Muslims hear the word "jihad," they may often picture a terrorist with an AK-47 assault rifle breaking down their door in the middle of the night. Well, that is not entirely untrue. But there is another element. The word jihad means "striving" or "exertion," and there are two types. Great jihad is struggle against inner evil, a personal struggle. Muslims believe a person will be tempted until they die and resisting Iblis and the jinn is a person's duty. This is called great jihad because all Muslims are called to it. Lesser jihad is the armed conflict in defense of faith against the perceived enemies of Islam, a community struggle. If a person is killed during lesser jihad, he or she becomes a martyr and goes directly to paradise.[25]

Allah is separate from creation. Muhammad stipulated this to wean Arabs away from worshiping nature as God or gods. But God's "signs" are in nature, and human reason can discover them through science (examining the natural world). Where there is conflict, our understanding is incomplete. We need to go back to the laboratory or the Qur'an and see where the disconnect occurred, because there should not be one. In the interest of full disclosure, there is a conflict between creationists and evolutionists in Islam, as in other parts of society.

Muslims believe that God created the world to be enjoyed. There is no asceticism, or denying yourself creature comforts. Other than not drinking alcohol and not eating pork, the world is yours to enjoy: get rich, buy homes and yachts, and so on—all of this is perfectly fine. Men are allowed up to four wives, if they can afford them. Women are only allowed one husband.

Muslims are monotheistic, as mentioned before. They believe that Allah is supreme, is sacred, transcends all, and is the same as the God of Christians and Jews. That is why Muslims say Christians and Jews worship Allah but just don't know it. However, they acknowledge that Christians do not have the same view of God. Muslims say God cannot be divided nor have a son. So they disregard the concept of a Trinity and the belief that Jesus is the son of God.

FIGURE 3.7 Minaret from which issues the call to prayer five times a day

FIGURE 3.8 A woman's dowry, here represented in coins, is sewn into her face mask among Bedouin women.

Mosques

Islam is not a temple-oriented religion. Muslims pray five times a day wherever they are. But Fridays are when Muslims are required to pray at the mosque because this is the holy day of Islam. An imam, a community member chosen for his knowledge and piety, leads believers in prayer. He is not a priest, because he is not ordained.

The call to prayer is by human voice, or a recording of it, from the mosque minaret. God said he preferred the human voice to a bell in a dream Zayd had. The mosque itself is sparse, with no furniture in the *musalla*, which means "place of worship." Shoeless faithful stand and kneel on rugs or carpeting facing the *mihrab*, the niche in a mosque's wall that shows the direction toward Mecca. Men and women worship separately, with women usually behind the men. A raised *minbar* (a kind of pulpit) is where speeches and sermons are given. Outside the *musalla*, in various forms—fountains to bathrooms—are the oblation areas where worshippers wash their hands and feet before entering the musalla.[26]

Women in Islam

Muhammad raised the status of women, but not as high as that of men. At the time, women were practically slaves, owned by their husbands or fathers. Muhammad outlawed female infanticide, as it was customary to kill girls in favor of boys. He taught that women were not property, so they could not be bought and sold as wives. He limited men to having four wives, but only if they could afford them. Husbands also had to be able to support their wives, and Muhammad believed more than four was untenable. Muhammad had more than that, but he was Islam's prophet and had special permission from Allah. Divorce was easy. A man just had to tell his wife that he was divorcing her to make the divorce final. But a divorced woman retained her dowry, the money that the groom gave to the bride at their wedding, so she would have money of her own. This was so a divorced woman would not be left destitute.[27]

Islamic Taboos

Halal is food that Muslims are allowed to eat, and this includes most food. Haram is food that is forbidden, such as pork, dogs, birds and beasts of prey, donkeys, mules, and alcohol. The proper way to slaughter animals for food is by cutting their throats and invoking the name of God.

Dogs are unclean and can only guard herds or property. Cats are okay as pets.

Muslims are not allowed to gamble. But in the interest of full disclosure, the Palestinian National Authority had started to build a casino in Jericho. However, it never opened, due to the Palestinian intifada (uprising) in 2000.

Branches of Islam

Islam is not a monolithic religion with a unified membership under a particular leader. It is a group of competing denominations and sects. They interpret the Qur'an and Hadith as well as Islamic law differently.

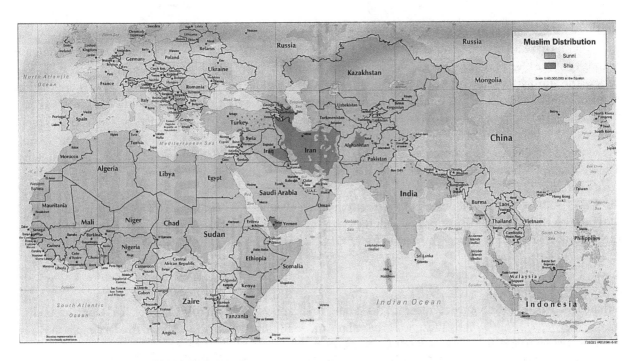

FIGURE 3.9 Map of Islamic branches

Sunni

Sunni make up about 85 percent of Muslims in the world. Their name comes from *sunna*, which means "way, manner of acting." They appeal to the Qur'an and the Hadith when interpreting Shari'a. They also use consensus (*ijma'*). There are different schools of Sunni, depending on how they interpret Shari'a.

- Hanifite is the earliest Sunni school of Islam, dating back to eighth-century Iraq. They used analogy and rational judgment when interpreting Shari'a. Analogy means comparing one example with another. For instance, one may want to know if the Qur'an permits sniffing crack cocaine. Well, there is no mention of cocaine in the Qur'an, because it is a modern drug. But the Qur'an prohibits the use of mind-altering alcohol. Cocaine also alters the mind. Therefore, by analogy, the Qur'an prohibits the use of cocaine.

- The Malikite school is more liberal, starting with the Qur'an and the Hadith before using consensus and analogy to interpret Shari'a.

- In the Shafi'ite school, equal authority is given to the Qur'an and the Hadith, but members tend toward the Hadith in disputes because Muhammad's settled disputes are recorded in the Hadith. This school deemphasizes reason but is stronger on consensus.

- The most conservative school, the Hanbalite, maintains that the Qur'an holds supreme authority, with the Hadith the only other recognized source of authority. This school also stresses individual responsibility to dictates of Shari'a.

Shi'a

"Shi'a" means "Party of 'Ali," and a member of the Shi'a is a Shi'ite. This Islamic group makes up about 15 percent of Muslims in the world. They believe that the fourth caliph, 'Ali, was the first legitimate successor of Muhammad, because Shi'ites believe one has to be related to Muhammad to be a successor. 'Ali was Muhammad's cousin.

The division between the Shi'a and the Sunni occurred when 'Ali was killed and his son Husain was executed. The commemoration of Husain's death is an important annual festival among the Shi'a, who cut themselves with knives and swords and whip themselves, grieving as if Husain had died the day before. Because of this, Shi'ites place a high importance on martyrdom for true faith.

Proper successors in the Shi'a tradition are imams ("he who stands before") rather than caliphs. They believe their imams have an infallible supernatural ability to interpret Shari'a, and they do not believe in the supreme authority of the Qur'an. The holy book of Islam is considered to be suspect because 'Ali is missing from it. Shi'ites believe the Sunni have removed Ali's name from the scripture, so their imams are able to point out where 'Ali was mentioned before his name was removed. Of course, Sunnis disagree that 'Ali was ever in the Qur'an.

In the Shi'a tradition, the imam is a central figure, such as in the case of the Seveners or Twelvers. Seveners believe there will be seven imams before the end of the world. They believe that the seventh imam is already living in the world but has not yet revealed himself. The Twelvers believe the same thing, except there will be 12 imams. The final imam, whether it be the seventh or 12th, will return as Mahdi ("the guided one"), or messiah, to restore purity of faith.

Shi'a also have men called Ayatollah ("sign or reflection of Allah"). These are men so righteous and steeped in true faith they can make independent judgments that carry the authority of imams. An example of this was the Ayatollah Khomeini of Iran, who helped found the Islamic Republic of Iran.

Sufi

Sufi means "wool clad," because members of this branch of Islam were known to wear wool. It is a mystical movement. They rejected the worldly lifestyle of the caliph and maintained that Muhammad lived a simple spiritual lifestyle without the riches and power of his successors.

Mansur al-Hallaj (858–922), a Sufi teacher, was dismembered after proclaiming unity with Allah: "I am the Truth," which was interpreted as him saying he claimed to be Allah. The theology behind his statement, though, was orthodox even by Sunni standards. Sufis believe that their ultimate goal is to become one with God. For instance, if water is absorbed by a sponge, does it not become the sponge? If a person is absorbed by God, does he or she not become God? That is the premise behind al-Hallaj's statement, which is compatible with the Islamic idea that people come from one soul, Allah. Sufis were striving to return to Allah in paradise. But the martyrdom of al-Hallaj and his followers forced the movement underground into secret brotherhoods.

Sufis pray to their saintly dead (wali), something that most Muslims do not do. Members of the community focus on becoming fakir ("poor" in Arabic) or darwish (Persian) from which whirling dervishes get their name. Calling themselves Mawlawis, they whirl in a meditative state.

The persecution of Sufis ended with the teachings of Al-Ghazzali (1058–1111), a former Sunni professor at the University of Baghdad. He was able to synthesize Sunni teachings with Sufi mysticism and explained the idea behind being absorbed by God. Thus, the mass executions of Sufis as heretics ended. Al-Ghazzali also took on Avicenna (980–1037) in a series of debates. Avicenna believed God could be proven through logic. Al-Ghazzali argued that this type of philosophy was alien to Islam and that faith was needed to discover God. Al-Ghazzali eventually won, and he put an end to the study of philosophy in Sunni Islam.[28]

Black Muslims

The mysterious Wallace Fard founded the Nation of Islam, the first Black Muslim group, in Detroit in 1930. He disappeared while in Detroit police custody and no one, including the FBI, could find him. Elijah Muhammad took over after Fard's disappearance and said that Fard was Allah himself who had come down in human form and returned to paradise. Muhammad urged Blacks to withdraw from White society and create their own institutions.

The Nation of Islam mosques established across the United States, mainly in African American areas because only Blacks were allowed to join.

The Black Muslim myth (religious story) is that humanity was originally Black, then an evil scientist named Yakub rebelled against Allah and created the evil White race. So Blacks must purge themselves of evil White influences by not using any intoxicants or tobacco, not engaging in illicit sex, praying five times a day, and observing a strict lifestyle and a pure diet.

Malcolm X, who dropped his last name because he said it belonged to slave masters, rose in the movement in the 1950s. He was converted to Islam while serving time in prison for burglary. He had also been a pimp and a drug dealer. Upon his release, he became a charismatic and militant exponent of the movement, advocating violence against White oppressors.

Malcolm X had a change of heart, though, when he made a hajj after the Saudi Arabian authorities let him into Mecca after determining he was a Muslim. After the hajj, Malcolm felt all people should be able to join the movement. He saw people of all races who were Muslim and thought the Nation of Islam was being xenophobic. So he returned to the United States a changed man. He told Elijah Muhammad of his dream to open the group to all Muslims. But Muhammad had it on good authority from Fard that Whites were evil. Malcolm then accused Elijah Muhammad of illicit sex, which turned out to be true. But for that reason, he was excommunicated and, when he was speaking in a theater, gunned down by two Black men, one a member of the Nation of Islam.

Malcolm's daughter says a former calypso singer, now named Louis Farrakhan, ordered the hit on her father. Farrakhan denies this, though he said he did not like the direction Malcolm was going.

After Elijah Muhammad's death in 1975, his son, Wallace Muhammad, took over as head of the group and did what Malcolm wanted, opening the group to all races, and renamed it the World Community of al-Islam in the West, and then later, American Muslim Mission.

Farrakhan objected to this new direction and organized a Nation of Islam for Blacks only. He sponsored the Million Man March in Washington, DC, in 1995 to emphasize that Black men must care for their children.[29]

Baha'i

It was founded in 1844 by Sufi-influenced Iranian Shi'ite Mirza Ali Muhammad, who proclaimed he was Bab-ub-Din ("gate of the faith"). He was a Twelver and claimed to be the imam who came to purify Islam as the Mahdi. For this reason, he was thrown in prison and executed. He is buried outside Haifa, Israel, where the Baha'i has its international headquarters. He was succeeded in 1852 by Mirza Husayn Ali, who proclaimed himself in 1863 a prophet and successor to Moses, Jesus, and Muhammad. Followers called him Bahu'u'llah ("the glory of God") and his religion Baha'i ("glory") Faith. Baha'u'llah spent the rest of his life imprisoned and persecuted. He was succeeded by his son, Abdul Baha ("servant of glory"; 1844–1921), who established branches in the United States and developed the teachings of his father.

Abdul Baha was succeeded by his son, Shoghi Effendi ("guardian of the cause"). After his death, the Universal House of Justice took over, but this created dissent among members who believed that only members of Balu'u'llah's family should be the head of the religion.

Although the Baha'i began as a branch of Shi'a Islam, it no longer considers itself Muslim. The Baha'i believe that all religions are true because they come from the same source: God. They also believe that God reveals himself to a prophet in virtually every age, not just during the time of Muhammad. Like Islam, the Baha'i believe modern science and religion must cooperate. Followers also believe in world peace, universal education, and a universal language so nations and people can get along. However, the Baha'i are nonpartisan, have no political party affiliation, and will not give money for political purposes.[30]

Holidays

The **Feast of Fast-Breaking** ('Id al-Fitr) follows Ramadan when Muslims break their month-long fast. All are required to break the fast, and those who have food are required to give it to the poor so they can also break the fast.

The **Feast of Sacrifice** ('Id al-Adha), during the Hajj, commemorates Abraham sacrificing a goat rather than Ishmael. Muslims believe Abraham almost sacrificed Ishmael, not Isaac, as stated in the Jewish and Christian scriptures.

New Year is the month of Muharram, believed to be the month of the Hijrah, the migration.

Muhammad's birthday (Mawlid an-Nabi) is the 12th day of the third month, although not all Muslims observe it.

There are other holidays that are not universal, such as those of the Sufis and Shi'a.

ENDNOTES

1   M. Lipka, "Muslims and Islam: Key Findings in the U.S. and Around the World," Pew Research Center, 2016, http://www.pewresearch.org/fact-tank/2016/07/22/muslims-and-islam-key-findings-in-the-u-s-and-around-the-world/.

2   "10 Countries With the Largest Muslim Populations, 2010 and 2050," Pew Research Center, http://www.pewforum.org/2015/04/02/muslims/pf_15-04-02_projectionstables74/

3   Lipka, "Muslims and Islam."

4   Lipka, "Muslims and Islam."

5   Lipka, "Muslims and Islam."

6   "Pre-Islamic Arabia," https://pdfs.semanticscholar.org/9edd/f4ac0a15ea6ecac94c0c580c52bedf9da938.pdf.

7   M. Kahn, *Islamic Medicine* ([need city of publication here]: Routledge, 2010), file:///Users/ellenrgorman/Downloads/9781134564712_googlepreview%20(1).pdf.

8   A. Knysh, *Islam in Historical Perspective* (New York: Pearson, 2011).

9   R. Bell, *The Origin of Islam in its Christian Environment,* Frank Cass & Co., 1968, file:///Users/ellenrgorman/Downloads/9781136260674_googlepreview.pdf.

10 Ahmed, Ahmed, *Discovering Islam* ([city of publication] : Routledge, 2003).

11 Ahmed, *Discovering Islam.*

12 *Islam: Empire of Faith.* PBS video.

13 "Muhammad's Biography (Part 3 of 12): The First Revelations," Islam Religion.com, 2013, https://www.islam-religion.com/articles/183/muhammad-biography-part-3/.

14 Ibraham Syed, "The Significance of the Hijrah (622 CE)" History of Islam, 2017, https://historyofislam.com/contents/the-age-of-faith/the-significance-of-the-hijrah-622-ce/.

15 Anahita Shams, "Does Shiraz Wine Come from Iran?" BBC Persian, 2017, https://www.bbc.com/news/world-middle-east-38771806.

16 "Islam From The Beginning To 1300," International World History Project, http://history-world.org/islam4.htm.

17 Matthias Kessler, director, *Dracula: The True Story,* 1997, Langbein & Skalnik.

18 "Collapse of the Ottoman Empire, 1918-1920," Ministry for Culture and Heritage, last modified January 13, 2016, https://nzhistory.govt.nz/war/ottoman-empire/collapse.

19 *House of Islam,* American Museum of Natural History, https://www.amnh.org/exhibitions/traveling-the-silk-road/take-a-journey/baghdad/house-of-wisdom.

20 John Moore, "The Evolution of Islamic Terrorism: an Overview," Frontline, PBS, 2014, https://www.pbs.org/wgbh/pages/frontline/shows/target/etc/modern.html.

21 Knysh, *Islam in Historical Perspective.*

22 Esposito [citation incomplete]

23 Esposito [insert shortened form of citation above]

24 Esposito [insert shortened form of citation above]

25 "Jihad: A Misunderstood Concept from Islam—What Jihad Is, and Is Not," The Islamic Supreme Council of America, http://www.islamicsupremecouncil.org/understanding-islam/legal-rulings/5-jihad-a-misunderstood-concept-from-islam.html?start=9.

26 Jeffrey Brodd et al., *Invitation to World Religions* (Oxford: [publisher name] , 2015).

27 Jeffrey Brodd et al., *Invitation to World Religions.*

28 W. Young, *The World's Religions,* 4th ed. (New York: Pearson, 2013).

29 "Nation of Islam," Southern Poverty Law Center, https://www.splcenter.org/fighting-hate/extremist-files/group/nation-islam.

30 "Bahá'u'lláh and His Covenant," Bahai.org, http://www.bahai.org/beliefs/bahaullah-covenant/.

CREDIT

JUDAISM

LEARNING OBJECTIVES

1. Understand why the Jews consider the area of Palestine their homeland
2. See how and why the concept and title of God changes in Judaic history
3. Explain the messages of the prophets.
4. Understand the Jewish scripture
5. Know why each holiday is celebrated
6. Examine what is a threat to Judaism today

> I will make you into a great nation,
> and I will bless you;
> I will make your name great,
> and you will be a blessing.
>
> I will bless those who bless you,
> and whoever curses you I will curse;
> and all peoples on earth
> will be blessed through you.
>
> —Gen. 12:2-3

Jewish Statistics

Estimates are that there were about 14.5 million Jews in the world in 2017. Israel has the largest Jewish population of any country in the world, with about 6.5 million, or 44 percent of all Jews in the world. The United States has about 40 percent of the world's Jewish population, with 5.7 million Jews.

Reform Judaism is the largest denomination of American Jews (about 38 percent) but has only a tiny presence in Israel. Conservative Judaism is the second-largest U.S. denomination (about 33 percent), and Orthodox the third (about 22 percent). According to opinion polls, half of all Israeli Jews consider themselves secular, around 35 percent consider themselves non-denominationally religious, and 15–20 percent consider themselves Orthodox or Ultra-Orthodox.[1]

Jewish Myth

The Jewish religion originated among the Hebrew tribes in the Middle East about four thousand years ago. The Jewish scripture, called the Tanakh (part myth, part history), relates the Jewish creation myth (which it shares with Christianity): God created Adam (man) and Eve (woman) in the Garden of Eden, but they were expelled for disobedience. Scholars do not know if there were two people or two groups of men and women, because Adam literally means man, and Eve literally means woman. To further muddy the picture, there are two creation accounts in its first book, Genesis. The first concerns Adam and Eve, who disobeyed God in the Garden of Eden. A second account, also ancient, merely states that "When God created man, he made him in the likeness of God, and he created them male and female. When they were created, he blessed them and named them man" (Gen. 5:1b-3). The Bible also mentions giants walking around. So exactly what happened back in the beginning of humanity is not really known, in that we have no living eyewitnesses.

Then God decided to hit the redo button—the "select all and delete" command—because earth had become so evil. So because of human sin, God destroyed earth—except for Noah, his extended family, and animals—with a flood. Noah may have been the earliest investor, because he kept his stock afloat while the whole world was in liquidation. God gave Noah and his descendants the rainbow to show he would never flood the world again. However, the rainbow policy does not cover coastal areas in case of global warming.

Judaism's History

Abraham 's agreement with God is seen as the beginning of the historical accounts of Judaism because the places and cities that historians knew actually existed are part of the narrative. Abraham came from Ur, and although several places claim to be that ancient Ur, historians believe Ur existed. Abraham made the first oral covenant with God, which made the Hebrews the promised people because Abraham was willing to sacrifice his son Isaac. Abraham's encounter with God was based on geography. People at the time believed gods ruled different areas. So Abraham did not bring his gods from Ur but worshiped the local god, El. El means "god." Abraham called him El Shaddai, which some scholars translate as "God of the Mountain." This encounter was unusual in the ancient world, because people usually picked their gods. This God picked Abraham (Genesis 17).

God's name changes when Moses encounters him in a burning bush. God identifies himself as Yahweh, which translates as "I am" (Exodus 3:14). So Hebrews started calling God that, using a tetragrammaton, four letters: YHWH. This follows the Jewish tradition of not naming God but addressing him by a title because naming someone gives one power over him or her, such as Adam naming the animals. After Moses (with Yahweh's help) liberated the Hebrews from Egypt, he received the first written covenant, the Torah (also the name of the first five books in the Tanakh), the Ten Commandments. Well, he actually ended up with the Ten Commandments 2.0, because he destroyed the original copy Yahweh had made for him when he caught the Hebrews worshipping a golden calf. So he had to carve his own set.

Moses later wandered with the Jews in the desert with the Ark of the Covenant, the symbol of God's throne. This ark, which carried the Ten Commandments, manna that Yahweh fed the Hebrews in the desert, and the staff of Aaron (which turned into a snake in Pharaoh's court, was used as a weapon to fry anyone who touched it, and afflicted plagues upon the enemy). It was instrumental in bringing down the walls of Jericho. Then it mysteriously disappeared before the Babylonian Captivity. James Strange, a professor at the University of South Florida, Tampa, found a stone replica of what might be the ark in Capernaum, Israel.

Promised Land. When the Hebrews finally got to the Promised Land, the land of Canaan, they found other people living there. Canaan was home to the Hittites, Moabites, Canaanites, and mosquito bites, and the Hebrews had to fight them to carve out a kingdom. Their charismatic king, David, conquered Jerusalem and made it his capital. But it fell to his son, Solomon, to build the first temple for the Ark of the Covenant (1 Kings).

The Hebrews started quarreling among their 12 tribes, so they split apart to prevent war from breaking out. Ten tribes would become the northern kingdom of Israel, and the other two formed the southern kingdom, called Judea or Judah, where Jerusalem was located. Foreigners called the Hebrews of Judah "Jews." Eventually, they started calling themselves that (1 Kings).

When the Hebrews moved into the land of Canaan, they started backsliding. They intermarried with the Hittites, Moabites, and Canaanites and began worshipping other gods, such as Ba'al, a fertility god. There is even a story that King Manasseh put a pagan idol in the temple where the ark was supposed to be (2 Kings 21:7)! That would be like painting a target on you and yelling at Yahweh, "Hey, smite me!" People hit. God smites. But Yahweh forestalled the smiting and sent prophets instead. Prophets do not foretell the future but are mouthpieces of God.

Prophets. Two of the first Hebrew prophets were Elijah and Elisha. They were northern-kingdom prophets in Israel. Elijah decided to take the battle right to the followers of Ba'al. Elijah challenged the prophets of Ba'al to a sudden-death showdown on Mount Carmel. Elijah told the priests to build a pile of wood and that he would build a similar pile of wood. Whose god lit the wood first won. The loser would die. This was a real sudden-death showdown. Elijah, to be sporting, told the Ba'al priests they could go first. So he sat in his easy chair and read his issue of *A Prophet Quarterly*. The prophets of Ba'al worked feverishly but couldn't get their pile lit. Around noon, Elijah challenged them, saying maybe if they yelled louder they could wake up their god. Later, Elijah got up and called the Israelites, telling them to fill their jars with water and wet his pile. It was saturated. Then the prophet asked Yahweh to show them who was boss (paraphrased), and Elijah's pile went "whoosh" up in flame (2 Kings). A statue of Elijah cutting the throats of the Ba'al prophets sits on Mount Carmel in the courtyard of the Carmelite nuns.

Elisha was known to slaughter idol worshippers wholesale. When a group of youth insulted him, a bear appeared and ate them. Lesson: do not mess with someone who has a pet bear.

Amos was also a prophet of the northern kingdom (Israel). His big beef, or goat, was that social injustice was a covenant violation. The merchants of the cities had been shafting the goat herders by not giving them what the goats were worth. They had been doing it to the little guy, which breaks a commandment ("Thou shall not steal"), as well as worshipping other gods. Amos also spoke against national apostasy: Israelites were worshipping other gods wholesale. Yahweh was sick of it.

Hosea was a northern prophet and a native, unlike Amos. He was a literary prophet and wrote in the form of stories. And he compared Israel to an unfaithful wife. Let us bring this story up to modern parlance for better understanding. There was this sugar daddy. This guy had cash out the wazoo. He burned cash in the fireplace in the winter to stay warm. He had more money than he had uses for. He had a wife who loved pink. She had hundreds of pink dresses, pantsuits, shoes, and bags that matched. She had three pink cars: a Rolls, a Mercedes, and a Maserati. When she went shopping, he would hand her a stack of credit cards: "Go knock yourself out, honey. No limit." One day, he was sitting in his blue

FIGURE 4.1 A modern sculpture by Italian artist Giovanni Fantoni of the Brazen Serpent, depicting the one set up by Moses, sits on Mount Nebo, marking the place where Moses viewed the Promised Land.

FIGURE 4.2 A statue of Elijah on Mount Carmel shows him killing a priest of Ba'al.

FIGURE 4.3 Shepherds, like Amos, still herd sheep in northern Israel.

recliner—the only chair that was not pink—watching the semifinals: the Hittites versus the Patriots. "Hmm, the ball looks a little flat." That was when the wife showed up, arms crossed. "I'm bored. I'm leaving you." And she walked by. And not only did she walk by; her servants also walked by carrying boxes of shoes, bags, and garment bags of pink outfits. He heard three pink vehicles and a pink moving van start up—he had no idea where she got a pink moving van—and he was left in an empty house because she had also taken the pink furniture, drapes, and rugs, leaving him with the chair she never liked and the TV. His first reaction was this: "What the ...?" Then he said, "I've given her everything, and this is how she treats me? What a hussy. Man, I'm going to limit her credit cards to $10,000 each: that will cramp her style. What a wench!" He knew where she had gone, though: to the wild party a block away. In a sexual orgy in a city just north, her name also came up. While he was standing in line at the drugstore, he looked over at the magazine stand and saw his wife on the cover of *People* magazine with the Kardashians. Now he knew she had hit rock bottom. But he could not go anywhere without guys teasing him: "Hey, man, saw your wife last night—me and six other guys." He had to wear a paper bag over his head, but people still knew who he was because he was the only guy wearing a paper bag over his head. So he stayed in and ordered Chinese delivery.

Even though he turned the TV up as loud as he could, he still heard the tour busses outside his house with loudspeakers announcing, "On our left, we have the biggest loser in the world; his wife is sleeping with the country." This went on for months. One night, during a storm, he was watching the final (Patriots versus Moabites) when he heard a tentative knock on the door. It sounded like someone was knocking on the door but he or she really did not want anyone to answer. Maybe it was a Girl Scout with cookie orders; maybe it was an Amway salesperson; or maybe it was a Jehovah's Witness. He didn't know. Looking out through the peephole, he saw his wife. Her makeup was running, her stockings were torn, one of her stilettos was broken,

FIGURE 4.4 Jerusalem relied on its high walls for defense, as seen in this model of the ancient city in Jerusalem.

and she looked like she was listing like the *Titanic*. She mewed plaintively like a kitten: "Honey, can I come in?" "Wow," he said, "what a presumptuous hussy! What a wench." But he let her back in. The moral of the story: Israel was like that unfaithful wife. Yahweh knew she had been sleeping around with other gods. But if she would return to him, God would take her back. But there was a time limit on this offer: if she didn't get her little pink tush in gear and get back soon, Yahweh would not let her back in. He would be moving to a different zip code soon and if she didn't hurry, she would be coming back to an empty house, cancelled credit cards, and a world of hurt.

Isaiah was an important prophet for the southern kingdom, or Judah. What Judah had that the northern kingdom did not was the great city, Jerusalem. It was a massive, well-defended city, and its occupants felt pretty complacent. They walked around saying "We don't need Yahweh, we've got high walls, barbed wire, an ADT security system, and pit bull puppies." Isaiah told them they were fools because their security was linked to their covenant faithfulness. No matter how many pit bull puppies they had, if they dropped their side of the covenant, the Ten Commandments, Yahweh would drop his end, no longer protecting them, and the city would be destroyed.

Isaiah also told the Jews that Yahweh was impatient with their rituals. The Jews knew God was mad at them, so they tried to appease him with sacrifices, like ancient religions did using magic. The prophet told them Yahweh was impatient with the attempts. Isaiah said that Yahweh was not like other gods: you could not use magic to manipulate him. This God had free will and could tell people where to get off, and he did.

Yahweh did give the Jews a glimmer of hope: he would make the Jews an example to the world of the power of Yahweh. Because God had picked them, it was his reputation that was on the line. Other kingdoms would think he was a loser god: "These Jews couldn't follow you out of a paper bag." So God was going to ensure that Jews succeeded even if he had to drag them through the briar bushes, kicking them with golf cleats. So the Jews could do this the easy way, or they could do this the hard way.

Micah was also a southern-kingdom prophet. Like Isaiah, he spoke against self-complacent prophets and the inviolability of Jerusalem. These prophets were walking around: "We don't need Yahweh. Jerusalem has high walls, barbed wire, ADT security systems, and pit bull puppies. We also have golf carts!" At school or the mall, don't you feel secure knowing somewhere on the property is an overweight, sweating security guard in a golf cart? *Vvvvvvvv.* That is the sound of freedom.

Micah told the Jews that it did not matter how many golf carts they had. If they did not uphold their part of the covenant, Yahweh would drop his, and they would be squashed flat (Micah).

The prophet also knew the Jews had been trying to appease Yahweh with rituals. Like Isaiah, he told the Jews that God wanted instead a quiet fellowship with them; one established a relationship by talking to someone, not by throwing goat burgers at them. The opposite of love was not hate but apathy, and the Jews were apathetic to the God who had brought them out of Egypt and placed them in Jerusalem in the first place. And that was what hurt: that the Jews were ignoring Yahweh—ignoring. It was akin to unfriending him on Facebook®.

Dispersal. The prophets warned Jews to remain faithful to God's covenant, but they did not do so. So that is when the smiting started. Israel fell to the Assyrians, and its people were dispersed. The Bible calls Assyria the unconscious instrument of God.

> Woe to Assyria! My rod in anger, my staff in wrath. Against an impious nation I send him and against a people under my wrath I order him. To seize plunder, carry off loot, and tread them down like the mud of the streets.
>
> —Isaiah 10:5–6

These Hebrews are called the Ten Lost Tribes of Israel. They would disappear from history, though periodically pockets of their possible descendants would show up in different parts of the world. The Mormons believe they came to America, but we will talk about Mitt Romney's religion in the Christianity chapter.

Judah, because it refused to bow to Nebuchadnezzar II and made a secret deal with the Egyptians, fell to the Babylonians. The temple in Jerusalem was destroyed, and the Ark of the Covenant disappeared from history. The Babylonian army dragged the Jews kicking and screaming off to Babylon (now Iraq), and the Babylonian exile began.

> Lo! I will send for and fetch all the tribes of the north, says the Lord, and I will send to Nebuchadnezzar, king of Babylon, my servant; I will bring them against this land, against its inhabitants, and against all these neighboring nations. I will doom them, making them an object of horror, of ridicule, of everlasting reproach.
>
> —Jer. 25:9

The Jews underwent a fundamental change in their beliefs after living with the Babylonians and then the Persians, who conquered Babylonia. The Persians were Zoroastrians. Zoroastrians were monotheistic: Ahura Mazda, the only god in the universe, was their god. The Jews' god was Yahweh, but they were polytheistic in that they did believe there were other gods and worshipped them. At the end of their captivity with the Babylonians, the Jews were truly monotheistic: there are no more mentions of other gods in the Bible after this point. The Zoroastrians also believed in a heaven and hell. The afterlife for Jews was Sheo'l, the valley of the shadow of death that runs from Jericho to Jerusalem. The Israeli army currently uses this inhospitable area for deep desert training. It was the only place where the author saw the skeleton of a camel. Greek Orthodox monks live in the walls of cliffs in carved-out monasteries. Everyone went to Sheo'l: good, bad, ugly, and indifferent. The Zoroastrians believed in a heaven and hell. After their captivity, the Jews believed the same, shelving Sheo'l. The Zoroastrians believed in Angra Mainyu, an evil opponent of their god who tried to dry out the land and launched demons. The Jews believed in an evil opponent too, but their devil was the little talking snake who approached Eve in the Garden of Eden. Later, he was a deer, a bird, or a woman. This was not too threatening. The Zoroastrians also had a hierarchy of angels that did different jobs: polish your car, clean your fenders, or put gas in the tank. The Jews' angels were just messengers, though occasionally they liked to wrestle (see Jacob). Angra also had a hierarchy of demons that did different jobs: dent your car, key your fender, and put sugar in your gas tank. A hierarchy of angels and demons was adopted by the Jews, too, during their captivity. And then there was the devil: he got steroids from Angra and became the powerful supernatural being known as Satan: *Snakes on a Plane.* So, although scholars do not have a smoking gun that said the Jews changed their religion as a result of their encounter with Zoroastrians in Babylon, there is certainly a lot of circumstantial evidence.

Return and the second temple. The Jews were finally released by the Persian king Cyrus, known as Koresh in Hebrew, in 538 BCE for their return to Jerusalem. He gave them money to rebuild their temple and practically gave them bus fare to get home. Koresh is spoken of in glowing terms in the Bible. However, when the Jews got home, they found another group of Jews already living on the Temple Mount. They were the descendants of the Jews who had escaped capture by the Babylonians. An argument ensued over who had the rights to the land. They would argue for a century before finally getting together and building the second temple.

Syrian invasion. Then the Syria-based Seleucid dynasty attacked and took over Jerusalem and the temple in 175 BCE. They defiled the temple. This ticked off the Maccabees ("hammers"), who led a revolt and kicked the Syrian tush out of Jerusalem. They rededicated the temple and relit the oil lamps, but there was only enough oil for one night. Miraculously, the lamps burned for eight nights. This event is commemorated by the Feast of Hanukkah ("lights"). In an ironic historical twist, this story can only be found in the Catholic Bible. This will be explained later in the Christianity chapter.

Roman invasion. Then the Roman Republic conquered and occupied Jerusalem in 63 BCE. There was a series of uprisings before the Romans appointed Herod king of Jerusalem. He rebuilt the temple by enlarging it. It was so large he had to have retaining walls to hold the dirt underneath it.

In 70 CE, the Zealots, a branch of Jews, threw off the Roman yoke in a revolt, which caught the Roman Empire by surprise. The Jews' freedom did not last long, and the Romans returned and pretty much destroyed the city and the temple and expelled the Jews. We have a first account by a Jewish historian, Josephus, who chronicled the outcome:

FIGURE 4.5 Herod's temple was built on an existing temple.

(Tiberius Alexander, governor of Jerusalem) sent out upon them those two Roman legions that were in the city, and together with them five thousand other soldiers, who by chance were come together out of Libya, to the ruin of the Jews. They were also permitted not only to kill them, but to plunder them of what they had, and to set fire to their houses.[2]

The only thing left of the temple complex was one retaining wall. This has become the most holy site for Jews: the Western Wall or Wailing Wall. Jews pray there and leave written prayers in the cracks between the wall's stones. Now sitting on the mount is the third-holiest site in Islam: the Dome of the Rock, built in the seventh century.

Diaspora. The Jews were thrown out of the city and forced to wander the world without a homeland. This is called the Diaspora, which is Greek for "dispersal." During this time, the wide use of the synagogue started when Jews were cut off from the destroyed temple. The Sadducees, priests of the temple, disappeared along with the temple. The Pharisees, the teachers, were transformed into the modern rabbis.

Judaism in the Middle Ages. Enmity between Christianity and Judaism grew during the medieval period. Christians and Jews did not get along from Day One. Christians were Jews who believed Jesus was the Jewish messiah for whom the Jews had been waiting. Other Jews were worried about losing their dispensation about worshipping the Roman gods (the emperor knew they never would, so to keep peace, he let them slide as long as they worshipped Yahweh). But with a new god, Jesus, seemingly added to the Jewish pantheon, the emperor might yank their dispensation. So Christians were kicked out of the temple. Early Christian writers said Jews even cooperated with Romans to hunt down and bring Christians to trial (or be fed to the lions and tigers and bears, oh my! in the Coliseum).

By the Middle Ages, Christianity had conquered most of the known world. Judaism stayed small because of the Diaspora. So the Jews were in trouble.

Jews were considered, at best, functional, such as working as bankers. Jewish bankers were the only people in many societies to lend money. Christians were not allowed to. "Owe no one anything, except to love each other, for the one who loves another has fulfilled the law" (Rom. 13:8). So Christians invested with Jews.

At worst, Jews were considered heretics, as per the statement attributed to them in the New Testament that they and their descendants were responsible for the death of Jesus (Matt. 27:24–25), and they were called "Christ-killers." Some German peasants on a Crusade to fight Muslims in Jerusalem made it a point to kill Jews.[3]

Ironically, Jews found some sanctuary among Muslims in Cordova, Spain, during the Islamic rule of that country. Many were evicted in 1492 when King Ferdinand and Queen Isabella also evicted the Muslims.

During the Middle Ages, Kabbalah, mystical Judaism, formed. Kabbalah, which had many rabbis through the centuries contributing to its beliefs, believed the Torah did not reveal all of its secrets at once. An example of this can be found in the main text of Kabbalah, the Zohar:

FIGURE 4.6 The Western or Wailing Wall, the holiest site for Jews, is all that is left of the Temple complex.

FIGURE 4.7 An ancient synagogue was discovered beneath the ruins of a Roman temple in Capernaum.

> She is like unto a beautiful and stately damsel, who is hidden in a secluded chamber of a palace and who has a lover of whom no one knows but she. … She opens a little door in her hidden palace, discloses for a moment her face to her lover, then swiftly hides it again.[4]

The Jews who fled Spain to the Middle East after they were evicted by Ferdinand and Isabella are called Sephardim ("Spanish"). Another group of Jews were evicted from Eastern Europe by the Russians in what were called pogroms (ever stay awake and watch the end of "Fiddler on the Roof?"). The Jews who fled from these areas, such as Poland and surrounding areas, to the Middle East were called the Ashkenazim ("Germans"). From the latter comes the Yiddish language, which is a combination of German and Hebrew. One of my favorite Yiddish words is "feh"! ("fooey"!) There are also at least eight words describing "crazy."[5]

During the Middle Ages, the Jews were offered an olive branch by the newly formed Protestants. Martin Luther, Protestantism's founder, admired the Jews' resistance to Catholics, such as during the Crusades. But the Jews rejected Luther, too, so he wrote a pamphlet entitled "Concerning Jews and Their Lies" in 1543, with paragraphs of disparagement.[6]

The 18th century saw the development of Hasidism, which involved the delightful storytelling faith healer, Israel Ben-Eliezer, also known as Baal Shem-Tov, "master of the good name." Receiving visions from God, this Jewish storyteller said God should be enjoyed through prayer, not just studied. This became a popular belief among illiterate Jews who did not know their scripture very well.[7]

During the same period, Moses Mendelssohn, a Jewish philosopher, encouraged Jews to blend into society. The time was the European Enlightenment, and discrimination on religious grounds was minimal. He told the Jews they should leave ghettos and assimilate into their countries' respective cultures.

Holocaust

The Holocaust did not come out of a vacuum but was built on generations of worldwide anti-Semitism, such as that of Henry Ford. When Ford was cranking out Model Ts, he was also cranking out a newspaper, *The Dearborn Independent*. The newspaper warned its readers about a plot by international Jews to take over the world. The paper differentiated between the Jews who were going to take over the world and those Jews who knew their place as domestic Jews.[8]

Adolf Hitler admired Ford's view of Jews as well as his view on cars, having created the Volkswagen himself. Hitler drew on pseudoscientific racial theories and wanted to purify the German Aryan race and all of Europe of Jews (*Judenrein*: "free of Jews"). Hitler said the Jews were not part of the Indo-Aryan race, the light-skinned people who used the swastika and settled Europe. He said the Jews had no legitimacy as a state because they created no original art, no social reform that was not borrowed from someone else, and no cohesiveness unless attacked.[9]

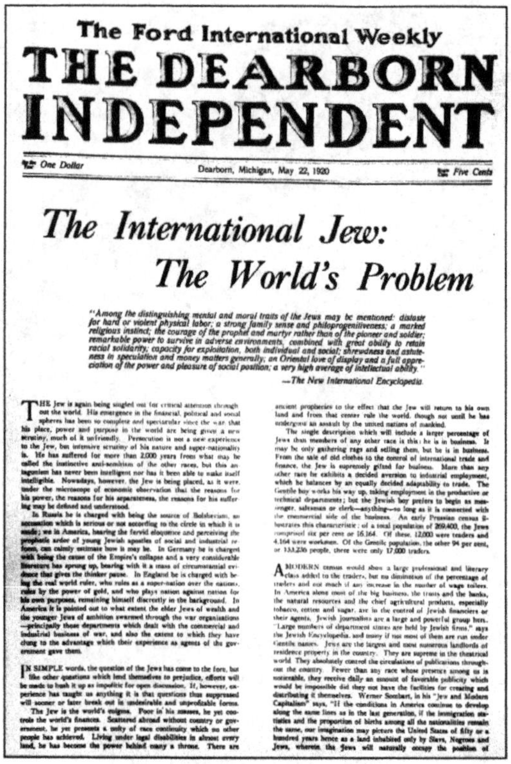

The Ford International Weekly

THE DEARBORN INDEPENDENT

One Dollar | Dearborn, Michigan, May 22, 1920 | Five Cents

The International Jew: The World's Problem

"Among the distinguishing mental and moral traits of the Jews may be mentioned: distaste for hard or violent physical labor; a strong family sense and philoprogenitiveness; a marked religious instinct; the courage of the prophet and martyr rather than of the pioneer and soldier; remarkable power to survive in adverse environments, combined with great ability to retain racial solidarity; capacity for exploitation, both individual and social; shrewdness and astuteness in speculation and money matters generally; an Oriental love of display and a full appreciation of the power and pleasure of social position; a very high average of intellectual ability."

—The New International Encyclopedia

THE Jew is again being singled out for critical attention throughout the world. His emergence in the financial, political and social spheres has been so complete and spectacular since the war that his place, power and purpose in the world are being given a new scrutiny, much of it unfriendly. Persecution is not a new experience to the Jew, but intensive scrutiny of his nature and super-nationality is. He has suffered for more than 2,000 years from what may be called the instinctive anti-semitism of the other races, but this antagonism has never been intelligent nor has it been able to make itself intelligible. Nowadays, however, the Jew is being placed, as it were, under the microscope of economic observation that the reasons for his power, the reasons for his separateness, the reasons for his suffering may be defined and understood.

In Russia he is charged with being the source of Bolshevism, an accusation which is serious or not according to the circle in which it is made; we in America, hearing the fervid eloquence and perceiving the prophetic ardor of young Jewish apostles of social and industrial reform, can calmly estimate how it may be. In Germany he is charged with being the cause of the Empire's collapse and a very considerable literature has sprung up, bearing with it a mass of circumstantial evidence that gives the thinker pause. In England he is charged with being the real world ruler, who rules as a super-nation over the nations, rules by the power of gold, and who plays nation against nation for his own purposes, remaining himself discreetly in the background. In America it is pointed out to what extent the elder Jews of wealth and the younger Jews of ambition swarmed through the war organizations—principally those departments which dealt with the commercial and industrial business of war, and also the extent to which they have clung to the advantage which their experience as agents of the government gave them.

IN SIMPLE words, the question of the Jews has come to the fore, but like other questions which lend themselves to prejudice, efforts will be made to hush it up as impolitic for open discussion. If, however, experience has taught us anything it is that questions thus suppressed will sooner or later break out in undesirable and unprofitable forms.

The Jew is the world's enigma. Poor in his masses, he yet controls the world's finances. Scattered abroad without country or government, he yet presents a unity of race continuity which no other people has achieved. Living under legal disabilities in almost every land, he has become the power behind many a throne. There are ancient prophecies to the effect that the Jew will return to his own land and from that center rule the world, though not until he has undergone an assault by the united nations of mankind.

The single description which will include a larger percentage of Jews than members of any other race is this: he is in business. It may be only gathering rags and selling them, but he is in business. From the sale of old clothes to the control of international trade and finance, the Jew is supremely gifted for business. More than any other race he exhibits a decided aversion to industrial employment, which he balances by an equally decided adaptability to trade. The Gentile boy works his way up, taking employment in the productive or technical departments; but the Jewish boy prefers to begin as messenger, salesman or clerk—anything—so long as it is connected with the commercial side of the business. An early Prussian census illustrates this characteristic; of a total population of 269,400, the Jews comprised six per cent or 16,164. Of these, 12,000 were traders and 4,164 were workmen. Of the Gentile population, the other 94 per cent, or 153,236 people, there were only 17,000 traders.

A MODERN census would show a large professional and literary class added to the traders, but no diminution of the percentage of traders and not much if any increase in the number of wage toilers. In America alone most of the big business, the trusts and the banks, the natural resources and the chief agricultural products, especially tobacco, cotton and sugar, are in the control of Jewish financiers or their agents. Jewish journalists are a large and powerful group here. "Large numbers of department stores are held by Jewish firms," says the Jewish Encyclopedia, and many if not most of them are run under Gentile names. Jews are the largest and most numerous landlords of residence property in the country. They are supreme in the theatrical world. They absolutely control the circulations of publications throughout the country. Fewer than any race whose presence among us is noticeable, they receive daily an amount of favorable publicity which would be impossible did they not have the facilities for creating and distributing it themselves. Werner Sombart, in his "Jew and Modern Capitalism" says, "If the conditions in America continue to develop along the same lines as in the last generation, if the immigration statistics and the proportion of births among all the nationalities remain the same, our imagination may picture the United States of fifty or a hundred years hence as a land inhabited only by Slavs, Negroes and Jews, wherein the Jews will naturally occupy the position of

The article that signaled the beginning of Henry Ford's seven-year hate campaign against the Jews. (COLLECTIONS OF THE HENRY FORD MUSEUM, GREENFIELD VILLAGE)

FIGURE 4.8 *Dearborn Independent*—"The International Jew." Ford's newspaper showed his opinion of Jews.

The Holocaust in Germany advanced in steps. In 1933, Jews were forced out of responsible positions, and their property was expropriated. In 1935, laws were passed identifying categories of "Jewishness," and discriminatory policies were institutionalized. Many Jews tried to escape Germany, but other countries—including the United States—would not accept them. In 1939, the Holocaust began in "liberated" areas—Austria and Poland—escalating from firing squads to killing centers. Jews were rounded up, initially forced into ghettos, and later sent to extermination camps such as Auschwitz, Poland, where they were gassed in showers with a pesticide, Zyklon B. About six million Jews had been killed by the end of World War II: two-thirds of all European Jews. Poland's Jewish population shrank from three million to 45,000.[10]

At the end of World War II, discovery of the full extent of the Holocaust caused Jews to do some soul-searching. Some gave up belief in an active God and adopted the belief that Judaism was just a cultural identity. Others believed that God did not have power to intervene in human history. A third group believed that the Holocaust was punishment for infidelity and called for stronger commitment to traditional Jewish ways and beliefs.

Modern Judaism

After the British allowed its independence in 1948, Israel fought and survived a series of military battles against its Arab neighbors to secure its existence. During these wars, which included the Yom Kippur War and the Six-Day War, Israel expanded its territory. From Egypt, it took the Sinai Peninsula, closing the Suez Canal for a time. From Jordan, it took the West Bank, which included East Jerusalem. From Syria, it took the Golan Heights. When Anwar Sadat became president of Egypt, he signed a peace accord with Israel, which returned control of the Sinai Peninsula back to Egypt. Israel received assistance from both the Soviet Union and the United States in its fight for independence.

Although Arabs protested the formation of a Jewish state in the middle of an Arab Middle East, so did Orthodox Jews. The latter believed Israel was a secular abomination. They were still waiting for the Messiah to reclaim Palestine, but the Orthodox Jews have gotten over it. The author learned this by witnessing a planeload of Orthodox Jews on their way to Tel Aviv in 2000.

The wars with the Arab nations set up the current land dispute and conflict between Palestinians and the ruling government of Israel. The Palestinians backed the Arab forces in the wars against the new Jewish state and were severely punished afterward by the victorious Israel. The Palestinians were forced to live in the Gaza Strip on the Mediterranean Sea and in the West Bank on the Jordanian border, with a lot of Israel in between. The Palestinians, however, strive for their own country with Jerusalem as its capital. Israel, of course, is set against that, particularly because Hamas in the Gaza Strip has been calling for the destruction of the Jewish state. To further complicate the Palestinian situation, a civil war broke out between Hamas and Fatah, so Palestinians are at war with each other.

Current Threats to Judaism

In the late 20th and early 21st centuries, there has been a resurgence of anti-Semitism. But most of the anti-Semitic fringe groups (neo-Nazis, skinheads, and the Ku Klux Klan), as well as lone gunmen, are not a threat to Jews as a whole. The countries of the world have learned from the Holocaust.

The greater danger threatening Jews as a whole is assimilation. Jews are assimilating into non-Jewish society and are no longer identifying themselves as Jewish. What the Holocaust and war could not do, peace seems to be doing. The liberal Jewish writer Alan Dershowitz states it well:

> The good news is that American Jews—as individuals—have never been more secure, more accepted, more affluent, and less victimized by discrimination or anti-Semitism. The bad news is that American Jews—as a people—have never been in greater danger of disappearing through assimilation, intermarriage, and low birthrates.[11]

There are cohesive forces that have kept Jews together: their shared history, scripture, and holidays. Their identity has been centered in these forces. Whether they are strong enough to resist assimilation, time will tell. There are already Messianic Jews who accept Jesus as the Messiah. And the Tanakh is the Protestant Christian Old Testament. We shall see.

FIGURE 4.9 A map of Palestine. Israel changes its borders over centuries. After 1967, Egypt got the Sinai Peninsula back.

FIGURE 4.10 Israeli bunker on the border of Lebanon.

Jewish Scripture

Judaism has many scriptures and scriptures that interpret other scriptures. Jewish scholars spent centuries interpreting the law of Judaism: the Torah. For instance, one law was that no one should work on the Sabbath. So if a person went to Lake Tiberius, bathed, and toweled off ten times, was that person allowed to bring all ten towels home? No, that was considered laundry, work.

Tanakh. The main Jewish scripture is the Tanakh. It contains the history of God's chosen people along with psalms and proverbs. The first five books of the Tanakh are called the Torah.

Mishnah. Mishnah in Hebrew means "repetition." This is a class of scripture that includes thousands of legal instructions drawn from the Torah.

Midrash. Midrash in Hebrew means "to search or interpret." These are interpretations of the Tanakh by rabbis of the first five centuries CE, with their commentaries. The Midrash is made up of the Halakah, another set of legal interpretations, and the Haggadah, stories and sayings.

FIGURE 4.11 A Jordanian soldier descends from his watchtower on the Israeli border. A fence runs along the border despite a peace treaty signed between the two countries.

Talmud. The Talmud is formed from several scriptures written over about five hundred years. One part is called the Gemara. It is a combination of the Halakah and Haggadah written during the first five centuries CE by Palestinian and Babylonian rabbis, with their commentaries. These Palestinian rabbis fled Jerusalem when the Jews were exiled by the Romans. They headed to northwest Palestine, approximately where Tel Aviv is now. After the Romans found them there, they snuck back south to Galilee and—right under the noses of the Romans—wrote the Halakah and Haggadah for half a millennium. The Babylonian rabbis were descended from the Jews who did not return to Jerusalem when the Persian King Cyrus liberated them, because they had jobs, a house, a satellite dish, and 2.5 kids. They didn't want to go home, so they stayed in place and wrote the Halahah and Haggadah. In the Middle Ages, Jewish scholars decided to combine the works of both sets of rabbis, and this created the Gemara. Now, take your newly formed Gemara and add Rabbi Judah's Mishnah that was written in 500–523 CE (it is a really good Mishnah), and now you have the Talmud.

FIGURE 4.12 The Dead Sea Scrolls, found in this cave in Qumran, include books from the Tanakh.

Jewish Theology

In Jewish theology, humanity is created in God's image. This assumes God has a close relationship with humans and assumes equality between men and women, although Jewish religious laws have assumed that men are superior. Humans are not inherently sinful, but they can follow "evil impulses" if they are religious Jews, or they can "miss the mark" if they are ethnic Jews. Unlike Islam, Jews have unfettered free will. They have a choice: follow the halakah or disobey God. Or if they are ethnic Jews, they can choose to abandon ethics.

There is an ardent hope among some Jews that the Messiah will come. This is called "Next Year in Jerusalem." In a year or less, the Messiah will come and redeem and save the Jews. If he does not get here this year, just you wait: he will be here next year. The author has a T-shirt with the saying on it. It is now more than a decade old. It is fading. A new one will have to be obtained. Still, just wait: next year. Or if a person is an ethnic Jew, next year will be a new and golden age for Jews, just you wait.

For many Jews, living obediently with Yahweh is following the Torah. The Torah is not a burden but a joy: it is God's gift to the Jewish people. It means he loves the Jews so much he gave them survival rules, such as kosher regulations. Obedience is a way of showing gratitude.

Speaking of kosher: vegetables are okay, but only animals with cloven hooves and dual digestive tracts can be eaten. Fish that have both fins and scales can be eaten. Forbidden birds include birds of prey or those without crops or gizzards. Gizzards with pebbles inside them are what veggie birds use to grind up the seeds and corn they eat. To prepare food in the kosher way, fish may be eaten when caught, but other animals must be ritually slaughtered, which requires specially trained butchers. All blood must be removed from meat as much as possible. Meat and dairy products should not be mixed when eating. The author ran into this in Jerusalem, where a buffet table of meat and bread was separated by the entire dining room from a buffet table of cheese and dairy products.

Branches of Judaism

Reform Jews

Jews who immigrated to the United States from Germany during the 19th century and who would eventually make up the largest branch of Jews in the country are now called Reform Jews. Reform Jews believe they should adapt to the changing world and rid themselves of beliefs that keep them apart from the rest of society. The belief that a messiah was going to someday arrive and redeem the Jews was dropped, along with the idea that Jews needed their own homeland. Reform Jews, like Mendelssohn advocated, should blend in with their adopted countries. They should not look different than anyone else. Strict adherence to dietary laws is also not necessary: no one has to remain kosher. Also not important is the written or oral Torah: only the ethical teachings of the Torah are important, because they are the laws of the land ("Thou shall not kill," "Thou shall not steal," etc.). Reform Jews also began the practice of bat mitzvahs, ceremonies celebrating when girls come of age at 12. Before, only boys' coming of age at 13 was celebrated, with bar mitzvahs. Reform Jews also broke the gender barrier by allowing women to be ordained as rabbis, not just men, as had been the tradition.

Orthodox Judaism

A reaction to Reform Judaism was Orthodox Judaism, which dismissed the changes adopted by Reform Jews. This branch of Judaism stresses strict observance of the Torah and the Ten Commandments. They believe that the Ten Commandments are not the "ten suggestions" but commandments to follow. Dietary laws also have to be followed: all Jews have to remain kosher. Orthodox Jews also allow only men to be ordained as rabbis; women need not apply. Only bar mitzvahs are allowed.

FIGURE 4.13 Hasidic Jews are Orthodox. They do not cut their hair and wear a tefillin, a box containing an excerpt from scripture, on their foreheads during rituals.

Conservative Jews

In the middle ground between the Orthodox and Reform Jews are Conservative Jews. This branch of Judaism, founded in the 19th century, applies the vernacular, not just Hebrew, to the worship service. Conservative Jews have a commitment to the Torah, which is stronger than the loosey-goosey approach of the Reform Jews but not as tight-fisted as the Orthodox Jews. Conservatives also apply historical study to teachings. For instance, Judaism only had male rabbis in the past because it was a patriarchal society. Conservatives argue that times have changed, so there should also be female rabbis and bat mitzvahs.

Reconstructionism

Reconstructionism developed out of the Conservative branch of Judaism in the 1920s and 1930s. These Jews view Judaism as a civilization or culture, and they place less stress on Judaism as a religion. Jewish literature, movies, and art are of interest to them. They tend to have Jewish community centers instead of synagogues. They also have the Havurah, a meeting in members' homes to discuss Jewish culture.

Zionists

The Zionist movement (*Zion* is the symbolic name for Jerusalem) evolved out of the idea that the toleration of Jews among non-Jews was short-lived and superficial. Sure, people will say some of their best friends are Jews. But when things got tough, historically, the Jews were the first to be thrown under the bus. The Zionists' main early supporter was Theodore Herzl, a journalist who covered the trial of Alfred Dreyfus, a French Jewish officer charged with treason. When Herzl discovered the charges stemmed from anti-Semitism, he realized that Jews were not going to get a fair shake in non-Jewish society, so he joined Zionism and became its chief negotiator. Zionists began to buy up land in Palestine and then part of the Ottoman Empire, and they established a new city (Tel Aviv) in 1909. By 1920, 50,000 Jews lived in Palestine. This Zionist-inspired influx of Jews worried Arab settlers. The British, who controlled Palestine after the fall of the Ottoman Empire at the end of World War I, encouraged Jewish settlement at first but then limited it, under Arab pressure, to 15,000 Jews per year.

The author's encounter with Zionism occurred 20 feet below the surface of Jerusalem in a souk, an underground marketplace in a long tunnel. Grabbed and jerked into an underground cave with fluorescent lights bolted to a rock ceiling, a film projector and screen, empty chairs, a book case, and a group of men chatting, the author was accosted by a very zealous man explaining why Jerusalem was for Jews only and that everyone else should leave. I replied, "Well then, so should I, because my tour group is disappearing down the souk." Still undeterred, he yelled, "Don't forget to tell them Jerusalem is for Jews only." It was then that a question popped into my head: He's 20 feet below the surface; where is he getting his electricity?

FIGURE 4.14 Theodore Herzl, Zionist spokesman, travels to Israel.

Jewish Holidays

The **Sabbath** is a weekly 24-hour holiday beginning Friday at sundown. Orthodox and Conservative Jews have Sabbath services on Saturday mornings. Orthodox Jews abstain from labor or driving on the Sabbath. This includes cooking, operating machinery such as a car, or even turning a doorknob or turning on a television.

Passover, or Pesach ("lamb"), is celebrated in the spring and is a seven- to eight-day celebration of deliverance from Egypt ("passing over") and deliverance in general.

Shavuot ("weeks") occurs five days after Passover and is marked by the bringing of the first fruits of harvest (Pentecost) to the temple, akin to when the biblical Abel gave his best harvest as his offering to God. This also marks the reception of the Torah.

Sukkot ("booths") is a seven-day autumn harvest celebration marking when the Hebrews wandered in wilderness and lived in booths or tents. It is celebrated in September or October.

The "high holy days," the holiest of Jewish holidays, include **Rosh Hashanah** ("New Year"), which occurs in September or October, beginning with shofar (a ram's horn) as a call to repentance and ten days of penitence.

Yom Kippur ("Day of Atonement") ends Rosh Hashanah with prayers for forgiveness and reconciliation. This is the origin of the term "scapegoat," when a goat symbolically holding the sins of the Jews is carried out into the desert. A scapegoat in modern times is a student who wrecked the grade curve by scoring a 100 and who the other students will blame for their bad grades and wait for him or her in the parking lot.

Hanukkah is the Feast of Dedication, which commemorates the rededication of the temple after the Maccabean revolution, and it features the lighting of candles on a menorah for eight days. Because it falls around Christmas, it has become a mini-Christmas for Jews. Now popular today are Hanukkah bushes with menorah ornaments hanging from their branches.

Bar or Bat Mitzvah are the celebrations of the rites of passage for 13-year-old boys or 12-year-old girls (in Reform and Conservative branches only).

SUMMARY

Judaism is a very old religion that has persevered over millennia. Its history is recorded in the Tanakh, which Jews use along with their traditions, rituals, and holidays. Judaism has had a rocky relationship with Yahweh, as we read in scripture, and faced many invasions and persecutions, such as the Holocaust. What Judaism is now facing is assimilation.

FOR FURTHER READING

36 Readings from Judaism, Robert Van de Weyer, ed., Pilgrim Press, 2000

Gates of Freedom Haggadah, Chaim Stern, Berhman House, 1999

Israel: A Concise History of a Nation Reborn, Daniel Gordis, Ecco, 2017

JPS Hebrew-English Tanakh, 2nd. ed., The Jewish Publication Society

Judaism, Arthur Hertzberg, George Braziller, Inc., 1961

Mein Kampf, Adolf Hitler, Haole Library, 2015

The Dictionary of Popular Yiddish Words, Phrases, and Proverbs, Freg Kogos, MJF Books, 1970

The Kosher Companion, Trudy Garfunkel, Birch Lane Press, 1997

The New Complete Works of Josephus, William Whiston, trans., Kregel, 1999

The Rise of Ancient Israel, Hershel Shanks, et. al., Biblical Archeology Society, 1992

The Vanishing American Jew, Alan M. Dershowitz, 1997

ENDNOTES

1 "Demographics of Judaism," Berkley Center for Religion, Peace & World Affairs, https://berkleycenter.george-town.edu/essays/demographics-of-judaism.

2 Josephus, in *The New Complete Works of Josephus*, trans. W. Whiston (Grand Rapids, MI: Kregel, 1999).

3 "Medieval Jewish History, 632 to 1650," My Jewish Learning, https://www.myjewishlearning.com/article/medieval-jewish-history-632-to-1650/.

4 S. Keller, ed., *The Jews: A Treasury of Art and Literature* (Fairfield, CT: Hugh Lauter Levin, 1992).

5 F. Kogos, *The Dictionary of Popular Yiddish Words, Phrases, and Proverbs* (New York: MJF Books, 1995).

6 M. Betram, ed., "Martin Luther: Concerning Jews and Their Lies," AAARGH Internet, 2009, http://vho.org/aaargh/fran/livres9/Luthereng.pdf.

7 H. Sachar, *A History of the Jews in the Modern World* (New York: Knopf, 2005).

8 N. Baldwin, *Henry Ford and the Jews* (New York: Public Affairs, 2001).

9 A. Hitler, *Mein Kampf* (New York: Reynal & Hitchcock, 1939).

10 "Jewish population of Europe in 1945." *Holocaust Encyclopedia,* Washington, DC: United States Holocaust Memorial Museum, https://www.ushmm.org/wlc/en/article.php?ModuleId=10005687.

11 A. Dershowitz, *The Vanishing American Jew* (Boston: Little, Brown and Co., 1997).

CREDITS

CHRISTIANITY

LEARNING OBJECTIVES

1. Understand the basic theology of the Trinity
2. Know and understand the teachings of Jesus
3. Understand the early hierarchy of the Church
4. Take note of early Christian persecutions
5. Know the Bible's evolution and versions
6. Know the historical leaders of Christianity and their accomplishments
7. Understand the different denominations, their origins, and their beliefs
8. Know the holidays and their meanings
9. Understand modern movements in Christianity

Go, therefore, and make disciples of all nations, baptizing them in the name of the Father, and of the Son, and of the Holy Spirit, teaching them to observe all that I have commanded you. And behold, I am with you always, until the end of the age.

—Matt. 19:29

Christian Statistics

With more than two billion members, Christianity is the largest religion in the world and in the history of the world. It makes up about 31 percent of the world's population. The largest denomination is the Catholic Church, with 1.1 billion, followed by Protestants at 376 million, Orthodox at 220 million, and Anglicans at 80 million (sometimes included with Protestants, sometimes not). Interestingly, Independent Christians not affiliated with any denomination are 427 million.[1]

Christian Myth

Christianity is the only religion in the world that claims God became a human being. There are religions that chronicle humans becoming gods (such as Chango, who was elevated from a king to a god in the Yoruba religion) or part god, part human (such as Hercules in Greek mythology).

The Christian myth shares the Jewish myth, as it addresses the creation of the world and the history of the Jews up until the beginning of the Common Era. Like Islam, Christianity views Adam and Eve, Noah, Abraham, Moses, and the other patriarchs and prophets as recognized messengers of God. Unlike Islam, Christianity sees the patriarchs and prophets as Jewish. Christians see Jesus, the founder of Christianity, as the Christ (Greek for "messiah") for whom the Jews were waiting and who was foreshadowed in Jewish scripture. Isaiah criticized King Ahaz of Judah after he tried to conquer Jerusalem—Jew against Jew. "Listen, O house of David! Is it not enough for you to weary men, must you also weary my God? Therefore the Lord himself will give you this sign: the virgin shall be with child, and bear a son, and he shall name him Immanuel" ("with us is God"; Isa. 7:13–14). Although some writers believed Immanuel referred to the birth of the future king Hezekiah—whose mother, during Isaiah's time, had been a young unmarried woman—consensus among Christians was Isaiah foreshadowed the coming of Jesus. Isaiah goes further: "For a child is born to us, a son is given us; upon his shoulder dominion rests. They name him Wonder-Counselor, God-Hero, Father-Forever, Prince of Peace," and he is from the line of King David (Isa. 9:5).

The location of the messiah's origins are also penned by the prophet Micah:

> But you, Bethlehem-Ephrathah, too small to be among the clans of Judah, from you shall come forth for me one who is to be ruler in Israel; whose origin is from of old, from ancient times. Therefore the Lord will give them up, until the time when she who is to give birth has born, and the rest of his brethren shall return to the children of Israel. (Mic. 5:1–2)

Christians also see Jesus's whipping and nailing to a cross for people's sins foreshadowed in the Jewish scriptures. Isaiah referred to the servant of the Lord as one "spurned and avoided by men" and "pierced for our offenses, crushed for our sins, upon him was the chastisement that makes us whole, by his stripes we were healed" (Isa. 53: 3, 5).

The nature of Jesus is described in the New Testament, which is the second part of the Christian Bible. John refers to Jesus as "*logos*," which means "word." John was drawing upon a Greek myth, which the Hellenized Jews knew, that asserted when the gods of Mount Olympus wanted to do something on earth, they sent their logos, it became flesh, did the job, and returned to Olympus. "In the beginning was the Word, and the Word was with God, and the Word was God" (John 1:1).

This would cause some consternation and arguments among early Christians: Who was Jesus? God? Human? Hybrid? John further states, "And the Word became flesh and made his dwelling among us, and we saw his glory as of the Father's only Son, full of grace and truth" (John 1:14). So Jesus is God become human. So which part was human, and which part was God? The human part apparently came from his mother, Mary, and the God part was from, well, God. But which part was which? The New Testament states that Jesus "emptied himself, taking the form of a slave, coming in human likeness, and found human in appearance" (Phil. 2:7). So when he was born in Bethlehem, he knew pretty much what newborn babies knew: nothing, nada, not much. He knew when he was hungry, cold, or colicky, but that was it. Like all humans, he had a human body and a human soul. Then the Bible says, "... the child grew and became strong, filled with wisdom" (Luke 2:40). Wisdom is a code word for the Holy Spirit. That is why the former church in Constantinople was named the Hagia Sophia ("holy wisdom"), the Holy Spirit. So the Holy Spirit is Jesus's second soul, telling him who he was and what his mission was going to be. So Jesus grew into knowledge of his Godhood. This is called the duality or dual nature of Jesus—he has two natures: human and divine.

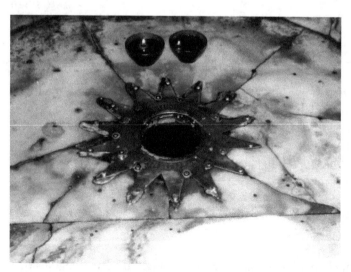

FIGURE 5.1 This star marks the spot of Jesus's birth in Bethlehem, now inside the Church of the Nativity.

Christian History

The founder of Christianity was Jesus of Nazareth. He was one of the Pharisees, the teaching class of the Jews, but he apparently did not get along with other Pharisees. He was born in Bethlehem during a census called by Caesar Augustus of the Roman Empire. His family was there because, apparently, members of the house of David registered there (Luke 2:1–5). Christians mark this as year one, the beginning of the Christian calendar, but this calendar was not codified until 1,500 years later. So the actual date is in dispute. Luke, the gospel writer, said the census during which Jesus was born was when Quirinius was governor of Syria. That would have put the census between 6–12 CE.[2] The gospel writer Matthew said Jesus was born when Herod was king of Jerusalem, which would have been between 37–4 BCE.[3]

Most of Jesus's life is not known. There are some Gnostic scriptures, such as the First Gospel of the Infancy of Jesus Christ, that were written in the second century ("The Lost Books") and came up with fanciful accounts that were rejected by early Christians. The Bible mentions how Jesus got separated from his family and ended up preaching in the temple as a youth. Then we see him again as an adult being baptized by John the Baptist.

As an adult, Jesus taught for three years and performed miracles. The reason Jesus performed miracles was for street credentials. He wanted people to listen to him. If I said, "Hi, I'm God. Follow me," you'd probably think I was getting paid too little to be God. But if I took a stroll on the local lake, cured

FIGURE 5.2 This icon shows times in Jesus's life and death.

everyone in town of AIDS, and then raised everyone from the dead at the local cemetery, would you listen to me then? Would you at least give me five minutes of your time? The Bible tells the story of Lazarus, who Jesus raised from the dead, as one of Jesus's miracles. Yet Lazarus eventually would die again, but Jesus's teachings, which are more important, have lasted more than two thousand years.

Jesus's teachings were radical, totally rad. They are more radical than just "being good" or "helping each other" sentiments in a greeting card. They are:

> Blessed are you who are poor, for yours is the kingdom of God. (Luke 6:20)

> [It is better to be poor than to be rich.] Truly I tell you, it is hard for someone who is rich to enter the kingdom of heaven. (Matt. 19:23)

So the very fact that you are attending college so you can get a high-paying job will probably condemn you to hell. It is a shame the student handbook never mentions this.

- Address God as your father ("Our Father who art in heaven ..."). Treat God as your dad, assuming you have a good relationship with your dad. He is not some distant ogre god but your father. Talk to him as you would your dad. He will give you what you need, not necessarily what you want (you can't afford the insurance on a Ferrari). He forgives, but he will also ground you if you disobey.

- Never fight back. "You have heard that it was said, 'An eye for an eye and a tooth for a tooth.' But I say to you, offer no resistance to one who is evil. When someone strikes you on your right cheek, turn the other one to him as well" (Matt. 5:38–39). So if someone attacks you, your family, your mother, your children, your cat, you are never allowed to fight back. Do you think you could handle that? Rad.

FIGURE 5.3 These are the original steps Jesus climbed to Herod's Palace for his trial.

FIGURE 5.4 Pontius Pilate, who sentenced Jesus to death, is credited on this stone for funding an amphitheater on the Sea of Galilee.

■ Love your enemies. "You have heard that it was said, 'You shall love your neighbor and hate your enemies.' But I say to you, love your enemies, and pray for those who persecute you" (Matt. 5:43–44). This includes terrorists, murders, thieves, rapists, and pedophiles. Rad enough?

Jesus taught for three years and then was crucified by the Romans, at the request of the ruling Jews, for treason. Before that, he instituted what is called communion, the Lord's Supper, or the Eucharist, depending on the Christian denomination.

While they were eating, Jesus took bread, said the blessing, broke it, and giving it to the disciples, said, 'Take this and eat; this is my body.' Then he took a cup, gave thanks, and gave it to them, saying, 'Drink from it, all of you, for this is my blood of the covenant, which will be shed on behalf of many for the forgiveness of sins.' (Matt. 26:26–28)

FIGURE 5.5 Ile-de-France students mass. Transubstantiation occurs during the mass, when the bread and wine change into the body and blood of Jesus.

Taking his body literally meant taking it and consuming it. This is called transubstantiation, the belief that the bread and wine at communion physically become the body and blood of Jesus. The early Christians practiced this, as verified by Eusebius in his accounting of *The Epistle of the Gallican Churches).*[vii] Most Christians of the world—Catholic and Orthodox—still practice transubstantiation. Protestants do not.

As we mentioned in the first chapter, cults often do not survive the deaths of their founders. Christianity was a cult. To survive, the pattern would be for Christianity to evolve into a sect. But something different occurred: it went from a cult to a cult, because Jesus came back from the dead. This is celebrated as Easter among Christians. Then Jesus hung around with his peeps for 40 days in the flesh and then ascended into heaven, never to be seen again in the flesh. This is called the Ascension.

Apostolic times. After the death of Jesus, the 12 apostles, Jesus's followers, were scared. The Jews and Romans were looking for them, and if they were crucified, they would stay dead because, unlike Jesus, they were not God. They were hidden in a place called the "upper room" when the Holy Spirit descended upon them. This is called Pentecost because it occurred during the Jewish holiday of Pentecost, but it's also known as the birthday of Christianity because the apostles went out to the known world and began preaching their ministry of the Gospel. (What is not the birthday is Christmas. Christmas is just the mass that celebrates the birth of Christ, and it's probably not even on the date of his birth.) The Holy Spirit gave the apostles and Mary gifts: courage (they would not be fearful anymore); wisdom (because that is what the Holy Spirit is) so they would know what to say or how to act in any given situation; and the gift of tongues so they could preach the Gospel to anyone—no matter what language that person spoke—and be understood. The apostles ruled the young church in Jerusalem with Peter as their leader; Jesus had given him authority over heaven and earth. Jesus had changed Peter's name from Simon and called him "Petra," which means "rock" in Greek:

> And so I say to you, you are Peter, and upon this rock I will build my church, and the gates of the netherworld shall not prevail against it. I will give you the keys to the kingdom of heaven. Whatever you bind on earth shall be bound in heaven, and whatever you loose on earth shall be loosed in heaven. (Matt. 16:18–19)

The apostles spread across the Roman Empire preaching the gospel. Peter preached throughout Asia Minor (now Turkey) and ended up as the bishop of Rome. There are legends about where the other apostles went, but this is subject to dispute among scholars. James, who was a relative of Jesus, became the first bishop, or episcopus (elder, supervisor), of Jerusalem.

Another important figure in early Christianity was Saul of Tarsus, a Jew. He hated Christians and had his own personal army he used to round Christians up for trial. Christianity was illegal at that time, and Saul considered Christians to be Jewish heretics. He heard there were some Christians hiding in Damascus, so he headed that way. On the way, he literally got "knocked off his high horse" and was blinded. He heard a voice: "Saul, Saul, why are you persecuting me?" Saul replied, "Who are you, sir?" The voice said, "I am Jesus, whom you are persecuting" (Acts 9:4–5). So Saul became a changed man. He changed his name to Paul, was baptized, and began preaching to the non-Jewish people of the Roman Empire: the pagans. The common consensus among the apostles was Jesus was the messiah for the Jews. Paul believed Jesus was the messiah for the whole world, Jews and non-Jews alike.

By the way, Paul was a tentmaker, so he had an income to pay his own expenses without being a burden to those to whom he preached. You could say Paul was "in tents."

Paul eventually ended up in Rome and was executed by beheading. Because he was a Roman citizen, he escaped the agony of crucifixion. Peter was crucified upside down: he requested this form of execution because he (having denied Jesus three times) did not feel he had earned the right to be crucified like the Lord. Peter's bones were found under

FIGURE 5.6 Emblem of Vatican City State; the keys of Peter, gold (for heaven), and silver (for earth) can be seen on the emblem.

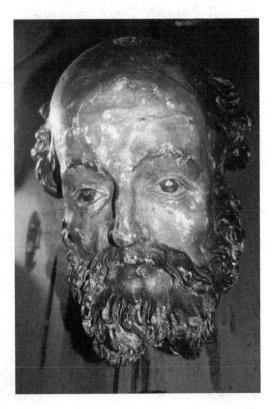

FIGURE 5.7 St. Paul was known as Saul before his conversion experience.

St. Peter's Basilica in Vatican City during World War II.[4] Paul's bones were found under the Basilica of Saint Paul Outside the Walls in Rome and authenticated in 2009.[5]

All the apostles, except for John, were martyred. James was killed when the Romans destroyed Jerusalem. John was exiled to the prison island of Patmos in Greece, where he wrote that strange Book of Revelation. He had scrolls smuggled off the island by visitors and wrote in code in case the Romans intercepted a scroll, so do not take Revelations literally. The number 12 means fulfillment: 12 tribes of Israel, 12 apostles. Seven is perfection. Six is short of perfection, and 666—the number of the beast or antichrist—is the exact opposite of the Trinity, 777. This number also spells a name: Nero. He was the antichrist about whom John was writing. Nero was notorious for having human torches illuminate his evening parties in the Roman circus. He was insane even by Roman emperor standards.

An account by Tacitus from the late first century goes into detail about how Christians were treated by the Roman Empire:

> Besides being put to death, they were made to serve as objects of amusement; they were clad in the hides of beasts and torn to death by dogs; others were crucified, others set on fire to serve to illuminate the night when the daylight failed.[6]

As mentioned, Christianity was illegal, so Christians went into hiding. Initially, they worshipped in synagogues because they saw themselves as Jews who accepted the messiah. But Jews were in danger of losing their dispensation from having to worship the Roman gods for harboring these Nazarenes, so the Christians were kicked out. Instead, Christians began to meet in people's homes. There were two parts of the service: the Liturgy of the Word and the Liturgy of the Eucharist. During the first, they would read a scroll from Paul or John, because the Bible had not yet been created. The second part would be the Liturgy of the Eucharist (thanksgiving) or Agape (unconditional love), when the bread and wine would be presented and transubstantiation would occur.

Post-Apostolic period. By 70 CE, the time of Jerusalem's destruction, the post-Apostolic period begins. Most of the apostles, except for John, were dead. The next generation of administrators come to power: bishops, who were the successors to the apostles; deacons (from *diaconate*, meaning "servant"), who did the grunt work—distributing wealth to widows and orphans and so on; and, when the church membership increased, priests (presbyters), who could do everything a bishop could do except ordain someone.

By the second century, the church needed to be clear about its beliefs because heresies had been cropping up. One of these heretics was Marcion. He was a presbyter who was very flamboyant: he had two men with trumpets announce his entrance when he came into town. Marcion wrote the first known Bible, consisting of Paul's writings as well as his own. He was kind of vain that way.

Gnosticism was a heresy that taught there were two gods: an evil Yahweh and a good Jesus, who married Sophia (the earth goddess) and beat up Yahweh. Oh, and a blind, insane angel who came down to earth and had sex with women, who then gave birth to giants. The reason you may not have heard of any of this is that gnosticism means esoteric knowledge. These Christians believed they had knowledge no one else had. The most important thing you should know about them was that they did not believe in the dual nature of Jesus: Jesus was God but not human. He only appeared to be human: he was God wearing a human suit. So Jesus did not die on the cross: he

FIGURE 5.8 The establishment of a hierarchy in early Christianity is evidenced by this tombstone for a deacon.

just slipped out of his human suit. This belief—Jesus escaping crucifixion—was passed on to Islam through the gnostic Nestorians, who communicated with Muhammad in Arabia.

In the eastern part of the Roman Empire, there was another heresy: Arianism. It was named after a presbyter named Arius who promoted it. Arians believed Jesus was neither God nor human, just a subservient creation.

The new Roman emperor, Constantine—who had legalized Christianity and funded its churches, clergy, and rituals—saw Christianity as a good way to unify his empire. But he heard Christians had different beliefs. So he called the Council of Nicaea (325 CE), told the bishops to decide on Christianity's belief, and said he would enforce it with his army. It was what emperors did. So the council affirmed the dual nature of Jesus, condemning both gnosticism and Arianism, and affirmed the use of the Greek-Roman tradition, or Alexandrine canon, as being the true Bible, therefore condemning Marcion's Bible. The Bible would be codified—what definitely got in and what got left out—during the Council of Hippo in 393 CE. The Nicaean council also created the Nicene Creed, which many churches still use in their services.

An early influential Christian theologian was Bishop Augustine of Hippo, Africa. He affirmed Christians were born with original sin—the sin of Adam and Eve—and needed to be baptized to be saved. He taught that only divine grace can save a person, not do-it-yourself salvation: you had to have faith for God to save you. He also affirmed the sacraments (such as baptism), saying they were outward signs of God's grace. He also affirmed the Trinity—the belief that God was three persons: God the Father, God the Son (Jesus), and God the Holy Spirit (or Ghost). Basically, 3 = 1. But this raised some questions about the dynamics of the Trinity that Augustine attempted to answer. Did God talk to himself? Did the Father die on the cross with the Son (they are one God!)? When Augustine was walking on the beach of Hippo along the Mediterranean Sea mulling this over, he passed a boy who was pouring a bucket of water into a hole he had dug in the sand. He asked the boy what he was doing. The boy, happy that he had been noticed, replied, "I'm putting the Mediterranean Sea into this hole." Augustine responded, "I can see you are trying to do that, but that hole is small, and the sea is big. How are you going to do that?" The boy responded, "I can put the sea into this hole before you ever figure out the Trinity." That is when Augustine realized what God was telling him: the Trinity is the mind of God—what he is apt to do as well as his feelings, dreams, and inner volitions. For one to understand that, one would have to be God. So Christians have accepted the Trinity on faith, not logic. Augustine wrote about his views on Christian theology in *City of God*.

Primacy of Rome and the Great Schism. Starting in the first century, early Christians deferred to the bishop of Rome in matters of morals because that bishop sat on the throne of Peter and was considered the successor to the head of the apostles. He was called by the title "father," "papa," or "pope" (*pappas* in Greek).

A lot occurred between the post-Apostolic period and the Middle Ages: Vikings and barbarians attacked and destroyed the Roman Empire; Christianity was nearly wiped out in Western Europe by the Norsemen, but the monks from the Monastery of Cluny reintroduced it. Pope Gregory Christianized most of Europe by marrying off orphans raised in convents to the kings of Europe. These pious women converted their husbands and kingdoms. And Gregory created the calendar we now use. But this is not a book on Christianity, so we must move on.

In 1054, Christianity was split in half over three words: "and the Son." This is called the filioque clause. Western Christians, centered around Rome, believed that the Father, the Son, and the Holy Spirit were equal because they were all God. So when the Holy Spirit was sent forth for baptism, for example, both the Father and the Son sent him. It was a collaborative effort. Eastern Christians believed the Father was superior to the Son and the Holy Spirit. So when the Holy Spirit was sent forth, only the Father sent him; he did not discuss the issue with the Son. The Western Church argued that all three were equal. The Eastern Church said the Bible clearly states the Father is superior. The Western Church argued that the clause was in the Nicene Creed: "The Holy Spirit proceeds from *the Father and the Son.*" The Eastern Church said the Westerners had snuck that clause in. The Western Church said it did not like baklava. The Eastern Church responded by saying "Your mama." Okay, the last two sentences are fictional, but the argument continued, resulting in the split between the Catholic Church (Western) and the Eastern Orthodox churches.

The Catholic Church became the new temporal power after the fall of the Roman Empire. People flocked to the church, which was the only governing body around for protection from the barbarians ranging across Europe. The pope needed to protect them, so he raised an army. To raise an army, he needed to raise taxes. To raise taxes, he needed to acquire land. So, in a way, the popes became like emperors.

During this period, an influential theologian was Thomas Aquinas (1225–1274). In his book *Summa Theologica,* Aquinas used the methods of the Greek philosopher Aristotle to defend Christian doctrine. Admiring how Aristotle arrived at truths through logic, Aquinas applied that same logic (using the prime mover theory) to prove God exists. To illustrate this theory, consider: When I move an object, such as a chair, what force is acting upon me? Gravity, so I don't fly away when I move the chair. Where does gravity come from? The earth. What gravitational force acts upon the earth? The sun. The sun is affected by the gravitational pull of what? The solar system. The solar system is affected by the gravitational pull of what? The Milky Way Galaxy. The Milky Way Galaxy is affected by the gravitational pull of what? Other galaxies in the universe. So the chain of cause and effect goes on. Now, there are two possibilities in this scenario. One: there is an infinite number of movers. But physics says that is impossible. One cannot have infinite mass or energy. The only other scenario is that there is one prime mover that moves everything but is not moved itself. All emanates from it. And, according to Aquinas, that prime mover is God.

Rise of Protestantism. Martin Luther, a Catholic German Augustinian monk, rebelled against the selling of indulgences. An indulgence replaces penance due for sin. When a Catholic went into the confessional and told his or her sins to the priest, the priest gave the penitent an act of penance to perform to show God true contrition. This could range from saying three Hail Marys or an Our Father to working in a soup kitchen or living with lepers, depending on the severity of the sin. If a person has undone penance at death, he or she gets a second chance: purgatory. There are three levels in the afterlife: heaven, hell, and purgatory. Saints go to heaven. Evil people go to hell. Most people are neither saints nor evil, so they go to purgatory. Anyone with sin cannot enter heaven because God and sin cannot coexist: sin is a rejection of God. Purgatory is a state of existence where souls can work off that penance and sin and then go to heaven. But it is not pleasant. Although it is not hell, one can see hell from the front door. So it is preferable to be sinless and have no penance left in this life.

One of the ways to receive an indulgence was to give to the church. This had always been the case. With St. Peter's Basilica being rebuilt, the popes needed money to pay people such as Michelangelo and Rafael and the laborers. The original basilica had been built by Constantine in the 300s. This was now the 1500s: the building was falling apart. So, if the faithful gave money toward the construction of the church, they received an indulgence. But in the minds of the peasants (and at least one priest), it was salvation at a price. Drop a coin in the tin (box), receive a paper that says you have an indulgence, and then carte blanche. Luther came out of church one day and saw one of his parishioners drunk in an alley. "Why were you not at Mass today?" Luther asked. The man said he had bought an indulgence so he did not have to show up. So Luther became incensed, particularly because his church had a display of saints' relics and asked for an admission fee that would buy an indulgence. So Luther wrote the 95 Theses, which were 95 reasons why the sale of indulgences was wrong, and he nailed them to the door of the Wittenberg Castle church. Unfortunately, he wrote them in Latin, so the general populace could not read them. A copy was sent to the pope, though, who allegedly said, "He's a German. He will change his mind when he sobers up." Luther became angry (he is called the "firebrand of Germany" for good reason), and he added his belief in the doctrines of *sola fide* (by faith alone is one saved; one does not need good works resulting in indulgences) and *sola scriptura* (by scripture alone is one saved; one does not need the church). After a series of confrontations, including a meeting with the Hapsburg emperor at Worms, Luther was excommunicated from the church. The German princes then kidnapped him to protect him from punishment, using his words in their attempt to secede from the Hapsburg Empire.

This was the beginning of the Protestant Reformation. The word "Protestant" comes from the Latin word for protest, because a Protestant protests against the Catholic Church. Other Protestant reformers thought Luther had not gone far enough. John Calvin, also a former Catholic priest, came up with the belief in the depravity of humanity: humans are so depraved they cannot save themselves; only God can save them. Calvin also believed in predestination: some of you are going to heaven and some of you are not going to graduate, and there is nothing you can do about it because God has already decided. Calvin also decided there was no transubstantiation at communion (which is why Protestants do not believe in transubstantiation).

Another break from the Catholic Church came when King Henry VIII of England wanted a male heir after marrying his brother's widow. When he and his wife were unable to produce one, Henry sought a divorce. At that time, only the pope could annul a marriage. Henry sent his request to the pope, who said no. In response, Henry created his own church, the Church of England, and he granted himself a divorce. Some scholars do not consider Anglicans (Church of England) to be Protestant because Henry had no problem with Catholic doctrine; he just had a personal problem.

Protestantism, having no central authority, would fragment into smaller pieces. Breaking off from the Anglicans was John Knox, who formed the Church of Scotland, and from them came the Presbyterians. Also breaking off from the Anglicans was a blue-collar movement, founded by John and Charles Wesley, called the Methodists. Another group that split off from the Anglicans were the Anabaptists, or rebaptizers. They believed their baptisms were the only valid ones, so converts to Anabaptism had to be baptized again. This would give rise to the Baptists, the Amish, and the Mennonites. A final group breaking off from the Anglicans were the Puritans, who wanted to purify Anglicanism of any remaining Catholic elements. They were also known as the Pilgrims. Also breaking off from the Church of England was the Society of Friends (Quakers), pacifists who sat in the Friendship Halls facing each other until someone stood up with a revelation. The Anglicans in the United States were forced to leave the Church of England after 1776 for political reasons: alignment with the enemy during the American Revolution was considered treason. They became the Episcopalians. Breaking off from the Lutherans were the Disciples of Christ and the Reformed Church.

The Great Awakening was a series of revival movements during which itinerant preachers would come to towns and preach in the open or in tents, creating a flurry of emotions. Emotion was seen as the way to truly connect to God. One of these preachers was Jon Edwards, who preached a sermon called "Sinners in the Hands of an Angry God." Out of the Great Awakening movement came the Holiness churches, which handled poisonous snakes because the Bible said one could: "They will pick up serpents (with their hands), and if they drink any deadly thing, it will not harm them" (Mark 16:18). Springing from the Holiness churches were the Pentecostals, who speak in tongues (which are repetitive sounds), employ prophesy, and are "slain in the spirit," falling to the ground like they are dead. A modern-day example of Protestant Pentecostals is the Assemblies of God church. Catholics also have Pentecostals, and they are called charismatics. Also coming out of the Great Awakening was fundamentalism, which is a literal interpretation of the Bible.

Protestant Reformers shortened the Bible by removing the following books—Tobit, Judith, 1st and 2nd Maccabees, Wisdom of Solomon, Ecclesiastics, Baruch, and parts of Esther and Daniel—as not canonical (i.e., the Apocrypha, or "hidden writings"). From his church's Bible, Luther removed the Epistle of James because it states that faith without works "is dead" (James 2:17), which seemed to reject *sola fide*. He called James "so much straw" that should be burned. In addition to James, Luther removed Hebrews, Jude, and the Apocalypse from the New Testament and placed them at the end of his Bible, but later Reformers reinstated them.

The Catholic Reformation was a response to the Protestant Reformation. A major part of it was the Council of Trent (1545–1563), when bishops met to determine what Catholicism believed in light of the Protestants' contentions. Protestants attended, too, but they were not allowed to contribute to the decision-making. In the end, the council rejected most everything Luther said. It reaffirmed that faith and works save (because it says so in Timothy) and that the Church has equal authority with the Bible because it created that scripture, so no *sola scriptura*. And it reaffirmed the books of the Bible that the Protestants had removed.

Another part of the Catholic Reformation was the formation of the Society of Jesus (Jesuits) by Ignatius of Loyola. The former soldier created a military order of priests to counter Protestantism. Candidates are ruddy in appearance, intelligent, and strong. Jesuits convert much of the Americas, Africa, and the Far East to Catholicism.

Modern Christianity

In the 19th century, the Catholic Church's First Vatican Council set the doctrine of papal infallibility. This holds that the pope can never be wrong when he is speaking about Catholic doctrine and morals and that he is speaking *ex cathedra* ("from the chair") of St. Peter. Because the pope is the primary teacher of the Catholic Church, if he is wrong, it would be a monumental catastrophe. The council also set doctrine (this means Catholics have to believe it) on something Catholics have believed for two millennia: the Immaculate Conception. This is the doctrine that Mary was conceived without original sin: Mary could not have been conceived with sin if she were to be the mother of Jesus (God), because sin is the rejection of God. Mary would be rejecting her own son if she had sin.[7]

The Second Vatican Council (early 1960s) changed many important aspects of the Catholic Church. The most notable was allowing the vernacular in worship services. Up until that time, the mass had been said in Latin;

after the council, the mass could be said in any language. The council also increased the role of the laity in the parish churches, emphasized ecumenism (unity among Christians) with other denominations, and stated that Jews were not responsible for the death of Jesus. The conference was called by Pope John XXIII ("Johnny Walker," because he liked to take strolls in Rome and surprise people), although it was concluded during the term of the next pontiff, Pope Paul VI.[8]

Pope John Paul II (1978–2005) helped fight European communism, promoted ecumenism (unity) among Christian denominations and other religions, and increased membership to record levels. Particularly successful in increasing membership were his World Youth Days, when he would travel around the world and meet Catholic youth in different cities. He was canonized a saint in 2016 along with John XXIII. Pope Benedict XVI (2005–2013) concentrated on ecumenism with the Eastern Orthodox (working to end the Great Schism) and Protestants. He was the first pope to resign in 596 years and the first pope ever to willingly resign. He was given the never-before-used title of pope emeritus. Pope Francis (2013–present), the first Latin American pope and the first Jesuit pope, brought to Rome his focus on the poor. He told Catholic bishops, priests, and nuns to refrain from having expensive homes and cars. He moved into a dorm for Vatican employees instead of the lavish papal apartments: instead, he allowed two Syrian refugee families to stay in the papal apartments. Francis also wanted the church to be more open to divorced people and homosexuals, but he made no changes in church doctrine: no homosexual marriages in the church. He has also been a world peace mediator, brokering normalization of relations between the United States and Cuba and serving as a peace ambassador between Israel and the Palestinians.

In the Orthodox churches, leadership is shared among several patriarchs and bishops ("equals" but with autonomous local sees). Unity has been a problem: the Russian Orthodox Church snubbed the Orthodox churches' "Great Council" in 2016, and split from the Patriarch of Constantinople over the latter's decision to remove the Ukrainian Orthodox Church from Russia's control. The Orthodox churches are organized along ethnic or national lines for the most part, and they place emphasis on mysticism: experiencing God instead of analyzing him (unlike Aquinas). For instance, religious icons are holier than statues. Icons are windows through which God's grace flows. If one touches an icon, one will receive God's blessing. By comparison, statues are not holy in the Catholic Church.

In modern Protestantism, an ecumenical movement led by the World Council of Churches brings different denominations together for charitable work projects in Third World countries. There have been some organic unions among denominations: the Methodist Church combined with the Evangelical United Brethren Church in 1969, creating the United Methodist Church. The Lamb of God Church in Fort Myers, Florida, was formed by the union of a Lutheran and an Episcopalian church in 2004. And the Evangelical Church stated in 2016 that there were no doctrinal differences between Lutherans and Catholics.

There are many more divisions in Protestantism than in Catholicism. Protestant churches have split into smaller and smaller groups, with the creation of storefront churches and nondenominational denominations. In 2016, the Episcopal Church USA was suspended from the Anglican communion with Church of England–affiliated churches over the issue of an active homosexual bishop.

The resurgence of Calvinism is occurring among evangelical Protestants. This next generation of Calvinistic churches has become more hard-line, with beliefs in predestination and the depravity of humans as well as no belief in transubstantiation.[9]

There have been some homegrown American Protestant religions. In the 1800s, there was a lot of talk about the impending end of the world. One of those supporting this belief was William Miller, who predicted that the end of the world would be between 1843–1844. After this "great disappointment," other religious groups sprang up. One of these was the Seventh-Day Adventists, an end-of-the-world denomination that meets on Saturdays, the original Jewish Sabbath.[10] They incorporate Miller's beliefs: there will be a rapture, a thousand-year rule of Jesus, and then a final battle with Satan/Antichrist. Many Protestants have adopted these beliefs. Catholics and Orthodox do not believe in a rapture.

Branching off from the Seventh-Day Adventists in 1934 were the Davidians, founded by Victor Houteff. He predicted that the start of the eternal kingdom of David would be soon. His widow, Florence, predicted the date would be in 1959. The Branch Davidians split off in 1955 from the Davidians. Vernon Howell joined the group and became its leader. He renamed himself David Koresh (Koresh is the Hebrew name of the Persian king Cyrus;

David is after King David) and began to "plant the seeds" of the new age by fathering children with congregation women. Koresh believed he was the anointed one to open the Seven Seals described in the Book of Revelation. The way he was going to do that was to write a commentary on it. That was when federal agents attempted a forced entry into his Waco, Texas, compound. Koresh saw this as the end of world, and people on both sides were killed in a shootout before most members of the cult died when their compound went up in flames. The FBI now uses religious scholars in dealing with people like this.

Oh, they're back. Charles Pace has created the New Branch Davidians, which has created dissent among surviving members of the original group who are waiting for Koresh to return from the dead and revive the group.

In 1866, Mary Baker Eddy founded Christian Science after she said she was spiritually healed of a spinal injury after a fall. She wrote about her beliefs in *Science and Health with a Key to the Scriptures*. She concluded that faith, not medicine, should be used to heal because disease and injury are caused by sin. Matter is illusion; only the mind and spirit are real. The Christian Science church has its headquarters in Boston, but it may be declining with the closing of its reading rooms across the country. In 2016, a count of its membership's online directory showed 1,750 members.[11]

Joseph Smith, the son of an evangelical preacher, founded the Church of Jesus Christ of Latter-day Saints (Mormons) in 1822. That year, according to Smith, the Angel Moroni led him to where the golden tablets were buried. Written on the tablets was a history of Christ coming to the Americas and converting the Native Americans descended from the ten lost tribes of Israel who had sailed over to the New World. Not all the Native Americans were converted, and after a big battle, the non-Christian ones (Lamanites) beat the Christian ones (Nephites). Moroni, the last of the Nephites, wrote the story on golden tablets, buried them, and came back several centuries later to tell Smith where they were. Smith dug them up and translated them into the Book of Mormon.

Smith headed west with his followers, but a lynch mob in Illinois killed him in 1844. His widow and his son, Joseph Smith III, formed the Reorganized Church of Jesus Christ of Latter-day Saints (now Community of Christ). Brigham Young led the rest of the church to the Great Salt Lake, Utah, territory in 1847, established the group's headquarters there, declared independence from the United States, refused to pay taxes, and practiced polygamy. When President James Buchanan heard about the Mormon activities, he sent the US Army to regain control of the territory. After initially holding off the army, the Mormons eventually surrendered and conceded on the issues of taxes, government control, and monogamy.

Mormons have different beliefs than other self-professed Christians. They view Jesus Christ as God of this world but also believe humans can be gods (of their own worlds). The latter is not doctrine, but several prophets (heads of the church) have said this. Mormons believe that the Trinity is actually three separate gods; that marriage is eternal; that baptism can occur after death; and that there are three levels after death: the Celestial, Terrestrial, and Telestial Kingdoms. The Celestial is the highest level, where faithful Mormon males can become gods. Again, although this is not official doctrine, several of the church's presidents have stated it. Leadership is through the prophet and a governing body called the Council of the Twelve Apostles.

Sacred scripture for Mormons include the Protestant Bible, the Book of Mormon, the Doctrine and Covenants (teaching of the prophets), and the Pearl of Great Price (Smith's own testimony).

The Jehovah's Witnesses were founded by Charles Taze Russell (1852–1916), son of Pennsylvania Presbyterians. Russell was a haberdasher in his father's men's clothing store. He believed the creeds of other Christian denominations had "elements of truth" but were buried under pagan teachings, like a hierarchy. The Jehovah's Witnesses began as an 1870 Bible study group. Then the group started publishing tracts, such as the *Watch Tower*. They believed that, according to the Bible, only 144,000 people will go to heaven, and then it will be full. The good will rise and live forever on an earthly paradise with Jesus. The evil will stay dead. They also believe Jesus Christ is not God but "a god," and their Bible, the New World Translation, has been rewritten to reflect their beliefs. So Jehovah's Witnesses have a different Bible than those of other Christians.

Also arising during the end of the 20th century was the Black liberation movement. A Baptist minister, Martin Luther King Jr., was a major proponent of this movement. King drew on his religious background to announce that Blacks are equal to Whites because God says so, not because of the government or Constitution. This divine right to equality is also present in liberation theology, which emphasizes power sharing between the rich and the poor. A more radical form of liberation theology in Latin America believes that the rich must share with the poor and that the poor can use violence to take from the rich if the latter are not willing. Pope Benedict XVI condemned this movement before he was elected pope because of the violence involved. Feminist liberation theology, another 20th-century movement, states that women are equal to men because God says so. She does. God is a woman, and men have been hiding that fact for centuries so they could dominate women. Ecofeminism, whose main proponent was Rosemary Radford Reuther, emphasized a love for nature because Gaia, the earth goddess, was a woman, too.

Christian Scripture

Christianity is one of the few religions of the world that has different versions of its scripture. Catholics, Protestants, and Orthodox have different books in their Bibles. Catholics have 72 books, Protestants have 66 books, and Orthodox can have up to 81 books. The reason has to do with history. By the second century, there were several translations of the Bible, the most popular being Old Latin or Itala. The Degree of the Council of Rome in 382 officially approved the books of the Bible. But mistakes were creeping in with each copy made by hand, so the pope commissioned Jerome to revise and correct it: the result was the Latin Vul-

FIGURE 5.9 Jerome translated the Bible into Latin, creating the Latin Vulgate, in this cell in Bethlehem.

gate, which would be the official Bible of Christianity for about a thousand years and translated into different languages. Protestants in the 1500s started writing their own, excluding the Old Testament books mentioned earlier. These included Luther's, William Tyndale's, Miles Coverdale's, and others: Tavernier's Bible, the Great Bible, and the Bishop's Bible. King James I of England had officials rewrite the Bishop's Bible, and this became the King James Bible, which many Protestants use. But because of mistakes, it was revised again in the mid-1800s and is known as the Revised Version. Catholics, in the meantime, created another Bible (called the New American Bible) in 1970 from original Greek, Aramaic, and Hebrew sources. Orthodox churches generally used the Catholic Bible before the Great Schism. But other Orthodox, such as Egyptian Christians, used other books as well, since they were read in their liturgy.[12]

Christian Beliefs

Humans can be separated from God due to sin, which is a rejection of God. The original cause of sin is original sin, the sin of Adam and Eve in the Garden of Eden. All humans inherit this sin, and baptism removes it. So no one is born a Christian; they have to be baptized first.

The ultimate goal is the kingdom of God in heaven as well as on earth. Christians want to go to heaven, not hell. Catholics also have the concept of purgatory as another afterlife option (though temporary), while Protestants generally do not believe in purgatory: the kingdom of God on earth is the mandate to convert the world to Christianity, as mentioned in the passage that opens this chapter. Some Protestants believe there will be a rapture on earth, with the good being taken up to heaven before the end of the world. Catholics and Protestants do not.

The means to get to heaven is through God's grace, faith that God can save one, and sacraments. Catholics have seven: Baptism, Reconciliation, Eucharist, Confirmation, Marriage, Holy Orders, and the Sacrament of the Sick. Most Protestant churches have two: Baptism and the Lord's Supper (communion).

Christian Branches

Catholicism

Catholicism is the largest branch of Christianity and the oldest, dating back to Peter as the first pope. Other popes followed for two thousand years. The religion has two major "rites." The Latin Rite is the largest and requires its priests to be celibate. The Eastern Rite reflects the local ethnicity of a community, such as the Greek Catholic or Russian Catholic Church. Loyal to the pope, its clergy can marry, though bishops and monks must be celibate. As mentioned before, the Catholic Church has seven sacraments, which are ritual actions through which God's grace is bestowed: Baptism, Eucharist, Confirmation, Reconciliation, Marriage, Holy Orders, and the Sacrament of the Sick (formerly known as Last Rites). Catholics believe in a communion of saints that can intercede for people on earth with God.

Protestantism

Protestantism does not have a common theology or structural organization, so there are literally thousands of Protestant denominations with different interpretations of the Bible. Some common beliefs include Luther's *sola fide* and *sola scriptura.* The supreme authority of the Bible is emphasized. Some denominations believe in the Trinity; some do not. Some denominations have consubstantiation; others believe the Lord's Supper is purely symbolic. Anglicans tend to have a communion of saints, while other denominations do not.

Orthodox

Orthodox Churches tend to reflect the national or ethnic makeup of its members (Russian, Greek, Romanian, Egyptian, etc.). There are 14 autocephalous, or autonomous, Orthodox churches, all of which are titled equal to each other, but the Ecumenical Patriarchate is titled first among equals. They consider themselves to be united in faith, but unity has been a problem with the Russian Orthodox Church, as mentioned earlier in this chapter. Orthodox have the same seven sacraments as the Catholic Church. They also have the communion of saints.

Christian Holidays

Christian holidays vary depending on the denomination. Some are universal.

Advent: four weeks before Christmas; the beginning of the liturgical (worship) year; observed by Catholics, Orthodox, and some Protestants; preparation spiritually for Christmas (Orthodox fast)

Immaculate Conception: December 8; commemorates the conception of Mary without sin; celebrated by Catholics

Christmas: December 25 for Catholics and some Protestants; January 7 for Orthodox (based on the Julian and not Gregorian calendar); celebrates the birth of Jesus, if not his actual birthday

Solemnity of Mary, the Mother of God: January 1; celebrates Mary in her title as the mother of Jesus; observed by Catholics

FIGURE 5.10 An altar was erected in what was once Mary's house.

Epiphany: the 12th day of Christmas in January for Catholics; celebrates the arrival of the three wise men to Jesus's home; January 6 for Orthodox, it celebrates the baptism of Jesus by John the Baptist

Ash Wednesday: about six weeks before Easter; the beginning of Lent, a period of fasting and abstinence from meat on certain days, penance, and preparation for Easter; for Catholics, Anglicans (Episcopalians), and Lutherans

Lent: about a six-week long preparation for Easter; for Catholics, Orthodox, and some Protestants

Palm Sunday: Sunday before Easter; commemorates Jesus's entry into Jerusalem and Jesus's passion

Holy or Maundy Thursday: the Thursday before Easter; celebrates the Last Supper by Catholics, Orthodox, and Protestants

Good Friday: the Friday before Easter; observes the crucifixion of Jesus; for Catholics, Orthodox, and Protestants

Easter: celebrates the resurrection of Jesus from the dead; for Catholics, Protestants, and Orthodox (though often on a different day for Orthodox)

Ascension: 40 days after Easter; observes Jesus's ascent into heaven; celebrated by Catholics

Pentecost: 50 days after Easter; observes the descent of the Holy Spirit upon the Apostles; celebrated by Catholics, Orthodox, and Protestants

Nativity of the Virgin Mary: September 8; celebrates the birth of Mary; for Catholics and Orthodox

Elevation of the Life-Giving Cross: September 14; observes the finding of the Cross by the Empress Helen (the mother of Constantine); observed by Orthodox

FIGURE 5.11 This church marks the spot where Mary was born.

Presentation of the Virgin Mary in the Temple: November 21; observes Mary's consecration to God by her parents; observed by Orthodox

Presentation of Christ (or Lord) in the Temple: February 2; observes the circumcision of Jesus; celebrated by Catholics and Orthodox

Annunciation: March 25; celebrates Gabriel's announcement to Mary that she will conceive a son; observed by Catholics and Orthodox

Transfiguration: August 6; observes Jesus's appearance to the apostles with Elijah and Moses on the mountain; God the Father tells them to listen to Jesus

Assumption (Catholic), Repose, or Dormition of the Virgin Mary (Orthodox): August 15; observes Mary's resurrection into heaven; Orthodox believe Mary's body was taken to heaven three days after her death; Catholics believe Mary did not die but was assumed into heaven bodily

Reformation Day: October 31; Protestants celebrate the Protestant Reformation

All Saints' Day: November 1; celebrates all saints in heaven; observed by Catholics; Orthodox celebration is on the first Sunday after Pentecost

FIGURE 5.12 Orthodox Christians believe Gabriel visited Mary at this well.

FIGURE 5.13 Pope Pius XII made the Assumption doctrine for Catholics.

ENDNOTES

1 C. Hackett et al., "The Future of World Religions: Population Growth Projections, 2010–2050." Pew Research Center, 2015, http://www.pewforum.org/2015/04/02/religious-projections-2010-2050/.

2 T. Johnson, "World Christian Database: Navigating Statistics on Religion," American Theological Library Association proceedings, 2014, http://ezproxy.lib.usf.edu/login?url=http://search.ebscohost.com/login.aspx?direct=true&db=rfh&AN=ATLA0001456958&site=eds-live.

3 W. Durant, *Caesar and Christ* (New York: Simon and Schuster, 1944).

4 *New American Bible* (Washington, DC: Catholic Biblical Association of America, 1970).

5 John Walsh, *The Bones of St. Peter: The First Full Account of the Search for the Apostle's Body* (Doubleday & Co., 1982).

6 Nick Squires, "Bone Fragments Confirmed to Be Saint Paul," *The Telegraph*, 2009, https://www.telegraph.co.uk/news/worldnews/europe/vaticancityandholysee/5685157/Bone-fragments-confirmed-to-be-Saint-Paul.html.

7 H. Bettenson and C. Maunder, eds., *Documents of the Christian Church*, 3rd ed. (Oxford, UK: Oxford University Press, 1999).

8 "First Vatican Council." *Encyclopaedia Britannica*, https://www.britannica.com/event/First-Vatican-Council.

9 Jordan Teicher, "Why Is Vatican II So Important?" National Public Radio, 2012, https://www.npr.org/2012/10/10/162573716/why-is-vatican-ii-so-important.

10 Lillian Kwon, "Resurgence of Calvinism is Real Despite Survey, Pastors Say," *Christian Post*, 2010, https://www.christianpost.com/news/resurgence-of-calvinism-is-real-despite-survey-pastors-say-47678/.

11 William Miller, *Christianity Today*, https://www.christianitytoday.com/history/people/denominationalfounders/william-miller.html.

12 *Christian Science Journal Directory*, 2016, http://directory.christianscience.com/search?query=&language=all&distance_select=any&manual_location=&location=.

13 M. Bonocore, "Why Does the Orthodox Bible Have More Books Than the Catholic Bible?" Catholic Bridge.com, 2016, http://catholicbridge.com/orthodox/why_orthodox_bible_is_different_from_catholic.php.

6

HINDUISM

LEARNING OBJECTIVES

1. Learn how Hinduism and Indian history are tied together

2. Understand the evolution of Hindu beliefs from Dravidians and Indo-Aryans

3. Know the social problems of India and how they are connected to Hinduism, including the caste system

4. Understand how Hindus can devote themselves to a god or be atheists and still seek salvation

5. Know the scripture of Hinduism and how it contributes to the belief system

> Not one of you, gods, is small, nor once a little child; all
> of you are truly great.
> Therefore you are worthy of praise and of sacrifice, you
> thirty-three gods of Manu, arrogant and powerful.
> Protect us, help us and speak for us; do not lead us into the distance far away from the path of our father Manu.
> You gods who are all here and who belong to all men, give
> far-reaching shelter to us and to our cows and horses.
> —"To All the Gods," Rig-Veda

Hindu Statistics

Counting Hindus is difficult because they belong to many different sects. Hinduism is actually a collection of religions that use the same scripture. It is estimated that there are 930 million Hindus in the world, most in India, with about 20 million in other parts of the world.[1]

Hindu Mythology

Hindus have a variety of myths and beliefs about their origins and what is desirable and undesirable in life. Students should be cautioned not to try to make sense of Hinduism: it causes headaches to do so. Hinduism is several

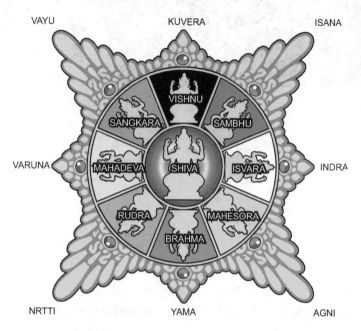

FIGURE 6.1 Hindu Gods Chart. "The Sun of Majapahit" is the emblem commonly found in Majapahit ruins. Displaying the image of eight-pointed sun rays. The emblem consisting of images of nine Hindu gods and eight sun rays also symbolizes Hindu gods arranged in eight cardinal points. The 17 Hindu gods represented in Surya Majapahit are: Shiva, Vishnu, Sambhu, Isvara, Mahesora, Brahma, Rudra, Mahadeva, Sangkara, Kuvera, Isana, Indra, Agni, Yama, Nrtti, Varuna, and Vayu.

religions with the same scripture lumped together. So think of the religion as a four-thousand-year-old vacuum cleaner that has sucked up everything and thrown nothing away: everything is still in the canister. There are different goals one can follow: one can become a millionaire, starve him or herself, or engage in orgies. All of these are okay.

The Rig-Veda, the oldest Hindu scripture, has varying accounts of the creation of the universe and the world. It asks, "Who knows?" No one was there at the beginning, not even the gods. But there may have been "seed-placers" who started life. But that is not for certain because no one knows.

In another account in the book, there is a Golden Embryo that arises and gives life and commands the gods. Other accounts say creation was a by-product of a cosmic battle or gods separating heaven and earth.[2] Then there is the account of the avatar Krishna being born and overthrowing a king to become leader of Mathura, defending Indians from enemies and advocating for the downtrodden.[3]

Krishna claimed to be the all-knowing one, "the Knower of the field," or the body, while talking to the warrior Arjuna. "I am the Knower of the field in everyone, Arjuna. Knowledge of the field and its Knower is true knowledge."[4] This is why a latter manifestation of Hinduism, the Hare Krishnas, consider Krishna as the supreme being.

Ultimately, there would be between 90 million and 330 million Hindu gods. This is just an estimate: no one knows how many gods there are. Hinduism is ecocentric, so most of nature is divine: rivers, mountains, and strangely shaped rocks. Every village has its own local gods.

FIGURE 6.2 Saraswati, the goddess of knowledge, music, arts, wisdom and learning, is sitting in the lotus position.

Hindu History

The history of Hinduism is the history of India. The religion draws on the many cultures that have occupied the subcontinent. As early as 2500 BCE, the Indus Valley civilization thrived. They apparently worshipped a fertility goddess or goddesses[5] and used the lotus position for meditation. So goddesses, like the rivers of India—including the holiest river, the Ganges—may have come from the Indus Valley civilization, along with the lotus position: a half-cross-legged position uncomfortable enough to keep one awake during meditation.

What happened next is a point of argument among historians, archeologists, and religious studies types. The Indo-Aryans—the light-skinned settlers of Europe, although this particular group came from Persia (Iran)—invaded between 1800–1500 BCE and destroyed what was left of the Indus civilization structures. The invaders encountered Dravidians: dark-skinned peoples who inhabited India. So speculation abounds as to what happened to the Indus civilizations. One theory is that they outstripped their food supply and returned to a more agrarian culture. The more technologically advanced Aryans drove the Dravidians into southern

India and dominated them in the rest of the country. Dravidians worshipped cows as a type of fertility goddess. This is why cows later on were sacred to Hindus.

The Aryans brought with them a work-in-development religion, the Rig-Veda, "the Veda of stanzas of praise," which eventually would have one thousand hymns to their gods. This is the oldest Hindu scripture, although the gods in the Rig-Veda are no longer worshipped today because they are too old. But passages from the scripture are still read at Hindu weddings.

The Aryans communicated with their gods using sacrificial fires instead of temples, which were used by the Indus civilization. In these sacrifices, animals, butter, and milk were burned. Horse sacrifice was the most costly and was done only for kings. Libations (drinks poured out in offering) were shared with gods, including the fermented juice of the soma plant, the exact identity of which is in dispute. Apparently, the best way to talk to the gods was by being rip-roaring drunk. Hindus have adopted this method of communicating with the gods, though they do not burn animals anymore.

FIGURE 6.3 The Indo-Aryans brought the Rig-Veda to India.

The heat from the sacrificial fires is called tapas, which is not to be confused with the appetizers in a Spanish restaurant that are also hot and spicy. In Hindu mythology, heat is actually the language of the gods, and as this sacrificial heat rises to the heavens, it takes Hindu supplications with it.

An early Aryan god was Indra, god of storms and ruler of the space between heaven and earth, because that is where storms occur. He was probably in charge of flying birds and any aircraft that had not yet been invented. He later may have become an aspect of Shiva, destroyer god and god of agriculture, because rain destroys and waters crops, according to at least one theory. This is an example of gods and symbols being recycled (recall the theories of Carl Jung in the first chapter).

The Aryans brought to India the tradition of henotheism, which is the elevation or worship of one god out of many. The Vedic (any religion that uses the scripture called the Vedas) and Hindu traditions are henotheism.

The Aryans also created the caste system and placed themselves on top. The following are levels of the caste system, starting from the top:

- Brahmins: priests who performed public and private ceremonies and interceded with gods

- Kshatriyas: rulers and warriors

- Vaisyas: common people, middle class, and merchants

- Shudras: servants and laborers

- Untouchables: a subcaste of the shudras who were lower than the low; members of this caste worked the most miserable jobs, such as shoveling cow dung off streets, removing dead bodies for cremation, and working with leather, which was disgusting because cows were sacred

FIGURE 6.4 Gods and spirits were often placed on elephants, since the latter were regular means of transportation in India.

What is considered good and evil in Hinduism is what kept people in their place. The religion stresses one should do one's *dharma*, or duty. If a person is a Brahman, he is the prayer and ritual leader. If a person is a warrior, he fights and/or rules. If a person is a merchant, his job is to make money through business (Donald Trump made the move from merchant to warrior when he was elected). If a person does not do one's duty as dictated by his or her caste, that person strays in to *maya*, which means illusion. Anything outside one's dharma or duty is illusion, and karma will punish that person severely in the next life. People in this state may come back as cockroaches eating stale crumbs behind a refrigerator. So the concepts of dharma and maya kept people in their place.

Tapas revolt. The Brahmans had the power to conduct rituals and communicate with the gods. Only the Brahmans had this spiritual power, which involved a ritual fire in which plant matter was burned, as mentioned before. But the lower castes, particularly the Kshatriyas, were upset at this monopoly of power and revolted against the Brahmans, because everyone had to pay to pray to the gods. The Brahmans defused the situation by letting everyone internalize tapas. Now people could pray to the gods directly because they had that spiritual power within themselves. Brahmans were still hired for public *pujas* and ceremonies, but families could do their private pujas by themselves. One group, who would later become the Buddhists, broke away from Hinduism at this point, not accepting the compromise.

Empire period. The people on the Indian subcontinent lived under several empires before being invaded by Muslims in the 13th century in a particularly bloody conflict. The Hindus responded by fighting back unsuccessfully against the Mughal invaders. By the 15th century, however, the Mughal Empire was well established in India. During this time, the Taj Mahal, a Muslim monument, was built by Mughal Emperor Shah Jahan as a tomb for his wife.[6]

By the 18th century, as the Mughal Empire began to disintegrate, the British Empire would occupy India, making it a colony.

Reaction to foreign influences varied. Some Hindus accepted Western traditions brought by the Muslims and British; other Hindus rejected them. One of those groups accepting them was the Brahmo Samaj (Brahmanist Society), founded by Ram Mohan Roy in 1828 in Calcutta. Roy examined Buddhism, Zoroastrianism, Islam, and Christianity and concluded God is at the essence of all of them. So they were okay for Indians to join.[7]

Hindus who were against Western traditions included the Arya Samaj (Aryan Society), a "back to the Vedas" movement founded in Bengal in 1875 by Swami (teacher) Dayananda, a Brahmin. This group rejected all non-Vedic religions— that is, any religion that did not use the Vedas as their scripture. Interestingly enough, Dayananda concluded there was one god behind the Vedas, not several, when they are properly understood. So this is an example of monotheism in Hinduism.[8]

FIGURE 6.5 Gods decorate the Hindu temple of Florida in Tampa. Before the Tapas Revolt, only the Brahmans could pray to the gods.

The mystical Christian-based philosophy called theosophy, founded in New York City, moved to India in 1878. It aimed to establish a unity, a "brotherhood," among all people no matter what their religious background was. Under theosophy, wisdom was transmitted to followers by masters or Mahatmas.[9]

Another group welcoming Western influences was the Ramakrishna movement. It was founded by 19th-century Hindu saint and seer Ramakrishna. He was born a Brahmin but accepted Western religious tradition. He studied other religions and even joined some of them, at least temporarily. He experienced Islam, Christianity, Jainism, Hinduism, and Buddhism and felt God was in all these religions. He was Muslim for two weeks and then heard church bells, had a vision of Mary and Jesus, and converted to Christianity.[10] Some of his friends were upset he had left Hinduism, but those in the know told them to wait: he was doing all of them.

Aurobindo Ghose, in the late 20th century, pushed "integral yoga" to enable one to become a superman or, if a woman, a superperson.[11] Supposedly, if you did his yoga correctly, you could buy a one-way ticket to India and just fly back yourself. Travel light: no checked bags.

Sarvepalli Radhakrishnan, the late president of India, showed cordiality to Western religion and philosophy and stressed mysticism as the heart of religion, not so much God. So he was accepting of Western religious traditions.

Opposing Western influence in India have been political and social groups, including the Mahasabha and Rashtriya Swayamesevak Sangh (RSS), "National Purity Service Organization," which pushed for a Hindu state in India. These groups supported Hindu nationalism: India for Hindus only. An RSS member assassinated Mahatma Gandhi because he dealt with Muslims when seeking India's independence from England.

Social reforms. Social reforms in India were hallmarks of the 20th and 21st centuries. For instance, the caste system has led to discrimination. Those at the bottom originally were not allowed to run for office. Nor could they get higher-paying jobs. As a national leader, Gandhi took up the cause of the untouchables: he promoted members of the lower castes in the government. By 2017, an untouchable was elected president of India. Legislation has also tried to eliminate the caste system, with limited effect. Another attempt at dismantling the caste system was called "opposition by withdrawal." Hindus created groups outside the caste system, giving each group the name of a color, which was similar to the original castes. But this ended up with more castes that refused to mix with each other. Another attempt was "reform from within." The idea was that castes should be seen as aptitudes, not status. A rocket scientist was just as important as the person who emptied the trash cans in the classroom, which is why you are going to school so you can ride the back of a garbage truck at 3 a.m., right? As you can expect, this argument broke down quickly, and people only paid lip service to it: "Sure, garbagemen are important, but my daughter is not marrying one." The problem has been that as long as the caste system is rooted in karma, and karma is a fundamental theology of Hinduism, it is difficult to get rid of the caste system. (Those Aryans knew what they were doing thousands of years ago!)

Child marriage has been another problem for India. Children are betrothed as infants because they can only be married in their caste. So you want to line up a spouse before all the good ones are taken. If parents wait until a child is of marriageable age to go spouse hunting, all that is left is two-ton Tommy, who weighs himself on truck scales, and Betty, who really does have a third eye (she keeps it covered with her bangs). The upside of arranged marriage is that it kept families united because they had a vested interest in the relationship working out and they would help each other in hard times. It also eliminated that messy dating scene. The downside is that there was no freedom to marry. And young widows are forbidden to remarry. In the past, to prevent widows from becoming burdens on their in-laws, it was customary for them to throw themselves on their husbands' funeral pyres. This is called "sati," bride-burning. They were encouraged to make an ash of themselves.

The Dowry Prohibition Act of 1961 reduced dowries because female children were being aborted or killed soon after they were born. Daughters were often seen as being too costly for their fathers because when the young women married, their fathers had to provide dowries. A typical dowry amounted to one year's living expenses. Boys made money when they got married; girls were often undesirable. But the 1961 law has had little effect. High dowries have been a way of demonstrating enhanced social status. Sex-selection laws have also been widely ignored. If amniocentesis determines a child is female, some parents still choose abortion or infanticide. To demonstrate the extent of this problem, there have been 7,000 fewer girls born each year in India than expected, according to a 2006 UNICEF report.[12] Another 2006 study found that in the past 20 years, there have been ten million fewer females born than the natural birth rate.[13] This still pales in comparison with the 750,000 abortions each year in the United States, but the Indian abortions usually target just girls.

India's population has boomed in the past two centuries and currently makes up 15 percent of the world's population. Birth control is a violation of the law of karma. Preventing someone from being born in their caste as dictated by karma is maya, which will bring punishment in the next life. Never mind about that little bit concerning parents killing their daughters. Karma can be removed with a dip in the Ganges River or through a temple ritual: after all, it's only a girl.

On the political front, in 1947, Mohandas Gandhi led India to independence from England using peaceful civil disobedience. This method, later copied by Martin Luther King Jr. during the civil rights era in the United States, encourages protestors to break the law but never be violent. Gandhi encouraged Indians to make their own clothes with their own spinning wheels instead of buying England-taxed fabric. More importantly, he encouraged them to make salt without the required English license to do so. The British licensing of the salt was guaranteed income, because no one could survive in the humid climate of India without it. Gandhi told his followers that making salt was the birthright of all Indians. In a memorable march on the Dharmapada Salt Works, Gandhi's followers were mercilessly beaten by security forces, but the marchers never raised a hand to defend themselves. The repercussions of this tragic event prompted the British to move out of the country and give India its independence.

Gandhi temporarily united Hindus and Muslims behind his effort, but after India's independence, Muslims found themselves to be a politically weak minority. So Muslims agitated for their own state. To prevent violence,

FIGURE 6.6 Gandhi. Through civil disobedience, Mohandas Gandhi won India's independence from Great Britain.

Gandhi gave them northwestern India—East Pakistan—and west central India—West Pakistan. Later, East Pakistan, at India's urging, became Bangladesh, and West Pakistan dropped the "West." Since then, in a dispute over the northern Kashmir region, India and Pakistan have maintained a hostile border, exchanging artillery fire and experiencing attacks by paramilitary forces.

Within India, many Muslims still live and occasionally fight violently with the majority Hindu population. For example, thousands have been killed in a dispute over a 16th-century mosque built on top of a temple to Rama. The Hindu Bharatiya Janata Party started this dispute after India won its independence. This Hindu nationalist group told the Muslim congregation that they had to move their mosque so the Hindus could rebuild Rama's temple. The Muslims refused. Hundreds of Hindus descended on the site, destroyed the mosque, and then began the temple construction. The flash point for violence occurred when the Hindu workers were returning from the temple site on a train. As the train pulled into the station, the Hindu passengers noticed Muslim merchants on the station platform selling their wares. The Hindus began yelling at them, "Rama, Rama!" Translated into English, that is the equivalent of saying "Your mama! In your face!" The Muslims torched the train, and the civil strife was launched.

Another group, the Sikhs, lost their homeland when Pakistan was formed. They also agitated for a homeland, but they were suppressed by the army sent by Indian Prime Minister Indira Gandhi. In retaliation, two of her Sikh bodyguards killed her in 1984. Now it might just be me, but if I am going to fight Sikhs, maybe I don't want them as my bodyguards, too. We will talk more about the Sikhs in their own chapter.

Hindu Scripture

Hinduism has a lot of scripture, developed through the centuries since the arrival of the Indo-Aryans in India. A large body of Hindu scripture is called the Vedas, which means "knowledge" in Sanskrit. They are the most venerated texts in Hinduism. Initially oral, they were written down between 1500 BCE and 400 CE, so they have a long development history.

The Rig-Veda ("the Veda of verse of praise") is a collection of more than a thousand hymns to the gods of the Aryan pantheon. As mentioned, these gods have faded from worship or been incorporated into other deities. The most prevalent god in Rig-Veda is Indra, god of thunder and ruler of space between the heavens and earth, which is where weather happens.

Other parts of the Vedas include books of rituals, hymns, and spells. They also include philosophical utterances called the Upanishads ("to sit nearby," which is how a student learned from his or her teacher). Every living creature has an immortal *atman* (soul). When one's soul is in union with the cosmic soul (Brahman, the creator god), it is Atman. When one's soul is mixed up with the world and its troubles, it is the karmic self (that which is acted upon) and is known as atman. Hindus also get the idea of the cycle of rebirth (reincarnation), *samsara*. In early Hinduism, there was no concept of reincarnation, so it was a later development. The ultimate goal of Hinduism, according to the Upanishads, is the release from the cycle of rebirth: *moksha*, when one achieves "true knowledge." It isn't a coincidence that the Vedas mean knowledge.

The Laws or Code of Manu, written between 200 BCE and 200 CE, are ethical and religious guidelines for society. Manu was the first man, and Hindus believe he left these rules for them. The first part of the code concerns the duty (dharma) of four principle classes or castes, as discussed earlier. The second part of the code describes the four stages of life for men in the top three castes: (1) student (*brahmacarin*); (2) married householder (*grihastha*); (3) forest-dweller (*vanaprastha*), who withdraws from the world, although he can take a wife; and (4) renunciant, who completely withdraws from the world, begs or preaches for food, and is celibate. Most Hindus stop short of becoming a renunciant, because that stage is difficult. Gandhi, for instance, was a forest-dweller.

Hinduism has long epics, too. One is the Ramayana, the story of Rama (a god-man or avatar), who saves his beloved wife from an evil demon using winged monkeys like those in the *Wizard of Oz*. The Mahabharata—one of the longest epics ever written—is seven times the length of the Greek epics *The Iliad* and *The Odyssey* combined. It traces a family up until the time of the climatic standoff mentioned in the *Bhagavad Gita* ("Song of the Lord"), which is the sixth book of the Mahabharata. The *Bhagavad Gita*, popular as an Indian TV show, is about Prince Arjuna on the eve of a great battle, hesitating to fight his kinsmen. Krishna, an avatar, representing the Triad of Gods (most important gods), tells him he must: he is a warrior. The moral of the story: do your dharma (duty) to your caste and avoid maya.

After the *Bhagavad Gita*, the Puranas came into prominence (about 400–900 CE). This scripture concerns the personalities and exploits of the Triad of Gods: Brahma, the creator, who is rarely worshiped because Hindus do not know much about him; Vishnu, the preserver, who comes in the form of avatars to help; and Shiva, the destroyer and agricultural god.

Hindu Beliefs

FIGURE 6.7 The triune godhead is pictured with three heads representing Braham, Vishnu, and Shiva.

Let us look at some Hindu vocabulary words, some of which have already been mentioned before in the scripture section.

- *atman*: one's soul or inner self

- *prakriti*: matter, including one's body and sensory and mental states

- Monism (nondualism): movement toward connecting matter and the universal spirit, Brahman, or creator god; Atman (universal soul) and atman are one

- Qualified nondualism: Atman and atman are connected and affect each other

- Dualism: matter and Brahman are separate; the universe is out to get you, so you need Vishnu, the preserver god, to keep you alive

- *om*: the essence of the ultimate; the sacred syllable; the sound the universe made when it was born

- *turiya*: pure consciousness, which comes about with union with Brahman, self, and the world held together in pure essences, stripped of distortion and illusion; being one with the universe

- *kalpas*: cosmic cycles of the universe being destroyed and reborn regularly; one life cycle is called a kalpa

- *samsara*: sequence of change and reincarnation; the soul is immortal (Upanishads), so humans and animals are reincarnated regularly, hopefully moving up to more knowledgeable beings

- *karma*: law that determines at what stage a person will be reborn, based on one's deeds in the previous life (one reaps what one sows); karma also shapes a soul and determines whether it is born up or down in the caste system

FIGURE 6.8 Elephants pull the wheel of life or rebirth on this temple carving.

- *moksha*: the ultimate goal of a Hindu; being released from rebirth and the wheel of life and entering paradise

Devotional Hinduism (*bhakti*) is practiced by most Hindus because it is easier than other forms. The way of devotion is an ardent love of a particular god or gods.

Common people usually have a favorite god, but they are not monotheistic. All supernatural beings are honored. Worshipers go from shrine to shrine as needed. For example, a worshiper might go to a shrine to Ganesh for overcoming obstacles; Hanuman, the monkey god, for attaining bodily strength; or Rama for help if a father is dying.

There are three different types of worship:

- Individuals can make devotional acts, which include visits to temples as needed.

- A priest or parents can say domestic rites for a family.

- A priest can conduct a ceremony of homage (puja) for the whole community.

Lately, Devi worship has been a movement among women for equal rights. Devi is the consort or wife of Shiva. Oftentimes gods have different manifestations. Devi is the loving mother of Ganesh (the elephant-head god) and wife of Shiva. She is also Kali the Black, a bloodthirsty goddess; Lakshmi, the goddess of wealth; and Sarasvati, the goddess of learning.

Another popular god is Ganesh, the mover of immovable objects. He helps families overcome difficulties and is known today as the kitchen or microwave god because his statue is often kept there, where the family gathers. Ganesh has the head of an elephant because of his dad, Shiva, the god of destruction. I will bring

FIGURE 6.9 Hanuman, the monkey god, is prayed to for bodily strength.

FIGURE 6.10 Having one's car blessed (puja) is part of devotional Hinduism.

this myth up to modern parlance: Devi gave birth to Ganesh while Shiva was off on a business trip doing death and destruction things. Gods grow up fast, so Ganesh was in his teens by the time Shiva returned home. Ganesh was guarding the house because his mom was taking a bath and apparently did not have a door on the house or bathroom. Shiva, tired and crotchety after a day's work, saw this kid blocking the entrance to his home. "Who are you?" he demanded. "Get out of the way." Ganesh had never met his father, but he had his same temper, and he responded, "Doesn't matter. You are not getting in." Shiva, being the god of destruction, chopped the kid's head off, opened a beer, sat down in his easy chair, and turned on the game. When Mom came out of her bath, she was somewhat upset that Junior no longer had a head. So at halftime, she made Shiva go down to earth and find where the

FIGURE 6.11 This shrine is of the Jory goddess: a snake representing rebirth, death, and mortality.

head had landed. He could not find the head by the third quarter, so he picked up an elephant head, brought it home, and stuck that head on the kid. And that is why Ganesh has a face only a mother can love.

Pilgrimages are also popular among Hindus. Common people need more than just domestic rituals; they crave visits to holy places. They will visit other communities' pujas and commercial fairs (*mela*) that feature religious and cultural exhibits and parades. There are two types of pilgrimage destinations: sacred places, such as mountains, caverns, and strangely shaped rocks whose inherent holiness inspired people to build temples on them; and places that become sacred after temples were built on them. A very popular pilgrimage site is the Ganges, the holiest river in India. "Mother Ganga" was believed to issue from Vishnu's feet in heaven and fell on—and flowed out of—Shiva's head far below. Bathing in her waters cleans bathers of karma. So the dead are cremated and ashes are dumped in the river. There is a saying: "The Ganges is so pure, not even a microbe could survive in it." That's because today it is basically an open sewer. Everybody and their brother, their town, and their city dumps human and industrial waste into it.

There are also four permissible goals in life:

- *kama*, the way of pleasure and sex (Kama Sutra is the scripture)
- *artha*, the way of money and power
- *dharma*, the way of the caste system
- *moksha*, the way of denial, starvation, and meditation (renunciants do this)[14]

The Vedic traditions of strength added three ways of salvation, *marga*, or *yoga*. Salvation could be attained through one of the following three ways:

- Way of works; selfless action
- Way of knowledge; trying to comprehend cognitively one's place in the Atman
- Way of devotion, *bhakti*; devotion to a god[15]

FIGURE 6.12 Shiva is the god of death, destruction, and agriculture and apparently has a temper.

Hinduism also has funeral rites for the deceased and his or her family. The Shaddha rites are recited for a dead ancestor and involve the burning of the *pinda* (balls of cooked rice and barley flour that include sesame seeds).

Earlier we mentioned the way of men in the top three castes according to the Laws of Manu. There is also a way for women, *Padmapurana*. Women must please their husbands, no matter how bad the husband is. A wife must eat only after her husband, standing nearby in case he needs something. In the past, because women were not allowed to remarry if their husbands died, it was customary for them to engage in sati, "bride burning." A wife was encouraged to throw herself on her husband's funeral pyre. If she didn't do this of her own volition, her in-laws would encourage her by any means necessary.

Following the horoscope has been important in Indian and Hindu life. An astrologer is consulted for the best days for weddings and other important events. The name of a child when it is born is also determined this way (incorporating the first letter of the name of a star under which the child is born). This does not explain why people in tech support call themselves Bob.

Cows have been sacred to Indians for centuries, beginning with the cow veneration of the Dravidians. Mahatma Gandhi called for cow protection, saying the protection of a dumb animal means the protection of the whole dumb creation of God. Only humans have the intelligence to address ecological problems. Cows usually do not, although they are out standing in their field. Cows are respected by Hindu gods. Shiva has one. Cows may be someone's mother-in-law reincarnated. So you can call your mother-in-law a cow, and because cows are venerated, you can tell her you meant that in the best possible way. Cow dung is still used as fuel, as a disinfectant to wash floors, and as a building material.

As per the caste system and the Laws of Manu, brahmins are holy and have sanctity above all others. Brahmins can be ignorant, but educated brahmins can be teachers (gurus), and they are highly honored brahmins.

Hinduism reveres other holy ones, including the yogins, who hope yoga will liberate them; and the sannyasins, the ash-smeared followers of Shiva with begging bowls. A sadhu is any sacred person. Displays of self-control are part of this holiness: they sit on beds of spikes and sit between fires with their heads down in smoke. Some holy Hindus display in public, whereas others do torments in private, such as on top of a mountain, because they believe their actions are sincerer without the adoration of a crowd.

Reflective models. Reflective models are used by Hindus who do not necessarily believe in God. That is right: you can be a Hindu and be an atheist. Most Hindus follow the way of bhakti, but some prefer the reflective models. Reflective models are used by Hindus to see the "real," meaning seeking out the truth beyond worldly illusion (maya) through intuitive searching instead of cognitive and objective study. They were developed between 500 BCE and 500 CE, and there are many. The six most-used models are the following:

- *The Sankhya System.* Its mythical founder, Kapila, is said to have been born before Buddha. Sankhya is atheistic and believes in two eternal categories of being: matter (the world) and souls or spirits (ourselves). The presence of souls activates matter, and the natural world becomes manifest. How good or bad a person is in life determines how the world forms.[16] So, if you are happy, the world is sunny, the blue bird of happiness is on your shoulder, and the squirrels are waving to you in the park. If you are a miserable person, it is raining, the blue bird of happiness has pooped on your windshield, and the squirrels are flipping you off in the park. You create the world around you.

- *The Yoga System.* Mentioned in the Upanishads, this system uses physiological and psychological measures to assist the mind in concentration, resulting in a state of pure ecstasy without thought and sensation. A later and more esoteric form, Hatha Yoga, activates a power center behind the genitals that uncoils like a serpent and shoots up to the head, producing illumination of the consciousness. Afterward, you may have a difficult time walking out to your car with your rolled yoga mat. Maybe you can light up a cigarette afterward.[17]

- *The Vendanta System.* This system, mentioned before, is made up of three versions of the world, claiming it is illusionary, or "maya," arising from primal creative energy.

- *Nondualism.* The world, the individual ego, and Brahman, although not absolutely one, do not really exist separately; they are "not two" or more. So one, for all intents and purposes, is one with the universe.

- *Qualified Nondualism.* The physical world, individual souls, and the ultimate reality or supreme being are each real, although not divisible. The first two make up the "body of the last." So you and the universe are not one but connected, affecting each other.

- *Dualism.* There is a difference between Vishnu and human souls. Souls are real, and so is the physical world. So the universe is separate from you and may be out to get you. Salvation comes through Vayu, the wind god, the vehicle of the grace of Vishnu and his son. He breathes life-giving power into those he saves.

Hindu Branches

Vaishnavis worship Vishnu and his incarnations as avatars, usually as Krishna or Rama. For Vaishnavis, absolute reality (*brahman*) is manifested in Vishnu, who in turn is incarnated in Rama, Krishna, and other avatars.

Shaivas worship Shiva (often in the form of the *linga*). Saivites esteem self-discipline and philosophy and follow a satguru. They worship in the temple and practice yoga, striving to be one with Siva within.

Shaktas worship Shakti, also known as Devi, as the supreme mother (especially Parvati, Durga, Kali). Shaktas use chants, real magic, holy diagrams, yoga, and rituals to call forth cosmic forces and awaken the great kundalini power within the spine.

Smartas worship five deities (Vishnu, Shiva, Devi, Ganesh, and Surya). Because they accept all the major Hindu Gods, they are known as liberal or nonsectarian.

Saivite Hindus worship the Supreme God as Siva, the Compassionate One. Saivites esteem self-discipline and philosophy and follow a satguru. They worship in the temple and practice yoga, striving to be one with Siva within.[18]

Hindu Holidays

Holi: dedicated to god Krishna; once was a fertility ceremony in February/March. Demons are also celebrated, and taboos are set aside.

Divali: festival lights; New Year; in November; Kali and Lashmi are honored.

Dasehra: nine days in October celebrating Durga's victory over the Buffalo demon. Presents are exchanged; dances and processions are held for the goddess. [19]

SUMMARY

Hinduism, as we have seen, is full of different, sometimes contradictory, traditions and beliefs. We have learned that not all Hindus practice all of Hinduism. It is like a big cafeteria of beliefs from which they can pick and choose. Its resilience and strength, though, lies in the fact that it is linked to Indian culture, as Durkheim said, with the religion being eminently social.

FOR FURTHER READING

An Introduction to Oriental Mythology, Clio Whittaker, contributing ed., Grange Books, 1998

Autobiography of a Yogi, Paramahansa Yogananda, Self-Realization Fellowship, 1993

Hindu Arts and Architecture, George Michell, Thames & Hudson, 2000

Hindu Writings: a Short Introduction to the Major Sources, Klaus K. Klostermaier, Oxford, 2000

The Bhagavad Gita, Kashinath Trimbak Telang, Digireads.com Publishing, 2017

The Complete Idiot's Guide to Hinduism, Linda Johnsen, Alpha, 2002

The Ramayana, Arshia Sattar, trans., Penguin, 1996

The Upanishads, F. Max Müller, trans., Digireads.com Publishing, 2018

The Vedas, Ralph T. H. Griffith and Aruthur Berriedal Keith, trans., Kshetra Books, 2017

The Science of Self Realization, A. C. Bhaktivedanta Swami Prabhupada, International Society for Krishna Consciousness, 1992

ENDNOTES

1   "Hindu Demographics," Hindu American Foundation, 2016, https://www.hafsite.org/hinduism-101/hindu-demographics.

2   W. Doniger, trans., *The Rig Veda* (London: Penguin Books, 1981).

3   L. Johnson, *The Complete Idiot's Guide to Hinduism* (New York: Pearson, 2002).

4   E. Easwaran, trans., *The Bhagavad Gita* (New York: Vintage, 2000), 69.

5   G. Mitchell, *Hindu Art and Architecture* (London: Thames & Hudson, 2000).

6   "The Mughal Empire," Bharatadesam, http://bharatadesam.com/history/mughal_empire.php.

7   "History of the Brahmo Samaj," BrahmosSajaj.net, http://thebrahmosamaj.net/history/history.html.

8   "Arya Samaj," *Encyclopaedia Britannica,* https://www.britannica.com/topic/Arya-Samaj.

9   Paul Johnson, *The Masters Revealed* (SUNY Press, 1994), https://books.google.com/books?id=bMVrr1XaADwC&pg=PA107&dq=Dayananda+Sarasvati+%28Swami%29+-inauthor:%22Dayananda+Sarasvati+%28Swami%29%22&cd=4#v=onepage&q=Dayananda%20Sarasvati%20(Swami)%20-inauthor%3A%22Dayananda%20Sarasvati%20(Swami)%22&f=false.

10   Gahananandaji, "Ramakrishna Movement, " as cited in Ramakrishna Vedanta Society of North Carolina, 1990, http://vedantanc.org/ramakrishna-movement.

11   Sri Aurobindo, Sri Aurobindo Ashram Trust, 2018, https://www.sriaurobindoashram.org/sriaurobindo/

12   UNICEF, "2006 Annual Report," https://www.unicef.org/publications/files/Annual_Report_2006.pdf.

13   "Millions of Missing Girls," Auckland Woman's Heath Council, https://www.womenshealthcouncil.org.nz/Womens+Health+Issues/Millions+of+Missing+Girls.html.

14   Jayaram V, "Purusharthas in Hinduism," Hinduwebsite.com, https://www.hinduwebsite.com/hinduism/h_aims.asp.

15   Tahira Basharat, "Hinduism and Concept of Salvation," University of Punjab, http://pu.edu.pk/images/journal/szic/pdf_files/1-%20tahira%20bashart.pdf.

16   Ferenc Ruzsa, "Sankhya," *Internet Encyclopedia of Philosophy,* http://www.iep.utm.edu/sankhya/.

17   Jayaram V, "The History of Yoga, References in the Upanishads," Hinduwebsite.com, https://www.hinduwebsite.com/upanishads/essays/history-of-yoga-references-in-the-upanishads.asp.

18   "The Four Main Branches," The Heart of Hinduism, ISKCON Educational Services, 2016, https://iskconeducationalservices.org/HoH/tradition/1200.htm.

19   L. Johnson

CREDITS

BUDDHISM

LEARNING OBJECTIVES

1. Learn about Buddha's life
2. Understand what was Buddha's view of life
3. Understand the ultimate goals of Buddhism
4. Explain the path to enlightenment
5. Learn how Buddhism spread after the death of its founder
6. Compare the differences between Theravada and Mahayana Buddhism

All that we are is the result of what we have thought: it is founded on our thoughts, it is made up of our thoughts. If a man speaks or acts with an evil thought, pain follows him, as the wheel follows the foot of the ox that draws the carriage. ... If a man speaks or acts with a pure thought, happiness follows him, like a shadow that never leaves him.
—The Dhammapada

Buddhist Statistics

There are about 488 million Buddhists worldwide, representing 7% of the world's total population as of 2010. Mahayana Buddhism is believed to be the largest because it is prevalent in several countries in Asia with very large Buddhist populations, particularly China, Japan, South Korea, and Vietnam. Theravada Buddhism, the second-largest branch, is confined to Southeast Asia for the most part in such countries as Thailand, Burma (Myanmar), Sri Lanka, Laos, and Cambodia.[1]

Buddhism Myth

There is no origin of the world in Buddhist mythology. Among the various schools of Buddhism, reactions vary: the world does not exist in the first place; the world is just people being reincarnated over and over again until they cease to exist; or there are 31 planes of existence one can wander through. Buddha rejected speculative philosophy: Why are we here, what is our purpose in life, and where do we go when we die? Buddha would answer that you, as a person, do not exist; there is no purpose to life except escape; and—if you are fortunate—you will cease to exist when you die. So any aspect of the Buddhist myth is tied to the historical life of Buddha and his sayings, which we will pursue instead.

Buddhism History

The founder of Buddhism was Siddhartha Gautama. He was born around 563 BCE as a member of the warrior caste (the second Hindu caste) near the holy city of Varanasi in what is now Nepal,[2] which is right beside the holy Ganges River. Siddhartha's father was a wealthy chieftain—warriors, if you remember, fight and rule—and wanted Siddhartha to be India's emperor. A soothsayer told him his son would be a great political leader or a homeless monk; nothing in between. Talk about extremes! So his dad protected him from the outside world and raised

FIGURE 7.1 Lumbini is the traditional site of Siddartha's birth.

FIGURE 7.2 Four Passing Sights. The Four Passing Sights convinced Siddartha that he needed to discover how to escape suffering.

him in luxury to keep him from becoming tempted to be a homeless monk. So Siddhartha's life was like that of a college student who never shows up for class: wild parties and drinking, dancing with girls, watching movies into the wee hours of the morning, and running and screaming around the campus. It was a 24-hour, seven-days-a-week party. If he got tired, he would retire and take a nap, and then he would rejoin the party still in progress.

But Siddhartha began to feel inner longing, emptiness, like "there must be more to life than partying all the time." Have you ever felt that way, feeling like you might want to get a job or, I don't know, take a class at a college? Did that ever occur to you? Well, it did for him. In the meantime, the Hindu gods—the same gods he would eventually hate—sent him "four passing sights" that represented his possible life outcomes: a sorrowful old man; a sick man; a dead man on a funeral pyre, with or without his wife on top; and finally, a content monk in a yellow robe. Siddhartha realized, despite his riches, he would grow old, get sick, and die. The monk was the only good thing he saw. So he wondered what that monk knew that no one else did. Didn't he know he was going to grow old, get sick, and die? So Siddhartha wanted to find out.

The problem was that Siddhartha had married his first cousin—yes, that was legal in ancient India like it is in modern Florida—and had a son. So it looked like he was attached to this world with no escape. But that was not going to stop him. So, despite the birth of a son, he decided to leave his wife and child. He snuck out one night, something Buddhists call "the great renunciation." It is also known in other societies as "second childhood," "male menopause," and "midlife crisis." So Siddhartha snuck out of his castle with a servant, took off all of his bling and rich clothing, clothed himself in a monk's robe, shaved his head, and headed out into the Indian jungle that night to begin a six-year quest to discover how to escape the inevitable suffering of material existence: you are born, you suffer, and you die. There must be an escape.

Siddhartha tried the Hindu brahmins' teaching, using a meditative approach in the Upanishads, but it did not work. Scholars believe Buddhists have this story because Buddhism was a break from Hinduism over brahmins and rituals. If you remember the Tapas revolt, the Buddhists were one group that did not accept the compromise offered by the brahmins. He also tried rigid asceticism, as in Jainism, living on one grain of rice a day. While living this way, Siddhartha attracted five followers who believed he was very holy because he was living on one grain a day and sunlight—like a plant—but he nearly starved to death.

He fainted from hunger and fell in a river, which revived him. He decided to give up this austere lifestyle and began to eat again. Food was readily available because the holy men of India were followed by groupies: women carrying baskets of food and, apparently, ice chests full of beer and freezers full of TV dinners—anything they needed. Siddhartha ate something just to stay alive; he didn't even taste it. But his followers left in disgust. They thought he was holy, but apparently he ate like everyone else did. Eating is a nasty habit. Once you start, you have to do it the rest of your life. Ever notice that?

Siddhartha was also disgusted. He had tried everything for six years, and he still had not escaped suffering. If anything, he had heaped more suffering upon himself. So he sat under a bodhi tree (a large fig tree), and he was determined not to move until he achieved enlightenment—until he figured out how to escape the

FIGURE 7.3 This Thailand figure of Siddhartha shows his emaciated form while living on one grain of rice a day.

inevitable suffering of material existence. While he was sitting there, Mara, the god of desire and death, appeared and tried to tempt him back to his old life: dancing girls, movies, and wild drinking and carousing. Siddhartha refused, and then he realized desire (*tanha*) causes suffering. When humans desire anything, they will always be disappointed because it will never live up to their expectations. He became Buddha, which literally means one who is "woken up," and became enlightened. Enlightenment is the realization that desire causes suffering. Then he entered nirvana. Nirvana literally means "blowing out." A better way to explain it would be unattachment: one is not attached or desirous of anything; therefore, one avoids suffering.

Now Siddhartha had to decide whether to keep quiet and let his karma dissipate, move beyond rebirth (Parinirvana), or teach others and stay. Buddhism has a different definition of karma than Hinduism. Hinduism believes karma affects everyone. Buddhism believes karma affects everyone but enlightened people. Once a person becomes enlightened, he or she is karma-proof. Parinirvana is the ultimate goal of a Buddhist. It is complete annihilation of the elements that make up a person: complete destruction—poof. Because if a person no longer exists, he or she cannot suffer, right? But Buddha chose the latter: he found the five followers who had left him, and, in Deer Park (the deer are still there), he gave them the Deer Park Discourse on the Four Noble Truths:

- Life is suffering.
- Desire causes suffering.
- We are not trapped; there is a way out.
- That way is the Eightfold Path.

So the fourth Noble Truth has eight more steps! They are as follows:

- Right belief
- Right aspiration

FIGURE 7.4 Faithful gather around the tree where tradition says Siddhartha achieved enlightenment and became Buddha.

- Right speech

- Right conduct

- Right means of livelihood

- Right endeavor

- Right mindfulness

- Right meditation

The steps of following the Eightfold Path must be done in order, and they get harder with each step. "Right belief" partly holds that a person has to acknowledge the true nature of existence: that life really does stink. "Right aspiration" is when a person gives up attachments, such as chocolate, ice cream, puppies, pony rides, and sex. "Right speech" involves no lies, which includes all jokes, because there never was a farmer's daughter; a rope never walked into a bar and said, "Frayed knot." There never were a priest, minister, rabbi, and imam on a desert island together. It never happened. So all jokes are lies. We will go over the Eightfold Path in more detail in the Buddhist Philosophy section.

The first five followers of Buddha became the sangha, the Buddhist order of monks. Others soon joined. Buddha's womenfolk showed up, including his wife: "Why didn't you send any child support?" According to legend, they also wanted to join, but he did not want women around because Buddhism is all about unattachment, and having women around would cause attachment issues. But his followers prevailed upon him, so he began an order of nuns. They shave their heads just like the monks do, though they are inferior in rank and in number.

Then Buddha drew up the Ten Precepts for followers: laypeople follow the first five, and monks and nuns follow all ten.

- Refrain from taking life (*ahimsa*)

- No stealing

- Chastity (no sex outside marriage)

- No lying or deceit (this includes jokes)

- No intoxicants

- Food in moderation, never after noon

- No gazing on dancing and singing

- No wearing of ornamentation

- No reclining on high or wide beds (a grass mat on the floor is good enough for you)

- No accepting of gold or silver (vow of poverty)

Buddha died after eating poisoned food. He was invited to a follower's house for dinner. The food had gone bad. Buddha knew it, but the host did not. But Buddha ate it anyway so as not to offend his host. Have you ever eaten something at a friend's house, knowing it might kill you, but you ate it anyway to avoid offending the friend? Or did you feed it to the family dog instead? (Stay away from the Bengali fish curry: Fifi just flopped over.) At least one doctor at the time of Buddha's death thought it was brought on by an existing medical condition: a hiatal hernia aggravated by eating too much curry. Anyway, Buddha achieved Parinirvana, beyond rebirth: he ceased to exist, "poof," the ultimate goal of a Buddhist.

Buddhism then fragmented into more than 16 sects when followers could not agree on the meaning of Buddha's teachings. At a second meeting of all the sects in 390 BCE, the conservative minority called the other Buddhists heretics. From this dispute, two major camps formed: Theravada (conservative) and Mahayana (liberal).

Buddhism spread when King Ashoka of the Mauryan Empire renounced violence and embraced Buddhism. Hundreds of people were killed when he expanded his empire, and this bloodlust made him chagrined. Ashoka exported Buddhism to Sri Lanka and as far away as Egypt and Greece. In the late third century, missionaries brought it to Myanmar (Burma), Thailand, Kampuchea (Cambodia), Laos, Malaysia, and Vietnam.[3]

There has been no great change over the centuries in Buddhist theology, and Buddhism almost became extinct in the Middle Ages. But the religion experienced a revival through contact with Christian missionaries who were able to translate the Buddhist texts. Buddhists had lost knowledge of Pali, the original language, so, ironically, the missionaries revived Buddhism. There has also been a conversion of Americans and Europeans to Buddhism in recent years, especially to the Mahayana Buddhist schools, in which the Dali Lama is very popular.

Since World War II, there has been a rise of Asian nationalism. Some Asians have embraced nationalistic pride in being Buddhists. This has given rise to violence, with Buddhists in Sri Lanka attacking Muslims and Buddhist monks in Burma protesting the country's ruling junta (the Saffron Revolution).

FIGURE 7.5 The reclining Buddha symbolizes his death, as in this sculpture in the Dambulla Cave Temple, Sri Lanka.

Japan has also experienced two major modern Buddhist movements: a terrorist organization and a national movement.

Chizuo Matsumoto, a blind Japanese yoga teacher, claimed in 1986 to have achieved enlightenment while meditating alone in the Himalaya Mountains. He returned to Japan and changed his name to Asahara Shoko. He founded the religious movement Aum Shinryko ("teaching of the supreme truth"). Shoko claimed to have received divine instruction to establish a spiritual kingdom on earth called the Shambhala Kingdom. Aum Shinryko also became a legal Japanese political party in 1989, calling its political branch Shinrito (Supreme Truth Party). It claimed political action was aimed at spreading truths to save the world. That is a pretty big boast. Unfortunately, not a single candidate from the party won an election for any post. The Japanese must be a skeptical people.

Sued by disgruntled members, Asahara said he would not be able to save the world and that members should prepare for an inevitable final battle in 2003 that would involve chemical weapons. This might be why we should have tort reform. He told his followers to build nuclear fallout shelters, practice rigid asceticism, and recognize Asahara as the absolute ruler. Most people may snicker if they were told to dig a fallout shelter. The Japanese took this seriously from their experience in World War II. While Asahara was at it, he announced in 1991 that he was Christ returning to earth as well as Shiva, the Hindu god of destruction, and the pope of Tokyo.

Membership in the group grew to about 1,100 disillusioned, idealistic young professionals who were upset about Japanese materialism. After World War II, Shinto, one of the religions of Japan, became focused on consumerism: the pursuit of wealth.

Asahara created the Lotus Village Plan. He said small villages were key for followers to survive the coming nuclear holocaust. He based this on the Lotus Sutra's teaching of an age of the destruction of dharma, which he saw as the end of the world as we know it. Followers could attain Buddhahood if they followed his teachings.

In 1993, Asahara ordered his scientists to create sarin nerve gas to defend against gas attack by the American military in Japan. In 1994, at Asahara's command, his followers released the gas from a converted refrigeration truck, killing seven and injuring hundreds in Matsumoto, Japan.[4]

That same year, Asahara proclaimed himself emperor of Japan. The gas attack was not linked to Aum Shinryko until the following year. The government raided the group's headquarters in Osaka, Japan. After that, followers released sarin gas into the Tokyo subway on March 20, 1995, killing ten and injuring thousands. Asahara and two hundred followers were arrested. After a seven-year trial (during which he refused to say anything), Asahara was condemned to death in 2004 and executed in 2018.

The national Buddhist movement of the Soka Gakkai ("The Society for Value Creation") came out of the Nichiren school. It was started by high school principal Tsunesaburo Makiguchi (1871–1944) before World War II. He was jailed with some followers because they rejected the call to exclusive loyalty to Japan's Shinto religion, as required by the state, and he died in prison.

Led by Makiguchi's follower Josei Toda, Soka Gakkai grew rapidly during the 1950s, and Soka Gakkai International was created in 1975. The group adopted the teachings of Nichiren and the Lotus Sutra and stressed self-improvement, which led to truth, beauty, and happiness. Everyone can become a Buddha by chanting "Hail to the Lotus Sutra!" and meditating on a personal worship object, a mandala with the names of principal Lotus Sutra figures at its center. Followers meet in discussion groups and are encouraged to destroy other religious symbols in homes: Bibles, Shinto kami shelves, and so on. Members believe that now is the time for world salvation through the Lotus Sutra, so they use "break and subdue" methods to try to win converts. The movement is also affiliated with a Japanese political party, the "Clean Government Party."

As we have seen, Buddhism is a unique religion with no heaven, hell, or afterlife. It emphasizes the big picture over the person, yet it excludes most elements outside a person as tools for the ultimate goal: Parinirvana. Breaking from Hinduism, it is one of the world's oldest religions. Our next chapter will look at another old religion that also broke from Hinduism but is a lot more austere.

Buddhist Scripture

Buddhist scripture includes the Pali Canon (Figure 7.6). It is a collection of major sacred Buddhist texts. It is also a total rejection of Vedic (Hindu) scripture, which is why it is written in Pali, not Sanskrit, since the Vedas were written in the latter. It is known as the Tripitaka ("three baskets") because it was probably carried around in three baskets: Buddhist scripture tended to be written on pages between unbound boards. The contents vary, depending on country or religion. The three baskets are as follows:

- Basket of disciplinary regulations (guidelines for monks and nuns)

- Basket of discourses (basic teachings of Buddha, including the Dhammapada)

- Basket of higher philosophy (analysis of the nature of existence)

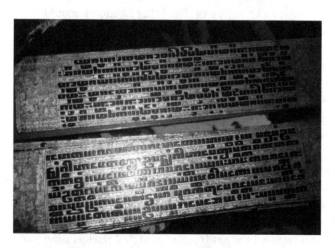

FIGURE 7.6 Buddhist scripture is traditionally written on unbound pages in Pali between two boards.

There are also different versions of the Dhammapada, Buddha's alleged sayings. It is unknown if the scripture contains the actual sayings of Buddha or was recreated later. In the 300s BCE, a famine killed a large part of the Indian population, and during that time, some scriptures were lost.

The Mahayana scriptures include the Lotus Sutra (the most popular, also called the "Lotus of the Good Law"), which contains the supposed sayings of Buddha and teaches the three ages of dharma: the age of the false dharma, the final dharma, and when a bodhisattva (we will explain what that is later) will come and reveal the true cosmic Buddha vehicle. The Diamond Cutter Sutra contains teachings on transcendent nondual wisdom (*prajna*), which is found in the emptiness of all distinctions and is beyond ordinal perception in its truest form. So nothing is the true nature of existence. The Heart Sutra, which addresses *prajna*, also identifies the source of the "wisdom that goes beyond" as the Bodhisattva Avalokitesvara ("the Lord who looks down with compassion"). So if a person prays to the Lord of Nothing, he will help a person achieve nothing, think nothing, and be nothing. Both the Diamond Cutter and Heart Sutras are called "wisdom sutras." The Garland Sutra reveals that the distinct forms of the world that we experience are delusions of our material minds.[5]

Buddhism Beliefs

Buddhism has no philosophy: zilch, zero, nada. That was easy. Actually, Buddha rejected speculative philosophy, as mentioned earlier. But the philosophy of Buddhism can be found in the Four Noble Truths and the Eightfold Path.

Four Noble Truths. The first Noble Truth is that life is suffering. Birth, decay, illness, and death all involve suffering. Buddha told the parable of the mustard seed. A woman in the marketplace came up to Buddha and exclaimed (in modern parlance), "Oh, great Buddha, I am really suffering. My husband and children left me, my dog ran away, my cat is living with the neighbors, my house has been foreclosed on, and I am living in a cardboard box underneath an overpass. Is anyone suffering as much as I?" Buddha, being the compassionate man he was, said, "Walk it off. Deal with it. Don't complain. Everyone suffers. Pick up a mustard seed (one of the smallest seeds in the world) and throw it in this crowded marketplace. I bet you hit someone who suffers more than you. Don't complain about it; address the suffering." Buddhists maintain they have a realistic, not pessimistic, outlook on life because life really does stink. To emphasize this, a Buddhist monk would meditate on a decaying corpse to emphasize that nothing is permanent in this life, this life is suffering, and one should not be attached (Figure 7.7).

FIGURE 7.7 Tibetan monks use this skull cap, called kapala, to hold an offering to a god. It represents the impermanence of a person.

The second Noble Truth is suffering is caused by desire or craving. Craving for sensual pleasure—cookies, ice cream, pony rides, and so on—causes one to be attached to this life and to be born again in this life, because attachment to this existence leads back to rebirth, then suffering continues. Suffering is caused by attachment to things or people who delude us as to their real nature, because problems and conflicts arise. Sure, that Ferrari looked good on the showroom floor, but when it breaks down on the highway at 2 a.m. with the top down in a rainstorm and the tow truck is two hours away, it loses some of

its shine, particularly when you start kicking the stupid thing. Or if you ever go on a date and the person looks fantastic, has mastered the art of sterling conversation, and dresses like a model in a catalog. You think, *Wow, there is perfection!* But if you go on a second date, or a third, you start noticing the little imperfections, such as the twitch in their left eye every time they talk, or their halitosis, which has become smellable. Or they suddenly have flatulence. That is when you notice—Rats!—they are just like you: imperfect. And you become disappointed. But do not try too hard to be unattached to anything, such as starving oneself or walking around naked. If life becomes too difficult, it can keep one from attaining the goal of enlightenment. It is like riding a bike: just go with it. Buddha stressed the Middle Way or Middle Path. Avoid extremes. Do not be a glutton nor starve yourself. Be like Goldilocks: choose what is just right.

The third Noble Truth is to escape craving and to achieve nirvana, unattachment. Buddha found escape by directly addressing his suffering. He told his followers to avoid things not directly related to our suffering, such as the man in the parable of the arrow. Two men were out hunting. One accidently shot the other. (Apparently, he was hunting with former US Vice President Dick Cheney.) The man who accidently let loose his arrow ran over to the other man on the ground and started a running dialogue: "Bob, how's the family? I saw your daughter the other day. She's starting college, right? Nice car, by the way. I like red. By the way, can I borrow your lawnmower on Saturday?" Bob will eventually yell out, "Will you shut up and pull the arrow out?" Suffering is the nine-hundred-pound gorilla in the room: don't ignore it; it won't go away. Address the suffering. When craving is extinguished, so is suffering and rebirth, and one achieves nirvana ("blowing out"), symbolized by a lotus flower. These flowers love to live in the darkest, blackest, scummiest ponds possible. They grow out of the scum at the bottom—representing suffering—and then blow out into a beautiful flower on the surface, seemingly unattached to the suffering they left behind.

The fourth Noble Truth is the Eightfold Path. The way to nirvana (not a state of existence but a wakening up) is through the Eightfold Path. Nirvana is not a hair and nail salon nor a band. Otherwise, you would be paying a lot of money for nothing.

Eightfold Path. The Eightfold Path is the Middle Way between self-denial and self-indulgence, a moderate and focused way of living. In Theravada Buddhism, one must work out one's own way to salvation using the Eightfold Path. No one helps anyone. You are on your own.

The first step in the Eightfold Path is to have the "right belief." This is when a person is encouraged to hold a correct view of the nature of reality: basically, life stinks. One should also recognize the "three marks of existence": *anatta* (no soul), *anicca* (impermanence), and *dukkha* (suffering). Ego is an illusion. You do not exist. You have no immortal part. There is no eternal self. What makes up a human person are the five shandhas, or "aggregates": form (physical factors), feeling, perceptions, volitions, and awareness, or consciousness. It is these shandhas that are reincarnated, not the person. This is called rebirth without transmigration: no soul transmigrates; just the five shandas do. All is impermanent; nothing lasts. So don't get attached to anything. The only reality is suffering. Address it, not the afterlife (no soul) or this life (impermanence). Observe dharma. Here, Buddhists redefine dharma from Hinduism. In Hinduism, dharma was the duty to one's caste. In Buddhism, there is no caste, so dharma is to the truth in the Pali Canon, proper conduct, and understanding reality's laws, such as the Buddhist definition of karma and the Chain of Causation. The latter is how a person becomes attached to this life. You are born. Then you become aware of your surroundings. Then you desire said surroundings. Desire causes suffering. Suffering leads to a painful death. Finally, you are reborn again. You need to break the Chain of Causation at the point of desiring your surroundings because you cannot keep from dying, being born, or becoming aware. And when you are suffering, it is already too late.

The second step is to have the "right aspiration." This occurs when one frees one's mind from sensual desires, greed, and malice and takes on thoughts of nonviolence, renunciation, and compassion. One replaces cruelty and unconcern with gentleness, benevolence, and goodwill. So, how does one show goodwill to others and still remain unattached? This is called metta, unattached love. You love everyone but couldn't care less what they think of you: "Have a good day. Talk to the hand." This love is a one-way street. That way, others' opinion of you will not become a barrier in moving forward on the Eightfold Path.

Having the "right speech" is the third step. This includes telling no lies. Lying also includes jokes because, as mentioned earlier, all jokes are lies. Here's an example about Fluffy the rabbit. A friend of mine was having dinner with a family when he noticed on the other side of their picture window that their dog, a wire fox terrier, had something in its teeth and was shaking it violently. "I think your dog has something," he pointed out. "OMG," responded the family in unison. "It is Fluffy, the rabbit from next door, and the little old lady who owns him is coming home tonight from a three-day cruise!" My friend thought for a bit. "We could go to the pet store and get another rabbit, but, uh," consulting a watch, "the store is closed now. I know! Let's get Fluffy, wash Fluffy, blow-dry Fluffy until Fluffy is all white and fluffy again, and put him back in his rabbit hutch. We will just say he died a natural death. Rabbits croak all the time." The family thought this was a splendid idea. The family members chased the dog around the yard until they grabbed hold of Fluffy, ripping it out of his teeth. They then threw the rabbit into the bathtub, poured detergent on it, scrubbed Fluffy, rinsed Fluffy, and then blow-dried Fluffy until he was all white and fluffy again. Then they returned him to the rabbit hutch in the old lady's backyard. Then they waited. The little old lady came home an hour later in a 1978 Dodge Monaco with screeching and grinding brakes. She slowly exited the car, leaning on her walker with a tennis ball on each metal leg. Then she slowly shuffled toward the backyard into the deepening gloom where the rabbit hutch was. Suddenly, the family heard a blood-curling scream. "OMG," they exclaimed together. "Maybe she's having a heart attack. Maybe we need to call 911!" They ran out of the house to the lady's backyard, and there they saw her: standing rigid, walker flopped over, hand over her mouth, eyes the size of dinner plates, pointing at the rabbit hutch. "Fluffy!" she screamed. "Fluffy!" The family pretended to peer into the hutch and exclaimed, "Oh, my, he looks like he died a natural death. I'm sure he wasn't in pain." The old lady looked at them. "No! I buried him three days ago!"

As mentioned, the second step is telling no lies. If you have any questions about that, feel free to reread the story above. Not spreading gossip is another element: "Did you see what she was wearing? Doesn't that dress make her look fat? I hear her parents had to tie a piece of meat around her neck so the dog would play with her as a child." Not using harsh words: "You cotton-pickin', no-good, low-down, raffen-rousing, no-good, fur-bearing varmint!" Not engaging in vulgar or prejudicial talk: "Man, his nose begins where a good nose ends." And no habit of useless chatter, of going on and on and not letting anyone get a word in edgewise, just talking because you want the conversation to be all about you, so you continue to talk and talk without actually saying anything, just to fill the room with your rather large ego, and you continue to speak, monopolizing all the attention because you don't want anyone to interfere with your personal glory and where you see yourself in the universe, so you continue to multiply words, like what this text is doing now, and yet, you, as a reader, are still reading this, no matter what comes next. See? Still reading, and so the words go on and on ... You get the idea?

The next step is having the "right conduct." You shall not kill (ahimsa). You shall not steal (grand theft auto). You shall not have sex outside marriage. You shall not use intoxicants, and no gambling. I'll bet you didn't know that. No, I won't bet. So all the fun stuff is off the table. No killing also eliminates employment as a farmhand, butcher, fisherman (or fisherperson), and slaughterhouse employee. Being a swinger, heavy drinker, and gambling man (or person) is also out.

The "right means of livelihood" is the next step. This includes a person not having an occupation that includes killing. So this is a rehash of the previous step. Also forbidden are occupations that engage in commerce or services for hire. So at this point, you need to tell your boss that you will now be working for free because you do not want to be attached to a paycheck. A person should not have a job involving trickery or deception: lawyer, real estate seller, and car sales person. No work is allowed that involves astrology, so palm reading is out. Astrology assumes there are powers outside a person that can influence him or her. Buddha was a functional atheist: although there are gods, they have nothing to do with them because they are Hindu gods, and they will keep you on the wheel of life because they are stuck there, too. They will jealously try to keep you from nirvana.

The next step is to engage in the "right endeavor." A person should avoid unwholesome action that will cause karma. You want to be rid of any actions that attach you to this life and resist distractions that might derail your journey, such as hot fudge sundaes with nuts, and whipped cream and a chocolate shell, with strawberries and sprinkles. Don't think about it! This helps develop one's mind. So you should remain alert to what you are doing and don't let your mind wander into ice crea—stop! So the moral is: not only actions can bind one to this world, causing suffering, but one's thoughts can do so, too.

With that in mind, "right mindfulness" is the next step. You should devote yourself assiduously to focused observation on self and others as you and they actually are, not as you would see them through a subjective, judgmental filter. One should be "fully present," seeing the true nature of things as they are. Contemplation begins by focusing on one's breathing to become aware of one's body and its impermanence and becoming aware of the ebb and flow of one's feelings, mental activities, and objects of one's mind. This is when you clean out all the cobwebs and dust. Every part of your mind is lit up. There are no dark corners. All your emotional baggage is stacked neatly and labeled. You are the master of your mind. If you say sit, your mind sits. If you say roll over, yes, it rolls over. To emphasize the impermanence of the body and the true nature of the world, it is time to dig out that decaying corpse mentioned in the First Noble Truth and meditate on its putridness. It probably is really smelly by now.

The last step is "right meditation." One's mind is brought into sharp focus because of right mindfulness. Calmness and peace results as one enters the state of samadhi, sainthood, with the breaking of all attachments. Nirvana is at hand with a flash of intuition, followed by a state of final bliss. Congratulations, grasshopper, you are enlightened.

Functional atheism. Functional atheism is what Buddha taught. As mentioned before, although there are gods—Hindu gods—you should have nothing to do with them because they are on the wheel of life, just like you. They have not escaped. And they are jealous of any success you may have in getting off the wheel of life, so they will try to interfere, like Mara did with Buddha. Functional atheism is different than theoretical atheism: the latter is belief in no god or gods. Buddhists believe that gods exist, but they act like they do not: they ignore them, defriend them on Facebook, and don't answer their tweets.

A branch of Buddhism, Theravada, closely follows Buddha's teachings in that they believe in not worshipping the gods, but shrines with images of Buddha are popular. The most important monuments are stupas that house relics associated with Buddha and early leaders. Buddhists visit these stupas, leaving offerings and showing reverence to them. So the question is: Are not Buddhists worshipping Buddha as a deity? Did they

FIGURE 7.8 Dhamekh Stupa, where the Buddha gave the first sermon on the Four Noble Truths and the Eightfold Path.

replace the Hindu gods with Buddha as their god? No, say Theravada followers; they are just simply showing reverence to one who has attained enlightenment. They are also showing that they are symbolically committing themselves to follow his example.

Speaking of Theravada, let us look at what they believe and compare and contrast that to the Mahayana Buddhists' belief.

Major Branches of Buddhism

The Theravada, the older of the two schools of Buddhism, received support from King Ashoka of India, and it spread to Sri Lanka and beyond. Theravada literally means "the way of the elders," though it is only one of several older forms to survive.

Theravada Buddhism

Theravada Buddhism believes in most everything Buddha taught: people have no atman or souls (anatta). Buddha looked inside himself and did not find one. There is no eternal self. What makes up people are the five shandhas, or "aggregates." It is these that are reincarnated, not the person. Theravada also endorses Buddha's Four Noble Truths and Eightfold Path as the way to enlightenment. There is no reality; everything is impermanent (anicca). This illusion can trap one with karma if one believes what is around oneself is real and one becomes attached to it or desires it. As mentioned before, Theravada Buddhists are functional atheists. Although there are gods, one should not have anything to do with them because they are also on the wheel of rebirth. They cannot help you. You are on your own.

FIGURE 7.9 Buddha in Mahayana Buddhism is traditionally portrayed as fat because he has been merged with the Chinese god of good luck. Good luck means one is not starving.

Mahayana Buddhism

The more liberal branch, Mahayana Buddhism, separated from the Theravada school following disputes after the death of King Ashoka when Buddhism's center in India moved northwest out of the country. Mahayana Buddhism moved into China, Korea, Nepal, Tibet, and Japan and set up monasteries.[6] Mahayana means "large method, vehicle, or raft" because achieving enlightenment is a group effort, unlike the Theravada school, where it is an individual effort (you're on your own). People receive help from bodhisattvas, people who forgo Parinirvana of their own free will and come back to help others achieve nirvana.

Buddha has three separate bodies or natures: (1) an earthly manifestation (Siddhartha); (2) several buddhas (Maitreya, Variocana, and Amitabha, or Pure Land, Buddhism, the latter being the most popular), bodhisattvas (such as the Dalai Lama), who achieve enlightenment but forgo nirvana to help others, and heavenly Buddhas called Dhyani "contemplative"; and (3) the cosmic body of Buddha (*dharmakaya*), who is present in all reality.

Sunyata is "emptiness" or "openness" in all things we perceive (nothing is real), and this can help one realize the freedom that Buddha taught. Your bills, family obligations, job, tests, and final exam do not exist. Boy, that is a load off. Sunyata cannot be grasped or desired, because then it will dissolve. Have you ever tried to hug nothing? The only way to discover this pure consciousness is to explore one's mind, and find—nothing.

There are several major Mahayana schools in East Asia:

1. **Pure Land** (devotional school) is based on a Sanskrit story about a celestial land known as the Western Paradise or Pure Land. One can be reborn in this land and prepare for nirvana and Buddhahood by belief in Amitabha (infinite light), who resides in the Pure Land.

2. **Zen** (meditation school) is focused on an Indian monk called Bodhidharma (c. 470–543) who brought it to China. This monk allegedly cut off his eyelids so he could meditate for nine years before a wall without falling asleep; he said all Buddhist texts are worthless, developed meditation by using word puzzles, and created art under the influence of meditation. He also created the tea ceremony (requiring many disciplined steps that must be done in order so one is eventually able to drink tea from an empty cup) and developed martial arts. Zen teaches everyone has the nature of the Buddha.

FIGURE 7.10 The stick of discipline is used as an aid to meditation. To meditate, one's mind must be absent of rational thought. Being hit by the stick accomplishes this.

3. **T'ien-t'ai, Tendai** (rationalist sect) was founded by a monk, Chih-l. This group uses reason and the study of the scriptures in addition to meditation. This sect believes that Buddha used different tools to speak, including Theravada and Mahayana Buddhism.

4. **Nichiren** (political school) was founded by Nichiren, a monk, who accepted the Lotus Sutra as the supreme Buddhist teaching after studying other forms, condemned forms of government and other forms of Buddhism, and picked Mount Fuji in Japan as the mountain where Buddha revealed the Lotus Sutra. Its followers claim that Buddha existed for all eternity and that when this age ends, it will be replaced with an era of cosmic harmony for those who accept the Lotus Sutra.

5. **Tibetan Buddhism** (Tantric school) originated in India but took root in Tibet. This school was brought to Tibet by the eighth-century Indian holy man Padma-Sambhava in the teachings of the Vajayana ("diamond" or "thunderbolt" vehicle). Padma-Sambhava taught that the union of male and female deities overcame the duality of life in samsara and that there were certain magic formulas that could be used to channel physical and psychic energy to experience sudden enlightenment. The school combined with the Bon tribe, mixing beliefs, gods, demons, and practices. Today this school teaches that there are five celestial Buddhas (with each at a directional point on the compass and one in the center); that one can merge with Buddha by fasting, meditation, and chanting; and that at the center of the religion are lamas ("superior ones") who possess special magic powers.

FIGURE 7.11 Inside the kapala is a symbol representing lightning. Tibetan Buddhists believe one can achieve instant enlightenment through magic and other means.

6. **Yellow Hat School** was created as a Buddhist reform movement in Tibet in the 14th century; followers wore yellow hats to set them off from other Tibetan Buddhists, who wore red ones. This school imposed celibacy on its followers. Because leadership could not be hereditary, the concept of the heads of monasteries being reincarnated was developed. After the death of an abbot, a search (which could take years) was launched to find a boy born 49 days after the abbot's death who—through magic and tests—could be identified as the reincarnated abbot. The Grand Lama

FIGURE 7.12 Monks from the Drepung Gomang Monastery in India make an ecumenical "peace" mandala using colored sand. The touring monks, some who are refugees from Tibet, stopped in St. Petersburg, FL, to sponsor the event.

FIGURE 7.13 The final resting place of a Buddhist monk would be in a reliquary like this, after his body is destroyed by cremation.

of the monastery in Lhasa took the name Dalai Lama, considered to be a reincarnation of the bodhisattva Avalokita ("ocean of wisdom" is another title given to him by Genghis Khan's sons). The most recent Dalai Lama has traveled the world to bring attention to the plight of Tibet since the Chinese conquest in 1959, and he won the Nobel Peace Prize in 1989.

Buddhist Holidays

Theravada Buddhists have as many as 40 holidays a year, but these are not celebrated by all Buddhists. All Buddhists celebrate the **new year**: three days in April. In a carnival-type atmosphere, Buddhists rededicate themselves and visit temples, washing statues with fragrant water with flower petals to honor gods who washed the newborn Buddha.

Buddha's birthday is celebrated on April 8 in China and Japan or on the last full moon in May in Southeast Asia. On this day, infant Buddha statues are washed. Sometimes there are processions of children dressed up as little Buddhas.

The **Festival of Souls** (Ullambana) is in July in Japan and August in China. On this day, souls are allowed to leave purgatory, and food is left for these wandering spirits.

The **Robe Offering** occurs at the end of the rainy season in November. The Theravada school celebrates the sending of first missionaries by Asoka. Monks receive new robes from laity. The mahakathina (great robe) is made, honoring Buddha's mother, who made his robe in one night while pregnant. This robe can cover a hillside.[7]

SUMMARY

As we have discussed, Buddhism's ultimate goal is Parinirvana, to escape suffering. Since Buddha's death, his followers have come up with different ways to do this. There is no central authority in Buddhism, so there are many competing factions. But a common element is the diminishing of the individual and ego (because they are illusionary) and embracing nothingness.

FOR FURTHER READING

A Concise History of Buddhism, Andrew Skilton, Windhorse Publications, 2004

Buddha, Karen Armstrong, Penguin, 2004

Buddhist Art and Architecture, Robert E. Fisher, Thames and Hudson, 1993

Freedom in Exile: The Autobiography of the Dalai Lama, Dalai Lama, Harper Perennial, 2008

Siddhartha: A Novel, Hermann Hess, Bantam, 1982

The Art of Tibet, Robert E. Fisher, Thames and Hudson, 1997

The Book of Buddhas, Eva Rudy Jansen, Binkey Kok Publications, 2004

The Dhammapada, Albert J. Edmunds, trans., Digireads.com Publishing, 2017

The Three Pillars of Zen, Philip Kapleau, Beacon Press, 1971

ENDNOTES

1   "Buddhists," Pew Research Center, 2018, http://www.pewforum.org/2012/12/18/global-religious-landscape-buddhist/.

2   W. Young, *The World's Religions,* 4th ed. (London: Pearson, 2013)

3   J. Esposito and D. Fasching, *World Religions Today,* 6th ed. (Oxford: Oxford University Press, 2017).

4   J. Sommerland, "Shoko Asahara: Who Was the Japanese Cult Leader Who Masterminded the Lethal Sarin Attack on Tokyo's Subway?" *Independent,* July 6, 2018, https://www.independent.co.uk/news/world/asia/shoko-asahara-japanese-cult-leader-aum-shinrikyo-tokyo-subway-sarin-attack-a8434241.html.

5   J. Fiester and J. Powers, *Scriptures of the World's Religions* (Boston: McGraw Hill, 2012).

6   M. Fisher, *Living Religions,* 4th ed. (Upper Saddle River, NJ: Prentice Hall, 1999).

7   J. Fieser and J. Powers, *Scriptures of the World's Religions,* 3rd ed. (New York City: McGraw-Hill Education, 2011)

CREDITS

8

JAINISM

LEARNING OBJECTIVES

1. Learn the history and myth of Jainism
2. Explain the Jain view of living things
3. Understand how nonviolence is incorporated into the religion
4. Know how unattachment is a large part of the religion
5. Examine how Jainism adapted to Western civilization

He who acts rightly, who does pious work, who practices no deceit, is called houseless.
—**The Agamas, Book One, Lecture One, Third Lesson**[1]

Jain Statistics

Jainism is a small religion (about 4 million members in India), and they are concentrated around Mumbai (Bombay), India. Although small, Jainism has had an impact on other religions with uncompromising ascetic ideals such as ahimsa, though other religions do not carry the concept as far as the Jains do.

Jain Mythology and History

Jain mythology and its history are wrapped around each other, making it difficult to separate historical evidence from the Jain myth. Jainism believes that within the current cosmic cycle (they have cosmic cycles like Hindus), there have been 24 teachers who have become tirthankaras, "crossing finders or markers." Tirthankaras have found ways to cross the proverbial river of life's many rebirths and have gotten off the cycle of rebirth.

Historically, though, evidence exists for only the last two tirthankaras. There is also some historical evidence of the existence of the third tirthankara. But we are pretty sure of the 24th's existence. He was Nataputta Vardhamana, born around 597 BCE. Scholars believe that Jainism, like Buddhism, was a revolt against Hinduism during the Tapas revolt. Jains believe that although they did object to Hindu theology during the Tapas revolt, their religion existed before Hinduism.

Nataputta's legendary life was so similar to Buddha's that scholars for a while thought they may be the same person. Nataputta was born in the warrior caste. Do you remember anyone else who was born in the

FIGURE 8.1 Jains believe there were 24 tirthankaras, or crossing finders, in the current cosmic cycle.

Hindu warrior caste? He became disillusioned with his comfortable life. Sound familiar? He left his wife and daughter when he was 30 years old. Okay, it was not a son this time. And instead of wandering for six years in a yellow robe, he wandered for 12 years naked through central India, abandoning worldly fetters that cause rebirth. He did not even want to be attached to clothes. And this was not a pretty naked; this was an ugly naked: because he was not attached to his body, he did not believe in personal hygiene. So one knew he was coming a mile away downwind, or otherwise the cloud of flies announced his presence.

Nataputta joined others who shared self-denial, but he thought this still showed too much attachment to others. So he took his dirty, naked, stinky self and headed back into the Indian jungle. Now that is a confirmed bachelor: he won't even hang around confirmed bachelors.

He rarely stayed in more than one place each night to avoid attachment to a place. "Oh, nice tree. Oops, getting attached. Better move on." He was not the first to practice ahimsa, but he carried it to the extreme. He swept his path with a broom so as not to step on bugs. He strained water through cloth to keep from drinking any living thing, no matter how small. That last idea may be a good one: he was the only holy man in India without dysentery.

Asceticism—denying oneself creature comforts—is not new, either, but Nataputta also carried it to the extreme. When it was hot, he meditated in the heat in summer. When it was cold, he meditated in the shade in the winter. And remember, he was naked, so he probably looked like a Smurf: he was blue. He shunned shelter when it rained. That is significant in that India has the monsoon season when it rains for months and floods. Instead, he sat out in the flood with water up to his neck, ignoring the bugs and spiders climbing up on his head for shelter. It was probably the only time he got washed.

Maybe because he would not talk to anyone—so as not to be attached to them—people abused him. They said, "There's that dirty, naked, stinky guy who is too good to talk to us. Let's sic the dogs on him." One tradition says people lit a fire under him while he was meditating to see if he would move and also stuck pins in his ears. But he remained oblivious. He probably had some pretty good scorch marks on the old patootie afterward.

After 13 years of practicing asceticism, Nataputta achieved his goal: he became a jina, winning victory over desire and attachment. So that is why a jina is a conqueror, conquering desire and attachment. Nataputta did what Buddha failed to do: through extreme measures, which took twice as long, he achieved unattachment. Remember when Buddha tried living on one grain of rice a day? Yeah.

For the remainder of his life, Nataputta taught, so he agreed to some sort of attachment. So if you are registering for classes and see one taught by N. Vardhamana and you have a problem with public nudity and a lack of hygiene, maybe you don't want to register for that class. Or you could take the online version.

He attracted followers to his lifestyle. So then there were a bunch of naked, dirty, stinky men walking around ringing doorbells and handing out pamphlets. Actually, the latter is not true, because Jains have no interest in converting anyone, about which we will talk later.

In about 527 BCE, Nataputta died of voluntary starvation, the ultimate act of self-denial. Jains do not consider this a violent outcome

FIGURE 8.2 Parshvanatha, the 23rd Tirthankara, is loved among Jains and had been reincarnated several times before becoming a tirthankara.

but a withdrawing of substance and attainment of ultimate unattachment. Hey, if you are not going to eat plants, what are you going to eat? He is called by his followers, with reverence, Mahavira ("great man" or "hero"). Tradition says his parents also starved themselves to death, but this may have been a retroactive story invented later to support the claim that he was so holy he came from a family who starved themselves to death.

The leadership of Jainism passed to Nataputta's first disciples, and the movement spread from central India to the south and northwest. King Ashoka of the Mauryan dynasty in the third century BCE gave state support to the movement. Remember how Ashoka liked Buddhism because of ahimsa? Well, Jainism was even more into ahimsa.

FIGURE 8.3 Mahavira sits to the right of Parshvanatha in the Jain Temple in Tampa, FL.

Modern Jainism

Jainism spread to the west with Indian immigrants who built temples. But this was a move into an alien culture where people ate meat and killed animals! Where one could go to a supermarket and buy a can of poison to commit genocide on insects! What a place! So organizations were formed to keep Jains from losing their religion in such an alien culture but not convert anyone. One of these organizations was the Young Jains of America, formed to support the religion of Jain youth. In 2017, their website claimed to have about ten thousand members who met in conventions in the United States and Canada.[2]

Jainism is changing, though, in the face of Western norms. For instance, Jains are not supposed to drive because it kills things like bugs and the movement causes karma. But the Western Jains are bending those rules, becoming more liberal in their thinking[3] while minimizing karma when they can. Jain youth are also adopting Jain beliefs to their new society. They have expanded the definition of ahimsa to encompass environmentalism, animal rights, and corporate business ethics; they have flocked to veganism, and they have volunteered alongside other faiths and learned about lobbying through political internships.[4]

FIGURE 8.4 Shvetembaras, "white clad," accept women, as seen with these two nuns.

One thing Jain youth have been warned against is starving themselves. The Young Jains website did have a question posted about monks and nuns starving themselves to death. The answer was that the religious Jains who took vows are different and that starvation had no place in the youths' lives. Then the question was dropped from the website after a redesign. Jain youth do not go to the extremes monks do: most will get married anyway and resign to stay on the wheel of rebirth until the next life.

Jain Scripture

Jainism developed quite a few scriptures over a long period of time. Collectively, they are called the Agamas, which means "tradition" in Sanskrit. They are religious and philosophical in character in that they tell a person about the afterlife

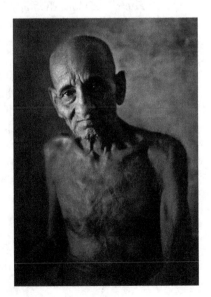

FIGURE 8.5 Digambaras follow Mahavira's lifestyle and are unattached to clothes.

FIGURE 8.6 Women decorate Jain temples, since women have always been an important part of Jainism, including as nuns and those who feed wandering Jain monks.

(unlike Buddhism, there is one in Jainism) and what he or she should do in this life to get there.

There is a disagreement as to the accuracy of the Agamas. The Shvetambaras say the Agamas are the remembered sermons and discourses of Mahavira. But the Digambaras say Mahavira's teachings are lost but their "essence" is preserved in the Agamas. The Digambaras may be right because of a famine in the 300s BCE that killed many Indians and during which a lot of scriptures were lost (maybe they ate it). So the Digambaras' Agamas do not have as many sutras as the Shvetembaras because they believed some are not authentic.

The scripture is seen as guiding a person to the right path. But unlike other religions' scriptures, they are not the complete truth. That is like a Muslim saying "Man, that Qur'an is something, but it just doesn't hack it" or a Christian saying "I wish the Bible had more." Why do the Jains dis their own scripture? Well, it is because they are consistent. Jainism teaches that there is nothing in the material world, including their scripture, that is capable of expressing pure knowledge.

Jain Beliefs

Jainism is one of the most extreme religions in the world. You may call it Religion X; that is how extreme it is. An overriding principle in Jainism is ahimsa, nonviolence. But unlike Hinduism and Buddhism, that nonviolence extends beyond humans and animals to plants, insects, and even microbes. Jains believe all living things have a soul, just as humans have. Therefore, one is not allowed to hurt any living thing. That raises a question: If Jains are not allowed to hurt any living thing, what do they eat? Even fruit is alive (it has living cells). In that vein, Jains also ultimately starve themselves to death. That is the only way to get to Jain heaven, known as the Dome or Nirvana.

"Jainism" comes from the Sanskrit word "jina," meaning "conqueror." Now these may be the most peaceful people on earth. So what are they conquering? To understand that, we will have to look at Jain mythology and history.

There is no Jain theology, because followers are like Theravada Buddhists: functional atheists. Jains believe the universe is shaped like a man with his hands on his hips. At the top is the dome or nirvana, Jain heaven. Below are the gods. These are Hindu gods, so one should have nothing to do with them because they are not allowed in the dome and might grow angry and try to keep you out, too. Below them are all life on earth: humans, animals, meerkats, microbes, plants, and college students. At the bottom is hell: one can be born into it or born out of it. The whole universe is called loka.

Every living being has a spiritual, eternal soul: a jiva. Jivas are by nature perfect, blissful, all-knowing, eternal, and infinite in number. So if jivas are blissful and all-knowing, and you are a jiva, why are you not always happy and acing every test? Well, the problem is that jivas get weighed down by karma, which is fine matter (like dirt). So we have a new definition of karma, different from Buddhism and Hinduism. Jain karma is actually physical, and it is always bad. It causes a jiva to be reborn at a lower level. Karma also limits a jiva's knowledge, bliss, and so on. It clogs your knowledge pores. So karma makes you stupid and unhappy.

All actions, not just desire, cause karma. Just walking around causes karma. So Jains have a commitment to inactivity or activity that focuses on liberation that will keep karma off, such as starving oneself.

A jiva that liberates itself from the bondage of karma is a jina, a conqueror. Jinas rise to the top or dome of the universe and dwell eternally in full consciousness, knowledge, and bliss, higher than the gods.

A jina is an "all-knowing one," which is known as a kevalin. Jinas have all karma removed, so knowledge returns to them. Jinas join all the other jinas (such as Mahavira) at the top of the universe, higher than the gods. But one has to go to extremes to be invited to this penthouse party at the top of the universe. The way to get there is through self-denial (so one is not attached to the world or karma) and to practice extreme ahimsa. Killing a bug by accident still causes karma. Ultimately, one must starve oneself to death to get to the dome.

Jainism believes in a dualism of reality: matter (*ajiva*) and spirit (*jiva*). *Ajiva* is evil in nature and obscures purity and the goodness of *jivas*. So anything physical is evil. This includes karma, which is physical. Jains believe karma sticks to one's *jiva*. One has to go to extremes such as starving and asceticism to remove it. So it would be good not to get too much karma on oneself.

Jainism believes the world is going to pot. We are currently in a period of decline that will last 21,000 years, during which Jainism and all other religions will fade along with human virtue. This will be followed by another 21,000 years, bringing an end to civilization. We will hit rock bottom. We will become virtueless, self-centered, egotistical, and self-serving: perfectly healthy cats. This will complete the downward spiral of the cosmic cycle, and then a period of ascendancy will begin. Civilization will come back. Virtue will come back. Religion will come back. And everyone will become Jains. This is why Jains are not worried about spreading their faith, because in about 42,000+ years, everyone will be Jains anyway. This is why Jains do not go around naked, knocking on doors with pamphlets: Jains are not interested in evangelizing.

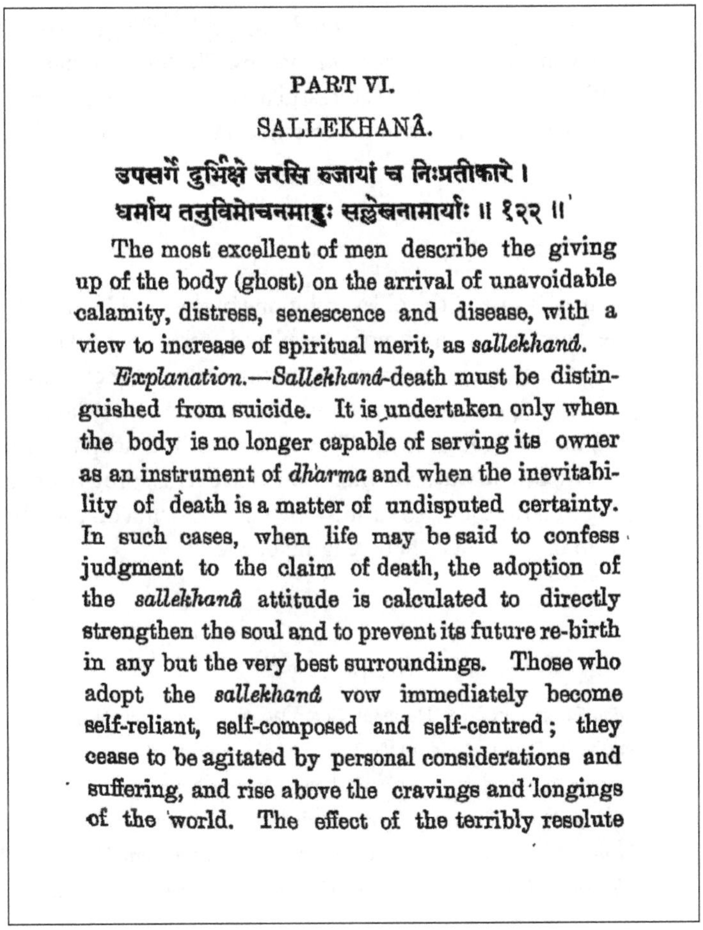

PART VI.
SALLEKHANÂ.

उपसर्गे दुर्भिक्षे जरसि रुजायां च निःप्रतीकारे ।
धर्माय तनुविमोचनमाहुः सल्लेखनामार्याः ॥ १२२ ॥

The most excellent of men describe the giving up of the body (ghost) on the arrival of unavoidable calamity, distress, senescence and disease, with a view to increase of spiritual merit, as *sallekhanâ*.

Explanation.—*Sallekhanâ*-death must be distinguished from suicide. It is undertaken only when the body is no longer capable of serving its owner as an instrument of *dharma* and when the inevitability of death is a matter of undisputed certainty. In such cases, when life may be said to confess judgment to the claim of death, the adoption of the *sallekhanâ* attitude is calculated to directly strengthen the soul and to prevent its future re-birth in any but the very best surroundings. Those who adopt the *sallekhanâ* vow immediately become self-reliant, self-composed and self-centred; they cease to be agitated by personal considerations and suffering, and rise above the cravings and longings of the world. The effect of the terribly resolute

FIGURE 8.7 This chapter from the Jain Agamas talks about starving to death.

Jain Branches

The religion would split into two factions: the Digambaras ("sky-clad" or "atmosphere-clad") and the Shvetambaras ("white-clad"). The Shvetambaras wear a simple white tunic. The Digambaras wear, at the most, a smile. They believe they have to be like Mahavira, including in his dress or, in this case, no dress.

FIGURE 8.8 Jain temples, such as this one in Chennai, India, are elaborate, and some are very old.

FIGURE 8.9 Tampa, FL, the Jain temple is more modest, but Jainism is relatively new in the United States.

FIGURE 8.10 Tampa's Jain temple was founded in 2008.

The Shvetambaras accepted women. The Digambaras did not, for obvious reasons. A room full of naked men and women causes attachment issues. The Shvetambaras became prominent in western and northwestern India, while Digambaras were successful in central and southern India. This was due to a practical reason: if you are naked, you may want to live in the warmer south. Gradually, though, Jainism faded in all areas except around Bombay.

SUMMARY

Jainism is one of the oldest religions in the world, and it's probably the most nonviolent one. It has incorporated the elements of an immortal soul and eternal life (like other religions) with functional atheism (like Buddhism). Jains are small in numbers, in that they do not seek converts nor rely on the birth rate to sustain their numbers.

Although small, Jainism has influenced other Eastern religions with its emphasis on ahimsa, though other religions do not go so far. There are even bird hospitals for pigeons operated by Jains.

Oh, by the way, Jain monks eat leftovers, going from house to house and begging for food. The food was not prepared for them, so eating it brings no karma on their behalf. But in the interest of unattachment, they do not claim to even own their begging bowls.

FOR FURTHER READING

Jaina Sutras: Part I & II, Hermann Georg Jacobi, Forgotten Books, 2008

Jainism: A Pictorial Guide to the Religion of Non-Violence, 2nd ed., Kurt Titze, Motilal Banarsidass, 2001

Jainism: An Introduction, Jeffrey D. Long, Penguin, 2009

Jainism: Art, Architecture, Literature and Philosophy, Haripriya Rangarajan, Sharada Prakashan, 2012

Living Jainism: An Ethical Science, Aidan D. Rankin and Kanti V. Mardia, Mantra Books, 2013

The Forest of Thieves and the Magic Garden: An Anthology of Medieval Jain Stories, Phyllis Granoff, trans., Penguin, 2007

ENDNOTES

1   H. Jacobi, trans., *Jaina Sutras (Part II),* 1884, http://www.sacred-texts.com/jai/sbe22/sbe2205.htm.

2   Young Jains of America website, https://yja.org/about.

3   B. Sacks, "Modern Jainism: One of the Fastest Growing Religions Is Changing Tradition," Annenberg Media Center, February 24, 2014, http://www.neontommy.com/news/2014/02/jainism-fastest-growing-religion-america.

4   G. Flaccus, "Jainism Religion Gets Updates for Modern U.S. Fit," SFGate, August 20, 2013, http://www.sfgate.com/news/article/Jainism-religion-gets-updates-for-modern-U-S-fit-4747658.php.

CREDITS

9

DAOISM

LEARNING OBJECTIVES

1. Compare harmony and disharmony, balance and imbalance
2. Learn about the origins of Daoism
3. Explain simplicity as a goal
4. Know what is meant by universal view

> **The Dao is like an empty bowl**
> **Which in being used can never be filled up.**
> **Fathomless, it seems to be the origin of all things.**
> **It blunts all sharp edges,**
> **It unties all tangles,**
> **It harmonizes all lights,**
> **It united the world into one whole.**
> **Hidden in the deeps,**
> **Yet it seems to exist for ever.**
> **I do not know whose child it is;**
> **It seems to be the common ancestor of all, the father of all things.**
> **—Tao Te Ching (Lao Tzu)[i]**

Daoism Statistics

Counting Daoist adherents is difficult in that Daoism is often practiced with other religions. It may not include atheists who attend Daoist rituals anyway. There are about ten thousand Daoists in the People's Republic of China, according to its government. That does not include Daoist congregations that may have not registered with the government. Other estimates range from 10,000 to 20 million worldwide.[2]

To clear up some initial confusion, you may have noticed that the word "Dao" as part of the title of this chapter, "Daoism," is spelled differently from "Tao" in the attribution to the opening quote of the chapter. Dao, a more modern translation of the word, is closer to what the word sounds like when spoken by a native Chinese. So, in literature about Daoism, you will see both Dao and Tao: they mean the same thing.

Daoism History

FIGURE 9.1 China's history is a series of dynasties, as seen in these coins from different kingdoms. The hole was threaded with fabric as a way of carrying the money.

Daoism and the other main Chinese belief, Confucianism, were born during a massive civil war in China called the Warring States Period (400s–221 BC). This was a civil war between six or seven kingdoms that lasted for almost two hundred years.[3] Addressing this disharmony were the main themes of Daoism and Confucianism, which were born during this time period. It should be noted that Chinese history is made up of a series of dynasties collapsing and/or being overthrown. Chinese explain this turnover as being the "heavenly mandate." This mandate is similar to the divine right of kings in Europe: kings rule because God gave them that right. Chinese emperors had the same right, given to them by Shang Ti, the head god of the Chinese pantheon of gods. So they ruled because the "heavens" said so. But this was a conditional mandate: it could be withdrawn and given to someone else if the emperor did not care for his people. So the emperor would send spies throughout his kingdom to make sure his people were fed and not starving. If they had cereal or an Egg McMuffin® for breakfast, all was well. But if they were eating something out of the local vending machine or had to resort to some secondhand sushi from a gas station for breakfast, the empire was in trouble.

An important fact to know about how Chinese maintained harmony has to do with their willingness to combine religions to do so. During the Sung Dynasty, Buddhism, Daoism, Confucianism, and neo-Confucianism received state endorsement. If one religion did not work, they had three more to fall back on. Daoism is rarely practiced by itself: it is almost always practiced with another religion.

Myth of Daoism

FIGURE 9.2 Lao Zi is riding an ox while reading a scroll in this Malaysian relief.

The legendary founder of Daoism was Lao Zi ("the old master" or "old boy"). Doubts abound about whether he lived or not. According to a biography written about six hundred years after his alleged birth in 604 BCE, he took a government post as a royal Chou Dynasty archivist, which was a record keeper. But he left his job because he said the government and laws distort simplicity of how humans should live. If you have ever filled out an IRS 1040 income tax form with the A, B, and C schedules, you know what he is talking about. And what about that intangible tax? How can anyone tax something intangible?

So Lao Zi left the center of government and moved to someplace more simple: a double-wide trailer with a window air conditioning unit in the town of Lutz. Okay, just kidding about Lutz, but it is the epitome of simple living. If you have never heard about this town, no worries: this knowledge is not necessary for your survival. The burg, located north of Tampa, Florida, used to be a Catholic mission and a train stop, although the train no longer stops there. Now it is God-honest country living. Excitement consists of counting the rock-hauling trucks headed north on US 41 toward Brooksville and watching the Budweiser® beer cans alongside the road slowly turn pink in the summer sun. All the squirrels in town actually have names because the residents had the time to name them.

FIGURE 9.3 Formerly called hell notes, this relabeled heaven bank note serves as a bribe for officials in the afterlife to care for one's ancestors.

It is so far out in the boondocks that sunlight has to be piped in. It has a sign, like most towns, at its city limits proclaiming "Welcome to Lutz." Unlike most towns, there is a second sign behind it that states "... if anybody cares." Most of the town members are named some version of Bubba, and everybody looks like they're related, to quote singer Bruce Ritter. So anyway, Lao Zi lived this simplistic life in a town that could be Lutz, but people continued to bang on his aluminum door, asking, "Oh great teacher, what is the meaning of life?" One can only say, "The magazine, the cereal, or the board game?" before it isn't funny anymore. So Lao Zi decided to move somewhere more desolate than Lutz. And the only place more primitive than Lutz was western China. People still lived in caves in western China. Back in the 500s BCE, it must have been like a Jurassic Park. People passed through the western gate and disappeared. But before Lao Zi disappeared, the gatekeeper convinced him to write down his philosophy of life. And so he did, on a cocktail napkin—that is, probably rice paper. This became the main scripture of Daoism, the *Dao De Jing*.

Modern Daoism

Religious Daoism can still be found mainly in Taiwan and Hong Kong, Malaysia, Thailand, Singapore, and the Chinese parts of San Francisco and Washington, DC. But it is a pale example of its glorious past. Daoist monasteries were closed in the People's Republic of China due to the Cultural Revolution. A Chinese dentist told me, as we were discussing Daoism, that the old religion had disappeared. Young Chinese were only interested in smartphones.

But individual Daoist practices still remain, such as "hell notes," *tai chi*, and *feng shui*. Hell notes—some have been renamed "heaven bank notes"—are the currency of hell or the afterlife. If someone buys them—and everybody and their brother sells them in Chinatown, not to mention on the Internet—and burns them, this currency goes to hell and bribes the officials in hell to take care of one's ancestors. It is a Chinese custom to bribe government officials to do their jobs, and there is no difference between earthly and hellish officials. So if one sends enough cash, one's ancestors will have three meals a day, air conditioning, a room with a view—wait, it's hell—a room without a view. If one sends enough money, one can make hell heaven. That way, one's ancestors will not cause disharmony by appearing at the foot of one's bed at 3 a.m. exclaiming, "Send money!"

Tai chi is a noncontact, very popular, martial arts series of exercises that facilitates the flow of *chi* and claims health benefits for those who practice them. The Taoist Tai Chi Society of the USA claims these benefits include improved circulation, better balance, and reduced stress as well as relief from other physical and mental ailments.[4]

Do you have a room that is not feeling it? Well, try feng shui, according to the home improvement channel HGTV. "Feng shui divides the world into five elements: wood, fire, earth, metal, and water. If you have a room that doesn't feel quite right, try balancing the elements to make it more comfortable."[5] This decorating method facilitates the flow of *chi* and keeps a proper balance of the Dao in one's living surroundings.

Daoist Scripture

The main scripture of Daoism may not have been written in the 500s BCE, as the legend says, but closer to the Warring States Period, about 475–221 BCE,[6] when Daoism was born and when the *Dao De Jing* appeared in history.[7] It may have been written even later, in the fourth or third century BCE.[8] In fact, the *Dao De Jing* was originally titled the *Lao Zi*, so it may have been a book in search of an author. So we really do not know who wrote it. But it is considered the founding document of Daoism.[9]

FIGURE 9.4 An excerpt of the Dao De Jing is displayed on a wall in Changchun Temple, Wuhan, China.

The *Dao De Jing* is a short work, with 81 brief chapters that have deep and esoteric sayings in them, mainly about the Dao or the sage—things like "The movement of the Tao consists in returning"[10] or "The Sage is self-effacing and scanty of words."[11]

The *Dao De Jing* may have originally been a how-to-run-a-government guide, but now it is interpreted with deeper philosophical meanings. This is probably a good thing, because politically, it was a failure: no Chinese government ever used it. For instance, the US government seems to be talking a lot about health care. Let's pick a chapter at random from the *Dao De Jing* and see what it says. "There was something undefined and yet complete in itself."[12] Hmm, kind of sounds like health care. Okay, let's talk about tax reform: "What is in the end to be shrunken, begins by being first stretched out."[13] Okay, I got nothing. That is probably why no government used it. Instead, its impact has been its teachings of natural, simple living, such as life in Lutz: name the squirrels in the backyard (harder than you think: they move around a lot and look similar).

Zhuang Zi ("Master Chuang" or "Chuang Tzu"), the legendary author of the book of same name, which was dated to 3–4 BCE, is another important author—assuming he existed—in Daoism. The book, the *Zhuangzi*, is second in importance after the *Dao De Jing*. It says the Dao cannot be understood rationally; one must let go of knowledge and words to live harmoniously. So we have a religion that defies being taught in class. The *Zhuangzi* also emphasized the spiritual freedom of the individual, and it said that the Dao was unlimited, as opposed to the limited potential of humans.[14]

So what is the Dao? And don't say stock market. The Dao, according to Daoism, is the original, natural equality of all things. It is also the nonliving mother of all life. So what is not alive but has all life in it? The universe! The Dao is the big enchilada, the double cheeseburger with fries, the large pepperoni pizza with anchovies! It is everything, and all is in it.

The *Dao De Jing* and the *Zhuangzi* seem to suggest immortality for those who live in harmony with Dao. This is a good thing, because in Chinese mythology, the afterlife is hell. Everyone goes to hell: the good, bad, or indifferent. So if a person can stay in this life forever, much better. So a religious branch of Daoism rises. By the second century CE, there were Daoist religious movements focusing on the pursuit of immortality and well-being, and this movement still continues today. But be careful: the first emperor of the Qin Dynasty, Qin, died when looking for an elixir of immortality from Daoist magicians.[15]

Daoist Beliefs

This claim of immortality is based on religious Daoism's idea that humans are not only part of the universe; the universe is in every cell of humans. Humans are a microcosm of the universe. In philosophical Daoism, this is the Unmanifest Dao, the source of all reality, the result of yin and yang forces interacting.

The Dao has a role in human and natural life: harmony is good, and disharmony is bad. The way one maintained harmony was to keep a proper balance between the two opposing forces in the universe: yin and yang in the Dao. Yin is dark, wet, cool, and feminine. Yang is bright, dry, warm, and masculine. Both are present in varying degrees in everyone and everything. Women are more yin; men are more yang. Fish are more yin; the sun is more yang. Ice is more yin; fire is more yang. For

FIGURE 9.5 Yin is dark, wet, cool, and feminine, while yang is bright, dry, warm, and masculine. As you can see, there is some yin in yang, and vice versa.

harmony purposes, a proper balance of yin and yang is good; an imbalance is bad. If the sun is more yang, we are fine. But if the sun is more yin, we will freeze. If the ocean is yin, great; but if it is more yang and boiling hot, we will cook.

Religious Daoism emphasizes breath (*qi* or *ch'i*), which creates the yin/yang dynamic. When qi divides yin and yang, death and disharmony occur. Harmony means life. So the way to live forever is to not stop breathing. It is that simple. How come no one has thought of this? So suck air in: it's free! So if one can keep the proper balance, qi will never dissipate, and a person can become a hsien (immortal being).

According to Daoism, there are different pathways to immortality. One is through alchemy, which is changing a base metal such as lead into gold. Then, from that gold, one can fashion a plate and a cup. Then after one eats off that plate and drinks out of that cup, one would become immortal. Another pathway is by drinking an elixir, a magic potion, which can be found somewhere on an island or some other inaccessible place shrouded in fog. If one finds that elixir and drinks it, one becomes immortal. There are also certain hygienic and dietary regimes that one can engage in to become immortal. Think: eat right and exercise! Have you ever heard that? (I could have had a V-8!). Breath control is another method to attain immortality. One only has a certain amount of breaths, and then one dies. So if one draws out every breath and makes it last, this extends life. There are also certain sexual practices one can engage in to become immortal. The specifics are outside the scope of this book, but an earnest student could probably do a scholarly search on the Internet and discover this knowledge (while in a closet or under the bedsheets).

Religious Daoism has an elaborate hierarchy of spiritual beings organized on the bureaucratic model of the Han Dynasty.

- Unmanifest Dao, the nonliving mother of all life, the universe, is at the top.

- Primordial chaos/*chi* is next. Primordial chaos is known as the undifferentiated potential. It is the "clay" from which

FIGURE 9.6 Dragons are considered good luck in China, scaring away evil spirits.

the universe shapes things. Some of these things need to be alive—people—so the universe breathes *chi*, breath, into them.

■ The final spiritual group begins with the three officials: the Jade Emperor, a popular emperor of the Han Dynasty; Lao Zi, the legendary founder of Daoism; and the Marshal of Supernatural Beings (who you would call other than the Ghostbusters). Below these officials are the nine ministers in the nine heavens and then humans, meerkats (and other animals), and demons.

All life on earth and in hell are at the bottom of this hierarchy. There is no upward movement. Humans are peasants in this structure and will always be.

The *Dao De Jing* says this about the Dao: "He who knows does not speak; he who is (ever ready to) speak about it does not know it." So if I know about the Dao, I am not going to tell you about it. If I do tell you about the Dao, it is clear that I have no idea what I am talking about. Once again, we have a religion that defies description in any cognitive way, such as in a textbook. Once again, we will have to plod through and explain it anyway.

Daoism states that all humans, like all reality, are part of the cosmic process known as Dao and yin and yang forces. One has to yield to the Dao for a harmonious life. Be one with the Dao. Resisting the flow of the Dao causes disharmony, as when we try to establish our own separate identities. Here is an example. In southern Colorado, there is a river called the Conejos, which means "rabbit" in Spanish. It is a fast-moving river with Class 5 rapids and is ice-fed, so the coldness compels a person to instantly need to pee. Your author was a whitewater

FIGURE 9.7 The Dragon Boat races in Tampa, FL, occur during the high-energy yang part of the year.

rafting guide on the river for a summer and lost only one customer (no worries, I found him again). Suppose you are in your own raft flowing downstream. You have your favorite beverage, magazine, and/or movie. You are just chillin'. How fast are you moving? Well, the speed of the river, subtracting some drag, is your progress. Now, downriver is Donald Trump. The Donald is set on establishing his own personal identity, so he is going against the river—something else no one would do. After the first mile he is wet, he may have peed in his pants, and his hair is on sideways. How fast is he going? Not very fast. Who is making the most progress? You, by doing nothing but going with the flow. And The Donald is never going to get to the beginning of the river, because it is more than one hundred miles away. He will end up in the same place you do. He will be ready for the emergency room, and you will be ready for your second nap.

For those people who succumb to the illusion of a unique permanent self, like Trump, and fall victim to desire and craving, the Dao eventually will roll over them. Think of the Dao as a big wave. No matter what a person wants to do, the Dao will eventually wash that person toward the way it wants to go. So a person can take the easy way or the hard way, but whichever way is taken, that person will always end up in the same place.

The goal in this religion is harmony with Dao, seeing both life and death as part of eternal Dao. Life is unending, so actually, there is no real "goal," because that involves striving. One either lives forever in this life or in hell, so life is immortal.

Going with the flow is called *wu wei*. Think of yourself flowing down the river, yelling "wu wei!" Now, how does one do this? How does one know which way the universe is flowing? There is that old traffic maxim: "If everything is going your way, you are in the wrong lane." In essence, seek the path of least resistance. Daoists say "Be yourself." Because you are a microcosm of the universe, and you are in every atom of the universe, if you can be "you," you can be the Dao. Still, this leaves a lot of decisions begging for guidance.

Daoism has some guidance for practical situations. In governments, Daoism supports noninterference with the population of the kingdom/country in general. In education, Daoism does not seek knowledge actively but passively, in an open and receptive way. This is a tendency among students, anyway: sit in the back of the room, slack-jawed, waiting to be fed information without pursuing it, kind of like goldfish in a bowl.

For the most part, it may be difficult to perceive the true way of the Dao because it is imperceptible. Dao is the "way," but it cannot be touched, named, felt, or desired. For example, picture our river again. The Conejos

River is lousy with trout: spotted trout, cutthroat trout, brown trout, and trout lining the banks waiting to get into the river. In the river, two trout are doing what trout do, which is basically sucking in water and flapping their fins. That is it. They look up and see you float by. They look downriver and see Donald Trump (snicker). And one trout says to the other—if trout could talk—"You know what? I really like water!" Well, the second trout would slowly turn on its fins and reply, "Duh, we're fish!" Now that is not something likely a trout would say, if trout could talk. A trout is hatched in water, grows up in water, and lives most of its life entirely in water. So it doesn't even notice the water, feel the water, or perceive the water. It probably doesn't even have a name for water. Water just is. It would be like you waking up one morning, sniffing, and realizing for the first time that there is air! "Air, air, omigosh! There is air today! Woo-hoo! I have to call my peeps: 'Hey, guys, get out of bed, there is air today! And it's free! Woo-hoo!' Sniff, sniff." You probably don't even notice the air. You are born into air, live almost entirely in air. Air just is.

And the Dao is just that way: it just is. It cannot be perceived, because one is one with the Dao. The only way to perceive the universe is to be outside it, and there is no outside! It is the universe! It is everything! Still, the way of the Dao seems nebulous. It does not have enough rules to practice by itself. It is like Jell-O®. Have you ever tried to nail Jell-O® to a wall? It is too soft and fluffy. It needs a frame or container. That is why Daoism is rarely practiced by itself: it is almost always practiced with another religion, such as Confucianism, Buddhism, or even Christianity.

Daoist Branches

Southern Daoism

Southern Daoism is an offshoot of Cheng-i Daoism, the only liturgical tradition surviving today. The modern Cheng-i tradition dates back to the 11th century. Its priests still perform liturgies like the *chiao*, believed to harmonize the local community with the cosmos. They also perform healing rituals and exorcisms in public. But these activities are frowned upon by "Northern" Daoists.

Northern Daoism

Northern Daoism grew out of the Ch'üan-chen tradition. It was founded in the 12th century by Wang Chu'ung-yang. It emphasizes moral and spiritual discipline and also continues self-preservation practices that date back to the classical Nei-yeh. Its headquarters are at White Cloud Abbey in Beijing.

Chin Tan

Golden Elixir Daoism—a tradition strong on meditation, or "inner alchemy." Much of this practice was absorbed into the Ch'üan-chen tradition.

Ch'ing wei

Clarified Tenuity Daoism—a complex of ritual traditions that trace back to a young woman, Tsu Shu. Its liturgies show practitioners how to link their physiological and mental well-being to spiritual enlightenment.

T'ien hsin

Heart of Heaven Daoism—a tradition of ritual healing based upon scriptures discovered in the early Sung period by a retired official, Jao Tung-t'ien.

Shen hsiao

Divine Empyrean Daoism—a liturgical tradition established by Lin Ling-su at the court of the Sung emperor Hui tsung (early 12th century).

T'ung-ch'u

Youthful Incipience Daoism—an obscure tradition of therapeutic rituals founded by a young man in 1121, claiming continuity with the Shang-ch'ing tradition.

T'ai i

Supreme Union Daoism—founded by Hsiao Pao chen in the 12th century, it stressed ritual healing and social responsibility.

Chen ta

Chen ta ("Perfected Greatness") or Ta-tao ("Great Way") Daoism—founded by Liu Te-jen in the 12th century. It combined the basic moral teachings of Buddhism, Confucianism, and Daoism and was patronized by the Chin government.[16]

SUMMARY

Daoism is an integral part of Chinese life. It concerns the balance of life's activities, from planting in the spring to balancing flavors in cooking. The religion concerns itself with harmony, avoiding disharmony, and keeping a balance between yin and yang. It is often practiced with other religions because that is the Chinese way and it has too few rules of its own to be a sole belief.

ENDNOTES

1   Lao Tzu, in J. Wu, trans., *Tao Te Ching* (Boston: Shambhala Publications, 1961).
2   K. Wenzel-Teuber, "People's Republic of China: Religions and Churches Statistical Overview 2011," trans. D. Streit, *Religions & Christianity in Today's China* 2, no. 3, http://www.china-zentrum.de/fileadmin/downloads/rctc/2012-3/RCTC_2012-3.29-54_Wenzel-Teuber_Statistical_Overview_2011.pdf.
3   "Warring States," *Encyclopedia Britannica*, https://www.britannica.com/event/Warring-States.
4   "Experience the Benefits," Taoist Tai Chi Society of USA Website, 2015, http://www.taoist.org/usa/experience-the-benefits/
5   S. McWilliams, "HGTV Presents the Elements of Feng Shui," HGTV, 2016, http://www.hgtv.com/design/decorating/design-101/the-elements-of-feng-shui.
6   "Warring States."
7   J. Yohannan, ed., *A Treasury of Asian Literature* (New York: Meridian, 1994).
8   X. Ji, *Facts About China* (Bronx, NY: Wilson, 2003).
9   Ji, *Facts About China*
10 Lao Zi, *Tao Te Ching.* (Shambhala, 1861), 93
11 Ibid, 35
12 Ibid, 53
13 Ibid, 81
14 Ji, 358
15 Ji, 362
16 R. Kirkland, "Subdivisions of Taoism," BBC, 2014, http://www.bbc.co.uk/religion/religions/taoism/subdivisions/subdivisions_1.shtml.

CREDITS

CONFUCIANISM

- Filial piety
- Ren or jen
- I or yi
- Li
- Great Ultimate
- Five basic relationships
- Leaders of character
- Five virtues
- De

LEARNING OBJECTIVES

1. Learn about Confucius's life
2. Understand the importance of virtue
3. Compare Confucianism versus Neo-Confucianism
4. Understand post-Confucianism
5. Explain the Chinese government's relationship with Confucianism

The Life of Pests

Let me describe the life of pests. When they are young, they are neither modest nor respectful. When they have grown up, they do nothing useful for others. And when they are old, they refuse to die.

—Kung Fu Tzu[1]

Confucianism Statistics

Like Daoism, Confucianism membership statistics are difficult to come by. Some censuses count self-proclaimed Confucianism members, while others include those who practice folk Chinese religion that has characteristics of Confucianism in it. So estimates range from six million to 330 million. These figures include people outside China.[2]

History and Legend of Confucianism

Confucius, the founder of Confucianism, unlike Lao Zi, actually existed, although he is surrounded by legends. Master K'ung (Confucius comes from the Latin version of K'ung fu-tzu—"Great Master K'ung") was born about 551 BCE in the feudal state of Lu in northwest China. His legend said his father died or was a wandering soldier who came through town, and 8½ months later, Confucius was born. Either way, when Confucius was born, Dad was nowhere around. So Confucius was raised by a single mom in a trailer park in Lutz. Okay, enough Lutz jokes. Still, only his mother raised him. This bothered him, and when he was old enough, he went looking for his father, certain he would recognize him if he ever saw him. Apparently, he never did.

At age 50, he said he was appointed to a high office but either resigned or was fired. He may have been a police commissioner in Lu who lowered the crime rate by instilling the virtues of citizenship—along with its

FIGURE 10.1 K'ung fu-tzu, known in the West as Confucius, came up with a novel way of structuring society.

FIGURE 10.2 Chinese paper cuts, such as this one showing the sky through it, are believed by some to date back to Confucius's time, but unfortunately, paper had yet to be invented.

responsibilities—and government accountability. Everyone knew their jobs and brought dedication and respect to their jobs. Few were "pests," as Confucius mentions in "The Life of Pests."

After his termination, he wandered for 13 years, starting at age 55. But, unlike some Indian mystics, he kept his clothes on. He also was not interested in finding enlightenment. Instead, he taught political and social reform. He was not interested in religion. He was a Poli Sci teacher. He could not care less about religion. And he did not start a religion. So, you are probably wondering why we are wasting time and trees on him, because this is a textbook on world religions. Well, we will get to that, eventually. Patience is a virtue.

At age 67, he returned to Lu and spent the rest of his life teaching and editing Confucian classics. Discouraged about his lack of influence on governments, he died about 479 BCE. Like the unpopularity of the *Dao De Jing*, Confucius's writings met the same apathetic audience, at least initially. But a band of followers remain committed to his teachings, which is why there is a chapter on Confucianism and why you are still reading this book.

Post-Confucius era. The followers of Confucius founded a loose school and eventually collected Confucius's writings (*Book of Filial Piety*) during the feudal-order breakup in the Warring States Period. Filial piety is respect for your father, your ruler, and your ancestors. You must respect anyone who has authority over you and keep him or her happy; otherwise, they can make your life miserable. Your father and ruler can punish you. Your ancestors can show up in your bedroom at night, moaning. Those you have authority over have to respect you in a similar fashion. If everyone follows this piety, they will have peace in society, because everyone knows his or her place.

One of these members of this loose school was Master Meng (371–289 BCE). He emphasized *ren* or *jen* ("humaneness") interacting with *I* or *yi* ("righteousness"), so a person's position in society dictates how humanely he is treated. For instance, the president of a college would be treated more humanely than a student because the president is in a higher position. Deans or provosts would be treated more humanely than students. Faculty and staff would be treated more humanely than students. Squirrels on campus would be treated more humanely—you get the picture.

Xan Zi or Hsü tzŭ (297–238 BCE), another member of this school, taught *li*, worth of rites, also known as propriety, as the most important virtue. Proper behavior, etiquette, is the most important virtue. For instance, did you know that it is customary to leave a party after the host or hostess serves the second cup of coffee? No? No wonder you get thrown out of parties. When your hostess pours that second cup, she is saying (without saying it), "Get out of here. It's late. We want to go to bed!" You see that second cup and are thinking, *The old biddy is trying to throw us out.* But what you say is "My, look at the time. We really must go." And she will say, "Oh, no, it is only 3 a.m. Maybe we can watch Lawrence Welk reruns." And you will say, "Oh, no, we must really get home. We hired a dingo as a babysitter, and it probably has eaten the children by now." That is what is called *li*, or proper behavior. Xan Zi said people are born evil and education fixes this. Babies do not know right or wrong: they throw up on anyone or scream at the most inappropriate times. They will also kick your seat nonstop on a transatlantic flight. As they get older, assuming they live that long, they are taught proper behavior. I am sure your instructor's syllabus said nothing about wearing clothes to class. What up? You can thank your parents.

Confucianism, for the next two thousand years (until 1905), would become the basis of the Chinese education system. Also, Confucius became an object of state piety. As early as the Han dynasty, the emperor performed sacrifice at the grave of Confucius in 195 BCE.

China's turn to the West in the early 20th century caused Confucianism as state orthodoxy to decline. It was abandoned as part of the education system, and religious worship declined. The Communist government, after 1949, banned sacrifices to Confucius, and Confucian classics (being considered part of the old feudal system) were burned. Confucianism was suppressed during the Cultural Revolution of 1966, and Confucius's birthplace was destroyed.

Confucianism was down but not out.

Neo-Confucianism. Neo-Confucianism emerged during the Sung Dynasty (960–1279 BC). If you remember, it was one of the four religions that had received state endorsement in China. Neo-Confucianism called for a return to the basic principles of Confucianism in response to growing Buddhism and Daoism in China. One of these Neo-Confucian scholars was Zhu Xi. He said that humans are essentially good and

FIGURE 10.3 During a period of prosperity during the Tang dynasty, illustrated by this ceramic Tang horse, Confucianism would battle with Buddhism and Daoism for the hearts and minds of the Chinese. As a result, Neo-Confucianism would be born.

that the Great Ultimate—the essence of all reality that can be studied and observed—gives humans *li* as a cosmic force. Humans have *li*—propriety—at their core. So what is this Great Ultimate? Well, as we mentioned before, Confucianism is not interested in religion. But it needs street credentials. So it invokes a nebulous power above as the reason why one should behave. So whatever that is, it wants people to use their inner *li* in interacting with society. Another Neo-Confucian, Wang Yangming, said the underlying rational principle of *li* can be discovered more by examining the mind than nature. Because cats don't have *li*. *Li* is a rational principle, a guiding light, an innate bearing toward goodness. It's that little voice you hear when you reach for a second brownie that says, "A moment on your lips, a lifetime on your hips." Yep, *li* becomes one's conscience.

So, we revisit the question we asked before. Why are we wasting time on Confucianism in this textbook if Confucianism is not a religion? Confucius was concerned more with ordering society than spiritual transformation. But principles such as *li* become cosmic and spiritual in Neo-Confucianism. And Confucius is transformed from teacher to spirit to be venerated in Neo-Confucianism. So is Confucianism a religion? No. But Neo-Confucianism is. This is why we have been spending so much time on the foundation of Neo-Confucianism: Confucianism.

As mentioned before, Confucianism was suppressed during the Cultural Revolution of 1966, and Confucius's birthplace was destroyed. But Confucius was rehabilitated in the late 1970s when the Cultural Revolution was discredited. Confucius's birthplace was rebuilt. The Chinese have always rewritten their history depending on who is in charge. The Cultural Revolution was believed to have been instigated by Mao Zedong, founder of the Communist People's Republic of China. Thousands of people were killed, temples and churches were destroyed, and many people who were believed to be capitalists became targets of the Red Guards. Mao, when the Cultural Revolution got out of control, sent the People's Liberation Army to restore order.[3] Although Mao was held partly responsible after his death for the slaughter, his widow and four associates were arrested for the damage.[4] So when the Cultural Revolution went out, Confucius came back in. The modern Chinese government has tried to draw on Confucianism's respect for authority and moral virtue to counter commercialism in the country today. Remember one of the main precepts of Confucianism: respect your ruler. In this case, the ruler is the communist government. So Confucius has become the spokesperson for the government: do what the government tells you. As part of this effort, the Chinese government has sent Confucian libraries—several shelves of Confucius's writings in Chinese—to major universities around the world as well as creating and cofounding Confucian Institutes in different countries as part of a "charm

FIGURE 10.4 A Chinese dragon, representing the Confucius Institute at the University of South Florida, meets the university's mascot, Rocky the Bull.

offensive."[5] Colleges are closing their Confucian Institutes amid accusations China can use them to collect intelligence. University of South Florida closed its Institute after a decade in 2018, citing low enrollment.

Confucian Texts

The Analects (Lun Yu) are the reputed sayings of Confucius. He did not actually write them in their current form. They were compiled by his followers from his writings after his death. In this book, there are sayings attributed to the "Master," or Confucius. For instance: "The Master said: a person who can bring new warmth to the old while understanding the new is worthy to take as a teacher."[6] The sayings focus on improving oneself as a member of society.

Great Learning (Ta Hsueh) summarizes the essential role of humans: to cultivate themselves through both their sincere intentions and their clear examination of things. In so doing, a person can help to establish order in both the family and the state.

Doctrine of the Mean (Chung Yung) describes the power of sincerity that emanates outward from humans to the cosmos itself. It describes the relationship between humans and the moral order.

Book of Mencius: third-century BCE collection of sayings of one of Confucius's principal disciples. It is a first attempt at a systematic philosophical statement of Confucius's teachings. In illustrates Confucius's teachings with discussions between Mencius and King Xuan of the Chi Empire on matters of defense and governance.

Five Classics: Book of History, Book of Changes, Annuals of Spring and Autumn, Book of Rites, Book of Poetry. These Classics set the pattern of what was to become a fully developed human being in the interaction with culture and politics.[7]

FIGURE 10.5 Knowing one's station in life, such as a Chinese farmer, and respecting one's superiors are integral parts of Confucianism.

Confucianism Beliefs

All people are part of society and must have proper social relationships for harmony, according to Confucianism. "No person is a rock. No person is an island," to quote Simon and Garfunkel, assuming the reader is old enough to remember them. One is related to someone else in some way: brother, sister, father, mother, aunt, uncle, pet, classmate, employee, employer, and so on. One is defined by one's relationships.

Five Basic Relationships. Confucianism's five basic relationships are the basis of all relationships in society. They are the most basic connections between people:

- Parent and child

- Husband and wife

- Elder and young brother

- Friend and friend

- Ruler and subject

These relationships have different social registers, and to have *li*, one must know them. Parent and child is probably familiar: "Be home at nine, or you're grounded for the week!" This is different than husband and wife: "Be home by midnight, or you're sleeping on the couch tonight!" Well, it should be different. Elder and younger brother: "Noogie! Wedgie!" This is not behavior you would engage in around the president, at least not without serious injury.

We are familiar with some of this type of etiquette concerning the differences between the sexes. If a man walked up to another man who was working on his car and said, "You still driving that piece of junk?" they would both laugh and open up a couple of cans of beer. However, if a woman said that to a man, he would be extremely offended, for she had just threatened his manhood. A woman can say to another woman, "You're looking good in those tight jeans." But if a man said to another man, "You're looking good in those tight shorts," that means something else.

FIGURE 10.6 Chinese ethics come from a variety of sources, since Chinese mix their religions. This shrine, in the Poshe Nails and Spa, includes Buddha, Heaven Notes from Daoism, and fruit. Apples are symbols of peace and luck.

Humanity also interacts with yin and yang to keep a proper balance and has earthly and heavenly souls. This latter is again Confucianism's attempt at street credentials. One has a heavenly soul telling the earthly soul how to behave. Does that mean one has two souls, similar to Commander Riker's transporter accident in *Star Trek* resulting in two Rikers? No, just an attempt at cred.

Social chaos is caused by breakdown in virtue, such as the Warring States period during which Confucianism was formed. During this period, people failed to follow their social roles. Rulers were not concerned with their subjects. Fathers were not concerned with children. The latter case was personal for Confucius.

According to Confucianism, what the world needs are leaders of character (*jun-zi*) who lead virtuous lives. These would be the good presidents, emperors, kings, governors, senators, dogcatchers, and whoever. All people must follow the Five Virtues. But leaders must follow the Five Virtues plus an additional virtue just for them.

The Five Virtues are split into the three inner virtues and two external virtues. The inner virtues are the following:

- *Ren* or *jen*: humaneness (we've covered this one already).

- *Shu*: reciprocity, the Silver Rule. Confucius phrased the rule negatively: "Do not do unto others as you would not have them do unto you." It means the same thing as the Golden Rule, but because it is phrased negatively, it is called the "Silver Rule."

- *Hsueh*: "self-correcting wisdom." This means no one has to tell you when you make a mistake; you figure it out all by yourself.

The external virtues are the following:

- *Xiao*: filial piety; respect for your father, ruler, and ancestors.

- Rectification of names: using the right names for the right roles in government. Only a bureaucrat would come up with this, and Confucius was a bureaucrat. The problem in the Chinese government was that no one did what their titles said they did. They did not want to be held accountable. Consequently, the average Chinese did not trust them. Confucius said if government officials did what their titles say they did, people would trust government.

The last virtue, which is not for everyone but just for leaders, is *de*, moral charisma. Leaders need to be both moral and charismatic. If a leader is charismatic, people will follow him to Lutz and back. But a leader also needs to be moral. For instance, Bill Clinton was a very charismatic president, but unfortunately, he had the morals of an alley cat. I am reminded of him when department stores have those President's Day sales: all pants half off, I think of Bill.

FIGURE 10.7 This bridge in the Forbidden City of China represents one of five of Confucius's virtues. Four other bridges do the same.

The most important aspect of Confucianism is life-giving, harmonious relationships. "We are our relationships." Therefore, humans make the Dao great through their harmonious relationships and not letting the Dao just happen, like in Daoism.

Branches of Confucianism

Mencius

Mencius had a branch of Confucianism named after him. He advocated the benefits of divisions of labor to exercise the mind as well as the body, and he believed that if a person truly lived in the mold of Confucius, he could not be corrupted by riches, conquered by power, or affected by poverty.[8]

Xunzi

Xunzi also had a branch named after him. He took the opposite stance of Mencius when he taught that human nature is essentially evil and virtue has to be learned. Society and laws played a part in that.

Dong Zhongshu

Dong was dedicated to scholarly pursuits, but he took a neutral stance on human nature, stating only that a person's actions have consequences in the universe. Dong used the five natural elements—fire, wood, metal, earth, and water—to form his version of Confucian cosmological theory.

Song Confucianism

Song Confucianism (960–1279): the men in this school of thought brought Confucian teachings back to what they thought were truer representations of Confucius and preached living a life of self-cultivation and balance between humanity and the cosmos. Their themes of balance and synthesis were so popular that Song Confucianism extended beyond China and into Korea and Japan.

Ming Confucianism

During the Ming Dynasty (1368–1644), scholars focused on uniting a person's mind with his actions and how they related to the earth instead of the heavens. Moral idealism, as originally taught by Mencius, was heavily promoted as Ming Confucians preached balancing Confucianism with everyday life.

Korean Confucianism

Yi T'oegye (1501–1570) took an intellectual approach to Confucianism by incorporating Mencius's ideas of basic feelings and emotions in his treatise, "Discourse on the Ten Sagely Diagrams," written to educate the king. Yi discussed how a person enters into a relationship with himself and others using Mencius's concepts of the four emotions—commiseration, shame, modesty, and integrity—and seven feelings: pleasure, anger, sorrow, fear, love, hatred, and desire.

Japanese Confucianism

In Japan, scholar Ogyu Sorai, a devotee of social and political reform, used four Confucian texts published in 1190, collectively called Sishu, to convert people to the ancient Confucian ideals and was so influential that by the late 1600s, most educated Japanese citizens had had some degree of education from them.[9]

Confucian Holidays

The birthday of Confucius is celebrated on September 28. This festival is held each year to pay respects to the founder of Confucianism.

Qingming occurs 106 days after the winter solstice. Adherents go to their ancestors' graves and give them offerings, such as paper money and paper cloths. Usually, food is offered after ceremonies; however, with Confucianism, they offer food during the ceremony.

Chongmyo Taeje honors the kings and queens of the Yi dynasty. This holiday takes place on the first Sunday in May.

Ching Ming is known as tomb-sweeping or ancestor day. It is celebrated on the 15th day from the spring equinox. During this ceremony, believers visit their ancestors' graves, present them with gifts, and sweep their graves clean.[10]

SUMMARY

Confucianism is all about virtue: interaction with other people and society in general. This also applies to government workers. The end goal is harmony through everyone's correct knowledge of what is expected of him or her. The purpose is not to create equality but a well-functioning society.

FOR FURTHER READING

Chinese Public Diplomacy: The Rise of the Confucius Institute, Falk Hartig, Routledge, 2017

Chinese Society in the Age of Confucius (1000–250 BC): The Archaeological Evidence (Ideas, Debates, and Perspectives), Lothar Von Falkenhausen, Cotsen Institute of Archaeology Press, 2017

Confucius: A Biography, Jonathan Clements, Albert Bridge Books, 2017

Confucius: And the World He Created, Michael Schuman, Basic Books, 2015

The Analects, Confucius and D. C. Lau, Penguin, 1979

The Four Books: The Great Learning, The Doctrine of the Mear [i.e., Mean], Confucian Analects, [and] The Works of Mencius, James Legge and Confucius, Andesite Press, 2015

ENDNOTES

1   R. Van de Weyer, *366 Readings from Taoism and Confucianism* (Cleveland, OH: Pilgrim Press, 2000).

2   "Demographics," Weebly.com, http://worldreligions.weebly.com/confucianism.html.

3   Ji, X. *Facts about China.* (New York: H. W. Wilson, 2003),555–556.

4   Ji, 527.

5   F. Hartig, "The Globalization of Chinese Soft Power: Confucius Institutes in South Africa," *Confucius Institutes and the Globalization of Soft Power,* Center on Public Diplomacy of the Annenberg School, 2014, https://uscpublicdiplomacy.org/sites/uscpublicdiplomacy.org/files/useruploads/u25044/Confucius%20Institutes%20v2%20%281%29.pdf.

6   R. Eno, *The Analects of Confucius: An Online Teaching Translation,* 2015, http://www.indiana.edu/~p374/Analects_of_Confucius_(Eno-2015).pdf.

7   M. Nylan, *The Five "Confucian" Classics* (New Haven, CT: Yale University Press, 2001).

8   R. Eno, *Mencius: An Online Teaching Translation,* 2016, http://www.indiana.edu/~p374/Mengzi.pdf.

9   C. Strynatka, "Different Sects of Confucianism," Classroom, 2017, https://classroom.synonym.com/different-sects-of-confucianism-12087403.html.

10 "Key Holidays and Festivals," Confucianism, https://10cpconfucianism.weebly.com/holidays-and-festivals.html.

CREDIT

SHINTO AND KOREAN RELIGION

11

NEW VOCABULARY AND CONCEPTS

- Shinto
- Miko
- Ryobu ("two-sided") Shinto
- Amaterasu
- Izanagi
- Izanami
- Kami
- Bushido
- State Shinto
- Shrine Shinto
- Musubi and chuto-hanpa

LEARNING OBJECTIVES

1. Learn how Shinto developed and how uniquely Japanese it is
2. Know about the indigenous religions
3. Explain the creation myth
4. Understand the role of the emperor
5. Examine the relationship between Shinto and Buddhism in Japan
6. Explain Japan's isolation and relationship with the United States
7. Understand harmony and disharmony and the role of individualism
8. Learn about the religions of South and North Korea

Death is a central aspect of the Way of the Samurai. When a samurai is faced with a situation in which he has to choose between life and death, his immediate, unhesitating choice is death. He must be resolute and not preoccupy himself with the thought that dying without realizing one's ambitions is an ignoble death. This is a glib excuse. Realizing one's ambitions is secondary when one is faced with the choice of living or dying.

—Yamamoto Tsunetomo[1]

Shinto Statistics

Shinto is a religion only for Japanese, but because Japanese practice Shinto and Buddhism, it is difficult to count membership. The Japanese Agency for Cultural Affairs reported in 2004 that 213,826,661 citizens claimed a religion. That number, which is nearly twice Japan's population, reflected many citizens' affiliation with multiple religions, particularly Shintoism and Buddhism. Many citizens practiced both Buddhist and Shinto rites. Furthermore, membership statistics kept by the agency were based on self-reports from various religious organizations.

Of citizens who claimed a faith, 51 percent were Shinto, 44 percent were Buddhist, and 1 percent were Christian. Shintoism and Buddhism are not mutually exclusive, and most Shinto and Buddhist believers follow both faiths.[2]

FIGURE 11.1 Izanami and Izanagi, standing on the heavenly floating bridge, stir up the brine with the jeweled spear to create the first Japanese island, Onogoro.

Myth of Shinto

The Shinto myth has a long oral history but was compiled in two books in 712 CE in the *Kojiki* ("Chronicle of Ancient Events") and the 720 CE *Nihongi* ("Chronicles of Japan"). According to these two books, the Japanese islands were created by two kami: the original male, Izanagi ("man who invites") and female, Izanami ("female who invites"). The two created the gods. Out of the left eye of Izanagi came the most revered sun goddess, Amaterasu. The storm god, Susa-no-wo, emerged from the nostrils of Izanagi: he blows right out of there. Other gods follow from other bodily orifices.

Susa-no-wo was constantly battling with Amaterasu over the control of the sky, which explains the weather: sunny or rain. This battle, though, caused disorder on the Japanese islands. So Amaterasu sent her grandson to rule. His great-grandson, Jimmu Tenno, was the first human emperor of Japan (660 BCE). Scholars do not know much about him because his name just means "divine might," but this is why the Japanese, at different times in the country's history, considered the emperor to be descended from the sun goddess.

The gods asked two original humans to "complete and solidify this drifting land." Japan was floating like a jellyfish or a BP oil slick on the water. It was not really solid. Some of the gods wanted to hunt, but there was no land to do so, and apparently they were getting tired of seafood. So the two stood on the heavenly floating bridge, lowered the jeweled spear, and stirred up the brine. Brine dripped off the spear, piled up, and then became the island Onogoro. And then they created the other islands in similar fashion.

The two humans came onto the island and erected a palace and heavenly pillar, and they began following each other around the pillar.

He asked her, "How is your body formed?"

She: "It has one place which is formed insufficiently."

He: "My body has one place which is formed in excess."

He then inserted excess into insufficiency, which gave birth to the Japanese. If you do not know what that means, ask your parents, or children.

FIGURE 11.2 The Izumo Taishakyo Mission of Hawaii is a Shinto shrine in Honolulu.

History of Shinto

In early Japan, there was no Shinto, just indigenous religions. Different periods of this part of Japan's early history included a Neolithic hunting and fishing period, and then around 250 BCE, agricultural farming began with the cultivation of rice paddies. Chinese records indicate southern Japan was run by women who were like shamans,[3] called mikos. Women would play a major role in Japanese history later as geishas.

The name Shinto was developed as a way to distinguish it from incoming Buddhism, which crossed the Korea Strait from Korea in around the sixth century, though they did begin to blend. When Mahayana Buddhism was introduced to Japan from Korea (imported from China) in the mid-sixth century CE, Shinto priests begin erecting Buddhist temples within Shinto shrines. This mixture caused arguments between Shinto priests and Buddhist monks. Shinto priests argued that the kami were "original substance" that made Japan first and Buddhist deities were "manifest traces," or leftovers. Buddhist teachers of course argued the other way around. In the street-level religious practice of the people, a mixed Shinto religion emerged, such as Ryobu ("two-sided") Shinto, combining gods such as Amaterasu with the Sun Buddha (Vairocana) from Mahayana Buddhism.

"Shinto" is composed of two Japanese symbols: Shinto = shen ("spirits") + dao ("way"). So Shinto means "way of the spirits." Chinese influence can be seen in Japan's history in that the word "dao" is being used. When the Japanese characters shen and dao are separate, they are pronounced kami-no-michi, "way of the kami."

Kami is anything or anyone inspiring awe, respect, and devotion—that is, anything sacred. This includes the sun, moon, Buddha and bodhisattvas, ancestors, heroes, and nature. Japan was a series of competing kingdoms throughout its history before being united under the ruthless and oppressive rule of the Shoguns. Throughout this history, a special type of warrior developed: the samurai.

A mixture of medieval Shinto with Confucianism and Buddhism created bushido ("way of the warrior"). Bushido virtues included loyalty and reverence to a feudal lord, courage, truthfulness, respect, justice, and honor. Death was preferable to disgrace. The warrior carried two swords: one for battle and one for ritual suicide (*seppuku*) in case one was shamed or captured.

Bushido reflects Confucianism's emphasis on filial piety, loyalty, and the five basic relationships; Zen Buddhism, with focus on self-discipline and spontaneity of action; and Shinto, in aesthetic appreciation of nature

FIGURE 11.3 The samurai warrior carried two swords: one for battle, one for ritual suicide (seppuku) in case one is shamed or captured.

and pride in one's ruler. Samurai traditionally were proud of their leader. They also wrote beautiful poems about cherry blossoms. It was not because they were wussy men but because they were engaged in the natural kami (spirits of Japan, including flowers and trees).

More modern versions of bushido were the kamikaze pilots and the courage among Japanese soldiers in World War II. During the battle for Okinawa, more than two thousand kamikaze flew to their deaths as suicide pilots, damaging or sinking more than two hundred Allied ships.

Ritual suicide and martial arts are also modern versions of bushido, as is absolute obedience to one's corporation. Until recently, one's CEO was one's shogun, and one obeyed, going into battle like a samurai carrying his two weapons: a briefcase and laptop. The businessperson's mission was not only to outsell the competition but to destroy it. Unfortunately, the downside is ritual suicide if one fails at an endeavor. Japan has a high suicide rate among teenagers who do not get into the college of their choice, bringing shame upon their families. The "forest of the ghosts" around Mount Fuji, a popular place for suicide, has signs asking people to call for help instead of killing themselves.

In the 14th century, Japan tried to revive Shinto and protect itself from foreign influence by trying to close off Japan. The country stayed in the Middle Ages while the rest of the world moved into the 19th century. Shinto scholars pushed for a return to the "Ancient Way" of a Shinto-dominated country. For instance, scholar Motoori Norinaga taught Japan was superior to other countries. Furthermore, the leaders of other countries had to give homage to the Japanese emperor because he was divine. Foreigners were considered dirty and corrupt. Japanese trying to flee the country were beheaded.

The United States wanted to trade with Japan, but Japan did not want to trade with the outside world. So Commodore Perry forced the reopening of Japan with American naval forces in 1853. The

FIGURE 11.4 A Yokosuka D4Y3 (Type 33), "Judy," in a suicide dive during a kamikaze attack against the USS Essex (CV-9) on November 25, 1944.

FIGURE 11.5 A Japanese print refers to the arrival of Commodore Perry's fleet in 1853.

backlash in Japan to this was to secure Shinto as national ideology (state religion). The Japanese Constitution of 1881 stated, "The Emperor is sacred and inviolable" (reference to his relative, the sun goddess). There was also a Japanese effort to force Buddhism and Christianity out of Japan. Christians were crucified.

There is a Christian saying, however: "From the blood of the martyrs grow the seeds of the Church." The death of martyrs in Japan only created more Christians through their inspiration. The Japanese government, after realizing that the effort to prevent the growth of Christianity was failing, established State Shinto as the state religion, though it was cast as a patriotic duty, not so much a belief. All Japanese were required to register at their local Shinto shrines, which were government supported. State Shinto believed that Japan was sacred and the center of the world. This was taught in schools as well as respect for the Imperial Throne, "coequal with

FIGURE 11.6 World War II ended with the signing of the instrument of surrender aboard the USS *Missouri*, September 2, 1945.

heaven and earth." Children learned it, their parents learned it, the children's grandparents and great-grandparents learned it, and so forth. Everyone knew this, and there was no one to teach anything different because Japan was closed off from the rest of the world. Although State Shinto was designed to be a state philosophy, it did become a religion with rituals.

Japan's defeat in World War II with the signing of the instrument of surrender aboard the USS *Missouri* on September 2, 1945, in Tokyo Bay, changed nearly everything about Shinto. Because Japan surrendered unconditionally, the Allies could tell the Japanese to do anything they wanted them to do: no conditions. One of the first things the Allies did was abolish State Shinto and replace it with voluntary Shinto, called Shrine Shinto. The number of shrines dropped because they were no longer government supported, and Shinto priests had to take part-time jobs after they lost their government subsidies.

The emperor also had to tell the Japanese that he was no longer divine and that they were no longer superior to everyone else in the world. The Japanese had just been attacked by two nuclear bombs; now they got hit with a psychological atomic bomb: everything they had learned the last several hundred years was wrong. And the person who would know, the emperor, was the one telling them that. It would be like a US citizen waking up one morning, listening to the news, and hearing that the Constitution and the three branches of government had been abolished the previous night and that co-dictators for life, Donald Trump and Hillary Clinton, now ruled the country. One would wonder if it was safe to even leave the house. That is what the Japanese experienced. So Shinto was gutted. It would have to evolve to remain viable and significant.

As a footnote, the bombing of Nagasaki wiped out most of the Christian population of Japan. Oops.

To survive in Japan, Shinto evolved into a consumerism religion: the pursuit of richness became the goal. Japan has a religion-driven economy. It is much like an Amway convention: God wants you to sell soap. Outsiders may look at the Japanese and observe that they are secular, but consumerism is their religion. The kami want the Japanese to be rich. Japanese still patronize Shinto and Buddhist shrines to keep the kami happy, though.

Shinto Scripture

Kojiki

The Kojiki is one of the two primary sources for Shinto, the Japanese national religion. It starts in the realm of myth with the creation of Japan from foam. Innumerable gods and goddesses are described. The narrative moves from mythology to historical legends and culminates in a chronology of the early imperial line.

Nihongi

The Nihongi talks about how the earth was split from the heavens and how the elements on it—water, wind, etc.—were created.[4]

Shinto Beliefs

Because Shinto myth viewed the Japanese islands and people as the land and people of the kami, there was strong interconnectedness among Japanese until the end of World War II. Everyone was part of the mutual admiration society, patting each other on the back for several generations.

As with Daoism and indigenous religions, the goal was harmony. The opposite was impurity and disharmony. Failure to maintain your relationship with the kami led to chaos for individuals, families, companies, and the entire nation. This chaos rippled out from one act of disharmony and affected others because Japanese were connected to each other like a network. Individualism was impurity and caused disharmony. This is why, even today, Japanese CEOs do not promote themselves in front of the public like American CEOs do. For instance, who is the head of Mitsubishi? Who is the CEO of Sony? On the American side, who founded Microsoft? Apple? Who had a TV show called *The Apprentice*, ran a real estate empire, and became president? See the difference?

One source of disharmony is the lack of reverence for the kami, caused by treating nature as lifeless and not alive, beautiful, and inspiring. So bulldozing a rain forest into a parking lot would cause disharmony. Disharmony happens when heroes and ancestors are forgotten. Disharmony happens when one loses pride in being Japanese. Having pride in being an individual would cause disharmony, but not being a member of the Japanese.

Like Daoism, Shinto's ultimate goal is cosmic harmony with all elements in balance. But that balance is to be attained in this world, not the next, as in Confucianism. Because in Shinto, one never escapes the wheel of rebirth. One always comes back to this life, hopefully in a better station. So Shinto is a religion of the living: getting ahead in life, making money, and becoming wealthy. When Japanese retire, they often convert to Buddhism because

FIGURE 11.7 The white torii in front of this Shinto temple in Hawaii is always open because the land inside the temple is as sacred as the land outside.

FIGURE 11.8 A temizauya awaits shrine visitors so they can purify themselves with water.

FIGURE 11.9 Shrine visitors ring the suzu to draw fortune from the kami and dispel evil spirits.

Shinto has nothing to offer them. And Buddhism does: a way off the wheel of rebirth, Parinirvana. So, to summarize, Shinto is a religion of the living; Buddhism is a religion of those who are retired or nearing death.

The principal path to harmony and purity in traditional Shinto is through temple rituals. The most popular shrine is the Grand Imperial Shrine of the sun goddess Amaterasu in Ise. It is a site of pilgrimage, like Mecca is for Muslims. But unlike Mecca, it is rebuilt every 20 years, reflecting renewal of nature and life.

Almost every Japanese village has a Shinto shrine; some of these are simply a little "toot-and-tell" along the side the road and designed for the busy Japanese professional. Suppose this professional is driving his or her Toyota to Tokyo to sign a deal for the new billion-dollar Play Station 5 with stand-alone 3D holographic—oops, did I just let out a trade secret? Anyway, the business professional needs to make sure the deal happens. So he or she pulls over to the roadside shrine, claps twice (to get the attention of the kami), leaves an offering, then heads off to Tokyo with the assurance that the kami are behind this deal and all will work out well.

Elements of a Shinto shrine. The elements of Shinto shrines dictate and assist a worshipper in the method of the appropriate ritual. The gateway of the shrine, if it is large enough to have a gateway, is called the *torii*, which literally means "bird nest." Japanese must have a sense of humor. The torii is always open, because the land inside the shrine is just as sacred as the land outside the shrine because both are the land of the kami. One then washes at the temizauya, which has ladles one uses for that purpose.

The outer shrine is called the *haiden*. Here the devout clap twice to get the attention of the kami—in the form of origami and statues—and get credit for their offering. Ringing the *suzu* (bells) outside bring fortune from the kami and dispel evil spirits (Figure 11.9). One building the laity do not enter is the *honden*, where the most sacred kami are kept. Only the priests are allowed in the *honden*. Once a year, these kami are taken out and paraded through the streets of the city.

Shinto Branches

Imperial House Shinto

It is Shinto for the Imperial Court; that is, the Imperial family, centered on the Three Shrines in the Imperial Palace.

Shrine Shinto

This is a type of belief putting an emphasis on the implementation of religious services and ceremonies, mainly by shrines and other organs consisting of Ujiko (shrine parishioners) and revering persons. This is different than the Shrine Shinto mentioned earlier in the chapter.

Sect Shinto (the 13 Shinto sects)

A religion based on religious experiences of a founder or originator of the sect. Sect Shinto is slightly different in character from other Shinto religions.

Koshinto

It is also called 'Minkan Shinto and Minzoku Shinto' (Folk Shinto and the Folk or Popular Shinto), and means things that have been continued by common people in Japan from the olden times and events of faith related to Buddhism or Sutra syncretized with Koshinto, such as Shugen or Koshinto incorporating the thoughts of Taoism.[5]

Shinto Holidays

Shinto holidays in Japan include local festivals in each town or city and national festivals.

Great Purification, June 30 and December 31, when the Shinto faithful are absolved of their offenses against the kami. Before the end of World War II, the Japanese emperor, as the manifest kami, would pronounce this forgiveness.

New Year, following the end of the year purification day, is celebrated with the Entrance Pine at the entrance to businesses, which acts as a greeting for the kami in the new year.

Coming of Age holiday is January 15. This is when 21-year-olds come to a Shinto shrine for the first time as adults, establishing their own relationship with the kami. Parents usually make the offering for their children.

Girl's (Doll's) Festival is March 3, and *Boy's Festival* (now Children's Day) is May 5.

Chrysanthemum Festival is celebrated with flowers (as natural kami) on September 9.

The Festival of the Elderly is celebrated on September 15. Respect for the elderly actually comes from China.

There are also agricultural festivals, such as the one celebrating the rice god. Rice is a main staple for Japanese, although this author prefers to drink his rice: sake, which is rice wine.

Shinto's ability to adapt has made Christmas a national festival with more of an emphasis on Santa Claus than Jesus Christ because Santa sells PlayStations while Jesus just pushes salvation. So Christmas is a consumer holiday in Japan. The blending of Japanese with a Western holiday occurs because of *musubi* ("creativity and production") and *chuto-hanpa* ("a little of this, a little of that"). This syncretism does not always work out well. Several years ago, several Japanese businesspeople had a great idea to sell to tourists. Their market research showed that many tourists were Christian, so they wore crosses around their necks. A hot-selling item at the time were Japanese Santa Claus dolls: tourists loved them. So these businesspeople decided to combine these two popular symbols into one selling item. It was a disaster, an unmitigated catastrophe. Apparently no one wanted to buy a crucified Santa.

Religion in the Koreas

Christianity in South Korea has taken root and grown significantly. But like Japan, though, it is significantly secular: only 25 percent of the population are religiously affiliated. Of that 25 percent, 70 percent are Buddhist and 30 percent are Christian.

North Korea is a different case: it is communist, so religion is outlawed. But a secular religion flourishes around Kim Il Sung (Great Leader), the founder of North Korea, son Kim Jong Il ("dear leader"), and grandson Kim Jong Un, the current and ruthless leader. North Koreans worship these leaders and their spirits from which all benefits flow.

The basis of this rule is on filial piety, as we learned in Confucianism. In a criticism of Nikita Khrushchev, Kim Ill Sung said the Soviet Union was faltering because Khrushchev had criticized Stalin, though he was "fathered" by that late dictator. That violated the respect for one's father and ruler, tenets of filial piety.[6]

SUMMARY

Shinto is a purely Japanese religion and has emphasized the superiority of the Japanese in the past. The goal is harmony by respect for the kami: nature, ancestors, and deities. The religion has also incorporated Chinese religion, such as respect for one's elders (Confucianism). Koreans are mostly secular, with a leader worship found in North Korea.

FOR FURTHER READING

Shinto: The Kami Way, Sokyo Ono and William P. Woodard, Tuttle Publishing, 2004

Shinto Shrines: A Guide to the Sacred Sites of Japan's Ancient Religion, Joseph Cali and John Dougill

Shrine Shinto After World War II, Wilhelmus H. M. Creemers, E. J. Brill, 1968

The Japanese Portable Shrine and Festival Handbook, Unosuke Miyamoto, Seibundo Shinkosha, 2017

The Kojiki: An Account of Ancient Matters, Yasumaro O (Author), Gustav Heldt (Trans.), Columbia University Press, 2014

The Nihongi, Yasumaro O (Author), William George Aston (Trans.), CreateSpace Independent Publishing Platform, 2013

The Samurai: The Philosophy of Victory, Robert T. Samuel, 2004

ENDNOTES

1   R. Samuel, *The Samurai: The Philosophy of Victory* (New York: Barnes & Noble, 2004).
2   "International Religious Freedom Report 2006," US Bureau of Democracy, Human Rights, and Labor, https://www.state.gov/j/drl/rls/irf/2006/71342.htm.
3   D. Noss and B. Grangaard, *A History of the World's Religions* (New York: Pearson, 2012).
4   B. Hare, ed., "Shinto Scripture," Internet Sacred Text Archive, 2010, http://www.sacred-texts.com/shi/index.htm.
5   "Classifications of Shinto," *Encylopedia Japan,* https://doyouknowjapan.com/shinto/.
6   C. Armstrong, "Familism, Socialism and Political Religion in North Korea," Totalitarian Movements and Political Religions 6, no. 3 (2005).

CREDITS

12

SIKHISM

LEARNING OBJECTIVES

1. Recognize the elements of Islam and Hinduism within Sikhism
2. Understand the blending of Hindu and Islamic cultures
3. Examine Sikhism's transition from a peaceful to a warrior religion
4. Understand the influence of the Singhs
5. Learn about the Guru succession of leaders
6. Explain who is the last and current Sikh leader
7. Know Sikh holidays and the incorporation of Hindu holidays

In the Amrit Vaylaa, the ambrosial hours before dawn, chant the True Name, and contemplate His Glorious Greatness. By the karma of past actions, the robe of this physical body is obtained. By His Grace, the Gate of Liberation is found. O Nanak, know this well: the True One Himself is All.

—Siri Guru Granth Sahib[1]

Sikhism Statistics

There are about 26 million Sikhs worldwide, but most of them, about 25 million, live in the Punjab area of India and in Delhi. Sikhs tend to crowd in the area that they want as their homeland. Others live in the United States, Canada, and Great Britain. Sikhism is the fifth-largest religion in the world.[2]

Sikhism Myth

According to a religious biography, Sikhism founder Nanak was a poet who tended toward religious musings. He would sit and contemplate the beauty of nature and write poems. Sikhs now have a collection of stories called the Janam Sakkis that include the legendary tales of Nanak's travels to holy men around Asia and his alleged supernatural powers.[3] Nanak's dad wanted him to follow the family tradition and go into business. Apparently, the family belonged to the merchant class of Hinduism, unlike the higher castes of the founders of Buddhism and Jainism. But Nanak, who was married with two sons, showed no proclivity for commerce. He wouldn't know a rupee (used by Mughals as currency) if it crawled into his lap and said, "Momma!"

Okay, so we had an Indian man with an overbearing father who wanted him to "grow up." He was married and had kids. I wonder how this is going to turn out. Hmmm. How about Indian holy men SOP (standard operating procedure)? Yep. So, like others before him, Nanak left his family and went on a spiritual quest. He joined up with a small band of musicians, including Mardana, a Muslim minstrel who played a mean sitar. And this band, singing hymns to God, wandered about, searching for the truth. This is similar to the 1970s wandering bands that drove from town to town searching for the truth: "We're searching for the truth, man. Anyone have the truth? We're looking for a gig, too, if you got one."

The turning point for Nanak happened when he turned 30. He was bathing in a river and suddenly disappeared. Those present thought he had drowned because he was gone for three days. This was a disaster: Nanak was their lead singer and lyricist! Drummers were a dime a dozen, but without a lead singer, they were washed up: they would have to become a karaoke band. But Nanak said he had been taken into the presence of God, who commissioned him to go and repeat the divine name and tell others to do so. And the true name of God was revealed to Nanak as "True Name." This was a neutral term that was neither from Islam nor Hinduism: Nanak did not call God Allah or Vishnu or Brahma. This was echoed when Nanak resurfaced and uttered his basic theme: "There is no Hindu; there is no Muslim." God also gave him a bowl of milk to drink, giving him the power of prayer, love of worship, truth and contentment.[4]

God told Nanak to remain unpolluted by the world and to practice charity (Islam's zakat), ritual bathing (done in Hinduism to remove karma), service (charity), and meditation (from both Hinduism and Sufi Islam).

Nanak then wandered about the region teaching anyone who would listen and sang with Mardana. Their lyrics had to do with the true love of God. His followers also wore a combination of Hindu and Muslim clothes. Basically, they were ecclesiastical cross-dressers.

When Nanak was near death, Hindu and Muslim followers debated on the fate of his body: Should it undergo cremation, as is the custom of Hindus, or burial, as is the custom of Islam? Nanak told his Hindu devotees to place flowers on his left side and his Muslims followers to place flowers on his right. Whose flowers remained fresh could have his body. He then drew a sheet over his body. In the morning, when his followers pulled the sheet away, both sets of flowers were fresh, and his body was gone. What is the moral of this story, other than Nanak is living with Elvis in a Lutz trailer park? Nanak's central theme: "There is no Hindu, there is no Muslim."

For 200 years after Nanak's death, his followers had human leaders. Does this raise a question in your mind? The religion is 500 years old. So, for 200 of those 500 years, Sikhism had human leaders. 500 – 200 = 300. Well? Yes! Who has been the leader for the last 300 years? Very good. Well, their leader is not human but alive! Baaa haaa! This will be explained later. The community became known as *Sikhs*, from the Sanskrit word for "disciple."

History of Sikhism

Sikhism may have never been born if the thirst for territorial conquest among the Muslim caliphs had been less than it was. By the 1500s, Islam had spread across the Middle East, Africa, and parts of Europe. It also headed east and was butting up against Russian armies. Then it went southeast, conquering northern India and launching the Mughal Empire with Islamic control over a vast Hindu population.

If there are two religions that are opposites of each other, they are Islam and Hinduism. Islam is a strict monotheistic religion with minimalistic rituals and sparse mosques. Hinduism has 330 million gods with almost as many rituals and temples filled with statues of the divine. But because these two religious traditions butted up against each other in India, *sants* (holy people) (Fisher 1999, 393) began to merge, creating a new religion. For instance, Islamic monotheism was applied to the Hindu *bhakti* (devotional) movements, resulting in a claim of liberation for the cycle of rebirth (*moksha*) by devotion to the one true God.

One of these reformers who began to meld elements of them together was Kabir (1440–1518). He was born a Muslim, but he accepted the Hindu view of reincarnation while rejecting the Vedas as a way to resolve it. Kabir combined *bhakti* with Muslim Sufi mysticism, and he taught a path of love of God, leading to absorption into the divine (the goal of Sufis). Also, he emphasized the need for a spiritual teacher, a guru, from Hinduism. He won many followers, and some still follow his religious movement.

But Kabir did not start Sikhism. The man he inspired did: Nanak (1469–1538). Nanak was born of Hindu parents in Talvandi⁵ in India's Punjab region (which is now part of Pakistan) during a time of hostility between Hindus and Muslims. During this period, Hindus were trying to overthrow their Muslim overlords.

The first *Guru* (as the leaders were known), Angad (1504–1552), compiled a collection of Nanak's and his own hymns. So the founders were very musical. Angad also started the custom of the communal feast for disciples, known as the *langar*. All people, even non-Sikhs, are invited to come and eat. The poor often come when they are hungry because the food is free. A warning: these people are Indians. So if you go to the nearest Sikh temple in Hillsborough County, know that everything—salad, entrees, desserts—is laced with flaming-hot curry! And the only substance that will put out the fire in the esophagus is Thousand Island salad dressing. The author knows: he tried everything on the table—water, juice, milk, bleach, gasoline—and nothing put the fire out but the Thousand Island salad dressing. So if you go, don't forget to BYOTHSD.

The fifth guru, Arjan (1563–1606), compiled the Sikh scripture, *Guru Granth Sahib* (also called *Adi Granth*). So this is probably an important item to know. He also had built the Golden Temple in the middle of a pool in Punjab known as *Amritsar* ("the Pool of Immortality"), which became the Sikhs' spiritual headquarters. Arjan helped establish a unique Sikh identity, and he functioned as the political and economic leader of the community. But this made the Muslim rulers nervous, particularly as Arjan became more political. So they arrested, tortured, and killed him. But before he died, Arjan left a message for his son to sit on a throne of "iron." Now many people prefer their thrones to be padded, or at least porcelain. An iron throne would be uncomfortable.

But Arjan's son, Guru Hargobind (1593–1644), apparently knew what Dad was talking about and took this message to heart and created the first Sikh army, leading them into battle against the Muslim Mughals. So this is when Sikhism made the transition from the peaceful "love of God" religion of Nanak to the warrior religion in which one kicks tush and takes names. So the Sikhs' relationship to Muslims would forever change.

The tenth and last human guru (there's that human thing again), Gobind Singh (1666–1708), created an elite military unit inside the Sikhs called the Singhs. Its formation is told in the account of the "Five Beloved Ones" (*Panj Pyares*) willing to surrender themselves completely to protect Sikhism. Gobind Singh came out of his tent on the eve of a battle with the Muslim Mughals. He reviewed his troops in formation while carrying his two-edged sword. He loved the sword because it cut both ways and made a cool sound—"snicker-snack"—when it chopped off heads. He announced to his troops: "I need five men who are willing to surrender themselves completely in order to protect Sikhism." One guy raised his hand: "Hey, over here." Singh motioned him to his tent: "Come with me." The two went into the tent, and then a few minutes later,

FIGURE 12.1 The first Sikh guru and founder was Nanak.

FIGURE 12.2 Nanak's successor, Angad, listens to Bhai Bala, who is narrating the Sakhis of Guru Nanak to the writer Paira Mokha. This was later called the "Bhai Bala wali Janam Sakhi."

FIGURE 12.3 Sikh pilgrim at the Golden Temple (Harmandir Sahib) in Amritsar, India. A Singh emerges from Amritsar, the "Pool of Immortality," which surrounds the Golden Temple.

Singh emerged, with his sword dripping with blood. "Next?" Four more guys volunteered. In the end, all five emerged unscathed from the tent. A lawyer would have picked out the loophole: they had to be "willing" to surrender themselves; they did not actually have to surrender themselves. These first five were called the *khalsa* (the "pure"), and then members of this fraternity, when initiated, became *singhs* ("lions").

After the end of the Mughal Empire, a Sikh empire (1801–1849) was formed in India, and it was tolerant of Muslims. Sikhs put up fierce resistance when England invaded in 1848, but they lost. However, their fierce fighting and pledge of loyalty after losing impressed the British, who incorporated them into its army.

While given autonomous rule, Sikhs wanted independence and backed Mahatma Gandhi's independence movement. Unfortunately, with the creation of Pakistan, Sikhs lost their homeland, and they were peeved. The Hindus got India, the Muslims got Pakistan, and the Sikhs, who also helped Gandhi, got the shaft. Sikhs were politically weak in India and became frustrated. Some called for an independent Sikh nation, *Khalistan* ("land of the pure").

Sikh Zail Singh was a symbolic president of India in 1982, and later, Manmohan Singh was India's prime minister from 2004–2014,[6] but more radical Sikhs formed paramilitary groups to attack Hindus. In June 1984, the Indian army attacked the Sikhs at their headquarters in Amritsar, killing 1,200 Sikhs. The Indian casualties numbered two hundred. Four months later, two of Indian Prime Minister Indira Gandhi's elite Sikh bodyguards killed her. Thousands of Sikhs were slaughtered by Hindus in retaliation. Indira's nephew, Rajiv Gandhi—who was in the Tampa Bay area several years ago promoting his book about his famous uncle, *In the Shadow of Gandhi*—signed a peace accord with Sikhs in 1985, but violence has continued to the present day.

More moderate Sikhs have migrated since then to England, the United States (mostly to the West Coast but also to parts of Florida, such as Palm Harbor—where this author's former accountant and his family, who are Sikhs, live—and north Hillsborough County, which is home of the only Sikh temple in the Tampa Bay area), and Canada.

There are about 23 million Sikhs, making the religion the fifth-largest in the world (after general groupings of Christianity, Islam, Hinduism, and Buddhism). The vast majority still live in northwest India, in the Punjab region, and in Delhi. Several hundred thousand Sikhs live in the United States, the United Kingdom, and Canada. Many of the taxi drivers in Victoria, Canada, are Sikhs (personal observation).

Sikh violence has diminished, although some Sikhs are still agitating for a homeland. But not all Sikhs are comfortable with this militancy. They emphasize the tolerance and respect taught by Nanak. They say Sikhism recognizes the truth of all religions, promoting unity instead of division.

FIGURE 12.4 Gobind Singh was the last human guru and created the Singhs.

FIGURE 12.5 This gurdwara is the only Sikh temple in the Tampa Bay area.

Sikh Scripture

The last human guru, Gorbind Singh, was assassinated and succeeded not by a human but by the Sikh scripture as guru. This was a pretty shrewd act, because a book cannot be assassinated: they will just print more, and there is the online version, too. *Adi* ("first") *Granth* ("guru") has been venerated by Sikhs since 1708 as their spiritual leader; the book is considered to be the embodiment of the ten human gurus. The *Adi Granth* is enthroned and also put to bed at night in a canopy bed, and it is given offerings, usually money, in the temple. Children are given names beginning with the first letter of a verse of the *Adi Granth* chosen at random. Also known as the *Granth Sahib* (*Book of the Lord*), the scripture includes about six thousand hymns by Nanak and the next four gurus, compositions by Kabir and other Hindu and Muslim poets. More than two thousand hymns are attributed to Arjan, who compiled the collection. And because the *Adi Granth* means first guru, you can say the first guru is the last guru. Poof: the sound of a mind blowing.

Sikh Beliefs

The Sikhs believe that all humans are good, like a pearl in an oyster; they just have to be opened. They may be ugly and gnarly on the outside, but they have a good spiritual nature on the inside. So, like an oyster, humans have a pearl inside. So all you need is a hammer and a pair of pliers—okay, so the oyster analogy breaks down at that point.

Living apart from God causes rebirth on the cycle of rebirth, which, if you remember, is a Hindu concept. People live apart because of egoism, leading lives that revolve around fulfilling their earthly desires, such as lust (for the last real Twinkie made by Hostess before it went out of business), anger (that someone got it and put it in a glass case in Mexico), greed (when you see it advertised on eBay), attachment (to placing the winning bid), and pride (that you own the last real Twinkie). New Twinkies have a shelf life of 45 days.[7] What do they put in them, formaldehyde?

The ultimate goal of Sikhism is to get off the wheel of rebirth (Hinduism) and be totally absorbed by God (Sufi Islam). The means to do this is through praise of God (*bhakti*) and compassion (Islam). Praise involves repeating God's true name: True Name.

FIGURE 12.6 The *Adi Granth*, covered, lies on a canopy bed next to Mohan Singh Rattam in the Tampa Bay gurdwara. The scripture is reverenced as the last and current guru. The sword represents Gobind Singh.

To reach God, one must penetrate *maya,* the "wall of falsehood" that surrounds God so people cannot see him. Like *maya* in Hinduism, *maya* is a negative term in Sikhism. In Hinduism, *maya* means "illusion," and in Sikhism it is the illusion that God does not exist. One must penetrate that wall of illusion to find God. And like Buddhism, the world can trap a person on the wheel of rebirth, but—unlike Buddhism—the world is real in Sikhism.

The Sikhs worship God in congregational worship (*kirtan*) in a house of worship, *gurdwara*—"house or gateway of the Guru." Do not confuse *kirtan* with *kirpan*, the Singh sword. They sound alike to specifically trap 21st-century college students. Do not fall into that trap! The house of the Guru is the house of *the* guru, the current and last leader: the *Adi Granth*. The *gurdwara* is patterned after the first temple Nanak built, the *dharamsala* (abode of faith).[8]

FIGURE 12.7 The Ik Onkar, the Sikh symbol for God, means "One with Everything," with *kar* referring to the Creator.

Following the *kirtan* is the *langar,* or feast, to which all, even non-Sikhs, are invited. The poor often come here when they are hungry. Just remember to BYOTHSD.

True Name is the ultimate, supreme, all-knowing, all-compassionate One (Islamic monotheism). The *Adi Granth* says: "God abides in everything. See him, therefore, in your heart."

Branches of Sikhism

Singhs are the most prominent part of Sikhism. Initiation into the order includes *amrit* (holy nectar) with sweets (compassion) being stirred by a sword (strength). This ritual, also called the Baptism of the Sword, emphasizes the two major aspects of a Singh. The edge of the sword facing the enemy is strength; the edge facing the Singh is compassion, because the sword cuts both ways. Singhs, who acknowledge their sword is an extension of God and therefore has divine qualities, follow the five Ks:

- *Kesh*, uncut hair
- *Kangha*, comb in hair
- *Kachh*, short pants
- *Kara*, steel bracelet
- *Kirpan*, sword

There are also the four cardinal prohibitions, called *kurahit:*[9]

- Cutting one's hair or having it cut
- Consuming meat that has been slaughtered according to the Muslim rite
- Extramarital sexual intercourse
- Using tobacco

Male Singhs also wear turbans over their long hair and snoods over their beards because they do not cut any hair. Neither do women who join. Men have always been invited to join; women have been invited more recently, and they are called *kaur,* "princess." All are known as fearsome fighters, used by British in both world wars, making Sikhs the finest soldiers in India. For instance, Sikhs are 1.5 percent of India's population but 30 percent of the Indian army. The US Army also has Singhs in their ranks, and they are the only soldiers without the regulation buzz cut. As long as they can get helmets over their hair and gas masks over their beards, they have exemptions from regular Army grooming regulations.

Singhs have had to make accommodations to Western society. Mohan Singh Rattam said he does not carry his *kirpan* with him in the Tampa Bay area, where his temple is. With the violence in Western society, he said wearing a sword might be misunderstood, so he keeps it at home. He said in India, though, he wears it in the open.

Despite reports in the media to the contrary, not all Sikhs are Singhs. The Udasis are an order of holy men. They are celibate and wear yellow garments like Buddhist monks or are naked like Jain monks. Sometimes it is difficult to determine a man's faith by his uniform if he isn't wearing one. They also frequently shave their heads and beards, which sets them apart from the naked Digambara Jains who pulled out their hair. So look for razor stubble. The Sahajdharis (conservative, slow-going) also reject the militarism of Gobind Singh and are clean-shaven so people do not confuse them with Singhs.

Sikh Holidays

Sikhism is a simple religion and does not have many holidays. Sikhs celebrate the Hindu Holi and Divali holidays with their Hindu neighbors. Unique Sikh holidays include the following:

- The **martyrdom of Arjan** is celebrated in June.
- The **birthday of Nanak** is celebrated in November.
- **Arjan's birthday** is celebrated in December or January.

FIGURE 12.8 A Singh does not cut his hair or beard, so a turban keeps it neat and in place, as seen with Mohan Singh Rattam of Tampa, Fla.

FIGURE 12.9 The sign of the Sikhs is the Kandha. The circle represents God, the two-edged sword in the middle is also known as the kandha (Gobind Singh's sword), and the crossed swords are the kirpan, representing truth and justice (which includes war).

SUMMARY

Sikhism is the newest world religion, having grown to the fifth-largest in merely five hundred years. Incorporating elements of Islam and Hinduism, Sikhs have created a new religion surrounding the lives of their gurus, ending with the scripture, the *Adi Granth*, being the last and current guru. Like other religions, Sikhism has divisions but basically believes in the goodness of humanity. Some members, however, are more militant than others, causing disagreement on what their future will be.

FOR FURTHER READING

From Guru Nanak to Guru Granth Sahib: Life Stories and Teachings of the Ten Masters (Sikh Gurus) and the Sri Guru Granth Sahib, Sawan Singh, Amazon Digital Services, 2011

In Pursuit of Empire: Treasures from the Toor Collection of Sikh Art, Davinder Toor, Kashi House, 2018

The Adi Granth: Or The Holy Scriptures Of The Sikhs, Abm Komers, 2004

The Sikhs, Patwant Singh, Image, 2001

Warrior Saints: Three Centuries of the Sikh Military Tradition, Amandeep Singh Madra and Parmjit Singh, I. B. Tauris, 1999

Zafarnama, Guru Gobind Singh, Penguin, 2015

ENDNOTES

1   S. Singh Khalsa, *Siri Guru Granth Sahib* 3rd ed. (Tucson, AZ: Hand Made Books, n.d.), http://old.sgpc.net/CDN/English%20Translation%20of%20Siri%20Guru%20Granth%20Sahib.pdf, p. 2.

2   "Sikhism Facts," Indiaonlinepages.com, http://www.indiaonlinepages.com/religions/sikhism/sikhism-facts.html.

3   Esposito et al., *World Religions.* (Oxford: Oxford University Press),. 288. [no full citation listed for this]

4   Fisher, M. *Scriptures of the World's Religions.* (Upper Saddle River, NJ: Prentice Hall), 394

5   J. Brodd et al., *Invitation to World Religions.* (Oxford: Oxford University Press) 220

6   K. Pletcher, "Manmohan Singh," *Encyclopedia Britannica*, 2014, https://www.britannica.com/biography/Manmohan-Singh.

7   M. Godoy, "The Science of Twinkies: How Do They Last So Darned Long?" National Public Radio, 2013, https://www.npr.org/sections/thesalt/2013/07/09/200465360/the-science-of-twinkies-how-do-they-last-so-long.

8   J. Brodd, p. 211

9   L. Vaughn, *Anthology of World Religions.* (Oxford: Oxford University Press), 224

CREDITS

- Figure 12.1: Copyright © John Hill (CC BY-SA 4.0) at https://commons.wikimedia.org/wiki/File:Guru_Nanak_at_Manikaran.jpg.

- Figure 12.2: Source: https://commons.wikimedia.org/wiki/File:Guru_Angad_listening_to_Bhai_Bala.jpg.

- Figure 12.3: Copyright © Paulrudd (CC BY-SA 4.0) at https://commons.wikimedia.org/wiki/File%3ASikh_pilgrim_at_the_Golden_Temple_(Harmandir_Sahib)_in_Amritsar%2C_India.jpg.

- Figure 12.4: Source: https://commons.wikimedia.org/wiki/File:Guru_Gobind_Singh.jpg.

13

NEW RELIGIONS

NEW VOCABULARY AND CONCEPTS

- Elohim
- Drawing down of the moon
- Second Adam and Eve
- Ganja
- Peyote
- Unitarianism
- Thetan
- Evolving belief
- Self-indulgence
- The Force
- Hermetic Order of the Golden Dawn
- Syncretism

LEARNING OBJECTIVES

1. Know how new religions develop
2. Understand why new religions develop
3. Examine the types of new religions

> Queen of the Moon, Queen of the Sun,
> Queen of the Heavens, Queen of the Stars,
> Queen of the Waters, Queen of the Earth
> Bring to us the Child of Promise.
> —"Witches' Drawing Down of the Moon" chant [1]

New religions have always been part of society: How else would any religion begin? So they are not a new phenomenon. Most new religions eventually die out; those that survive become the major religions of the world. For this chapter, we will look at the new religions of the first part of the 21st century. Some of these religions are more than one hundred years old (which is relatively new, compared with the 500–4000-year-old world religions). Some are newer. A couple involve aliens from outer space (time to tighten up border control). One believes that God came down in human form in the 20th century. And one believes its founders are the second Adam and Eve.

Why Do New Religions Form?

There are varying reasons why new religions form. Some emphasize individualism. Founding members want a religion that serves their interests and fulfill their wants and needs. They create a religion that revolves around them. Some are looking for an alternative communal atmosphere. For example, they want a religion with electric guitars or more after-service social time. Others are alienated from traditional religions. These alienation reasons could stem from divorce, homosexuality, abortion, or lifestyle changes that are not accepted by a particular religion. Some people want to return to the "true teachings," whatever those are. There are actually no religions out there that advertise: "Come Join Us! We Have False Teachings." But some new religions claim they have found the true teachings that other religions have missed or disregarded. And the last group has concerns about the future. Did the world really end in 2010? Am I really going to graduate? And, oh, what is going to happen to the human race? These types of new religions tout that they have the answers to those questions. (Though if you are concerned about graduating, you may want to save some money on an offering or two by checking your GPA first.)

Many new religions in the United States came out of the spiritualist movement, which used mediums to talk to the spirit world. The idea of communicating with the dead or spiritual entities was incorporated into new religions.

Types of New Religions

Scholars have categorized new religions based on the stated purpose or main thrust of the religion. Some emphasize improving this life; others emphasize the end of this life.

There are what are called apocalyptic religions. They have end-of-the-world beliefs that the end is imminent. These groups believe that humans have finally committed their last and fatal folly and the approaching end will have a satisfying crunch to it as these *Homo sapiens* idiots get what they deserve. International Raelian is one of these religions, and it believes the end of the world began with the atomic bomb attacks on Japan during World War II. Now that is one long, dragged-out end.

Other new religions claim that they will heal you in some way from your physical and/or mental afflictions. They will increase or expand your awareness. Or they will renew you in some way, perhaps like a library book. One's full potential has not been realized so far in this life, so one needs to try the renewal or improvement exercises or rituals. There are religions that call on healing angels to come and bring God's healing from heaven. Paradoxically, Satanism believes that healing comes from the devil.

There are ecological-based religions that see the powers of the universe as nature based. These powers can be withdrawn and used in one's life, such as for luck or intelligence or love. An example of an ecological-based religion is witchcraft, which includes a ceremony called drawing down of the moon, when witches gather spiritual power from nature. Neopagan religions also tend to be nature based, with the seasons, plants, and animals being part of a spiritual force with which one can communicate.

Some new religions are liberation types that claim to liberate a person from some sort of oppression or detrimental force. Scientology claims to be one of these, clearing one's thetan (we will get to what that is later) of emotional baggage that can prevent a person from being happy and successful in life.

FIGURE 13.1 Adam, Eve, and extraterrestrial Elohim are pictured in this Raelian picture.

International Raelian Religion

French car magazine editor and race car driver Claude Vorilhon said he was visited by extraterrestrials (ETs) called Elohim (Hebrew for "those who came from the sky") in a flying bell. In a video on the Raelian website, Vorilhon said he was driving when he saw a UFO on December 13, 1973. After stopping, he saw a door open, and stairs emerged. He said he was waiting to see if anyone came out with a weapon so he would run, but a small man with "love" in his face approached him instead. Initial drawings of the aliens on the Raelian website showed them as bald green translucent creatures. The latest illustrations reveal that they are almost identical to the late Michael Jackson.

Vorilhon said the aliens named him Rael and told him humans were created by genetics on another planet. When humans became too aggressive to handle, the aliens dropped them off on earth. The Garden of Eden Genesis story in the Bible was just our memories of the Elohim's laboratories. Apparently, there was a potted plant near our petri dish.

Rael said the aliens asked him to build an embassy in Jerusalem so they could come and visit their earthlings. (Apparently, the aliens have better service between their planet and earth than United Airlines has between Miami and New York.) So far, the government of Israel has declined to permit construction of such an edifice. Since then, they have invited other countries to bid for embassy sites.

Rael also said the aliens told him that Buddha, Moses, Jesus, Mohammed, and Joseph Smith were all prophets of Elohim and that Rael was just the latest.

Raelian is an apocalyptic religion in that it believes the end of the world is near. The age of apocalypse began with the atomic bomb attack on Hiroshima, Japan, in 1945. But if you want to survive the end, you need to clone yourself. Only this guarantees eternal life, not the soul. Your brain would then be transferred to this new clone. This is called the art of celling yourself. Okay, I heard that joke in a single cell bar.

So for this religion, DNA experimenting is important. The Raelians claimed to have cloned a human in 2004 (a girl named Eve), but they never produced her. There is a certain amount of skepticism that a human was ever cloned.

Raelians claim to have about 70,000 members in 97 countries, although there is no word that its members are actually just one person cloned 70,000 times.

Rael, though, must have a sense of humor. He was suspended from Facebook for posting a picture of a vegetable that looked like the posterior of a woman.[2]

Unification Church

Founded as the Holy Spirit Association for the Unification of World Christianity, or Unification Church, the church was established 1954 in Korea before that country was divided by war. Its founder, Rev. Sun Myung Moon, said Jesus appeared to him in 1936 and told him to establish the kingdom of God on earth. The Unification Church (just don't call them Moonies) opened its international headquarters in New York City in 1959.

The religion's sacred text is the *Divine Principle,* which interprets the true meaning of the Bible. The true meaning of the Bible is this: God's harmony will be restored when a second Adam and Eve pay the price for human sin. Jesus was the second Adam, but he died unnecessarily before he was married because John the Baptist did not properly prepare the way for him.

Moon and his wife considered themselves the spiritual parents of followers, so they held tight control over their followers. They were accused of brainwashing. Still, they traditionally arranged mass marriages for their "children." One met one's spouse for the first time at a wedding ceremony attended by literally hundreds of other couples also getting married. Consequently, the church is a strong supporter of family values.

Several years ago, at a party for the US House of Representatives, Moon and his wife crowned themselves messiahs and then moved back to South Korea, where they declared they were the second Adam and Eve. "Adam" died in 2012. This caused a split in the religion caused by family members who are fighting among themselves for control.

Ras Tafari Movement

Known as Rastafarianism, this movement began in 1930 when Crown Prince Ras Tafari became Emperor Haile Selassie of

FIGURE 13.2 Rev. Sun Myung Moon. Sun Myung Moon blessed couples at a mass marriage.

FIGURE 13.3 Ethiopian Emperor Haile Selassie

Ethiopia. This seemed to fulfill Black Jamaica nationalist leader Marcus Garvey's 1916 prophecy of a Black king who would redeem Black Jamaicans. (Selassie denied this.) Consequently, followers of Rastafarianism believe that Selassie was the living God and that Blacks are superior to Whites. The latter can be seen in the Nation of Islam, of which Rastafarianism is a close cousin. Malcolm X's parents were followers of Marcus Garvey.

Rastafarianism also teaches that Jamaica is hell and Ethiopia is heaven. Blacks in Jamaica originally came as slaves from Africa, hence the hell designation. The emperor, who was God, lived in Ethiopia; hence, it was heaven. Proponents of Rastafarianism teach that they must free their people from the "Babylon" of the oppressors: England, the United States, and the government of Jamaica.

But when Ras Tafari died in 1974, enthusiasm in the movement began to wane. A musician closely associated with the movement, Bob Marley, also died. So there was a split: an old school that wanted to return to Africa and a new school that wanted to improve the quality of life in Jamaica.

Men who are followers wear dreadlocks to look like a mane of a lion, the symbol of a natural life, to pattern themselves after the Lion of Judah, the symbol of Jerusalem from which many Ethiopians claim descent. Their religious rituals are famous, or infamous, for using *ganja* (marijuana). There has been a movement in the United States for legalization of marijuana on religious grounds, but it has been unsuccessful. However, in several states, one can light it up on recreational grounds. So just get your story straight when the police raid your house: "No religion here, officer. I'm just a pothead."

Native American Church

Speaking of controlled substances, Native American religion followers ingest peyote. The church is a consolidation of Native American nature-based religions and Christianity. So members believe peyote, a hallucinogenic drug from a plant of the same name, became "flesh of God," the symbol of Christ, just like the bread during transubstantiation in Christianity.

Followers of this religion organized when their rituals were outlawed so they could battle the laws legally as a corporate entity. The church has been successful to an extent: a federal spending bill allowed the use of peyote, but only on Native American reservations.

The organization claims to have more than 250,000 members, but it also allows all people to attend its ceremonial fires during its rituals.

Unitarian Universalists

This religion has its roots in early Protestantism (in the 1600s), and the church broke away from the Protestants after the Protestants broke away from the Catholics. Followers rejected the Trinity, saying that God is one person, not three.

The followers organized in their current form as the Unitarian Universalist Association in 1961. The Unitarians were rich Bostonians who did not believe in the Trinity. The Universalists were poorer Bostonians who did not believe in the Trinity. They did not overcome their class distinctions until the 20th century.

FIGURE 13.4 A Native American drums under the influence of peyote

The Unitarian Universalists interpret the Bible "rationally," not literally. They follow Jesus's example (although he is not God) and have devotion to serve humanity and right wrongs in society. The one thing the organization does not have is a central creed. Children in the religion are encouraged not to believe in any one doctrine. A Unitarian minister once told this author: "A Unitarian is someone who knocks on your door and then has nothing to say."

The only Unitarian Universalist church in Tampa is in north Tampa, according to its pastor, Patricia Owen, though there are others in the Tampa Bay area. The Unitarians use the flaming chalice as their symbol. Hans Deutsch, an Austrian artist, first brought together the chalice and the flame as a Unitarian symbol during his work with the Unitarian Service Committee during World War II. To Deutsch, the image had connotations of sacrifice and love. Unitarian Universalists today have many different interpretations of the flaming chalice, including the light of reason, the warmth of community, and the flame of hope.[3]

FIGURE 13.5 Patricia Owen lights the flaming chalice, the symbol of Unitarian Universalists, in her church in Tampa, FL.

Scientology

Created by science fiction writer L. Ron Hubbard, Scientology is a combination of beliefs in mind science, Eastern philosophy, and extraterrestrial life. A World War II veteran, Hubbard said he cured himself of psychological and physical battle injuries by using a process called Dianetics. Scientology is based on the premise that people are actually thetans, spirits of an alien race killed by evil aliens who have come to earth. These evil aliens captured these good aliens, stuffed them into volcanoes on earth, and then blew them up with thermonuclear devices.

FIGURE 13.6 L. Ron Hubbard, 1950

The spirits of these good aliens entered the bodies of humans but are trapped by emotions and bad experiences. This is called spiritual entrapment by mest, or matter.[4] Despite being blown up in a volcano, these were happy-go-lucky aliens, and humans were a pretty morose lot of cavepeople. And if your thetan is not happy, you are not happy. Thetans are actually a colony of alien spirits that live in one person and see themselves as an individual, taking on the person's identity.

Thetans are freed by auditing, when a person becomes "clear" by reciting past experiences and having an auditor utter "clear." It takes a while, and a lot of money, to clear away all these experiences, because a person has been reincarnated many times since the cavepeople days. "Scientology teaches that salvation is attained through increasing one's spiritual awareness."[5] Some Scientologists sign a million-year membership contract.

Scientologists currently distance themselves from the alien story, emphasizing the struggle between thetan (spirit) and mest.

The religion's services consist of a pitch for more auditing sessions by members on a stage next to a bust of Hubbard. There are also offers of trips on Hubbard's yacht with more auditing sessions. In a recent Ybor City branch service, two uniformed members pitched opportunities to an audience sitting in a hall with tables

FIGURE 13.7 The Flag building in downtown Clearwater, FL, is the spiritual headquarters of Scientology.

FIGURE 13.8 Scientology buildings can display the religion's symbol: the S for Scientology, the top triangle for knowledge, responsibility, and control, and the bottom triangle for affinity, reality, and communication.

of refreshments behind them. "Scientology quite logically sees worship not so much in the mode of celebration and devotion but in the mode of meditation and instruction, which stresses awareness, enlightenment, or, to use the Scientology term, 'Clearing'."[6]

Scientology has its international spiritual headquarters, known as "Flag," in Clearwater, Florida, and its Religious Technology Center in Gilman Hot Springs, California; it has attracted some celebrities such as John Travolta and Tom Cruise. In Clearwater, members of the Sea Org, a monastic type of Scientology order, can be seen walking the streets. These members have given away nearly all that they own to the church and then live and work full-time for its various ministries.

Jehovah's Witnesses

A partner in his father's men's clothing store, Charles Taze Russell (1852–1916), wanted to determine what the Bible really said about Christianity. Ultimately, his mission would end up with rewriting the Bible. The son of Pennsylvania Presbyterians, Russell believed that creeds of other Christian denominations had "elements of truth" but were buried under pagan teachings, like having a hierarchy. He started a Bible study group in 1870 that would eventually become the Watch Tower Society.

When Russell died, Joseph Rutherford was elected president of the Watch Tower, but this created dissention and schisms as his detractors accused him of being autocratic and secretive. The official history of the Jehovah's Witnesses glosses over this point and maintains that Rutherford was not really the recognized head of the religion and that it was God's work that Rutherford did reorganize the religion into a modern structure with officers.[7]

FIGURE 13.9 Charles Taze Russell

FIGURE 13.10 Osliy Vega, pastor of the Kingdom Hall in north Tampa, says his sanctuary has no statues because it believes in worshipping God alone, not venerating saints.

The Jehovah's Witnesses believe that, according to the Bible, just 144,000 people will go to heaven, giving a literal interpretation to the passage in the Bible's Book of Revelation (Rev. 7:4). The religion does not believe in a Trinity. Followers believe Jesus Christ is not God but "a god" (a rewrite of John 1:1). They believe that the angel Michael became Jesus and then returned to his angel form after the resurrection.

The Jehovah's Witnesses pride themselves in having an evolving belief instead of a fixed creed. Its early members "were not creed-bound; they were progressive."[8] Their Bible evolves. Originally, they used the Protestant Bible, then the *Emphatic Diaglott* version (1942), which was copied from the Catholic Bible and included the phrase that Jesus is God, not "a god." Recently, they have been using the *New World Translation* of the Bible, which has been rewritten once already and is published by the Watchtower Publishers. The most recent version goes back to Jesus being "a god."

The evolving belief of Jehovah's Witnesses also accounts for end-of-the-world predictions by church members in 1873, 1874, 1878, 1914, 1925, and 1975.

Satanism

Satanism is all about self-indulgence: if it feels good, do it. Various groups formed from a tradition in the late 19th and early 20th centuries. The key figure was magician and author Aleister Crowley (1875–1947), who emphasized a hedonistic rejection of Christian morality. They use the upside-down pentagram (witches use it right side up) and a goat. They refer to themselves as left-handed neopagans, though other neopagans refuse to include them in the neopagan group.

Anton LaVey organized the Church of Satan in San Francisco in 1966 to counter the hypocrisy of "good Christians" who followed their natural desires to sin during the week and then go to church on Sunday. LaVey said he created a church where people could go sin. (It was his house, painted black.) He wrote rituals, such as the "black mass," a parody of the Catholic Mass with Satan at its center. The altar would be draped with a nude woman, often with LaVey's boa constrictor. Curses, instead of prayers, would be shouted. Most of this is written in his book, *The Satanic Bible.*

Different Satanic temples have taken to the Internet claiming to be the true followers of Satan, and there is not a lot of Christian charity among them. Many of the postings are very derogatory toward rival groups.

Despite their claims of different beliefs, Satanists can be categorized into general groups. One is spontaneous Satanism. It can be seen in a temporary profession of faith in Satan. It can be found in heavy metal rock music and seen at concerts with such bands. Followers sober up, climb out of the mosh pit, and return to their lifestyles afterward.

Another group of Satanists are called formal. They practice the religion full-time. One type sees Satan as the evil opponent of God, and they worship him as the true power of the universe. Avoid these people: they will hurt you. They are psychopaths who fill prisons and insane asylums. A second group believes Satan is a heroic rebel against evil God and that Satan just needs a better public relations firm. Most Satanists fall in the third category: Satan as an intelligent entity does not exist. Satan is just the name for the natural life force, to do what one wants to do and to be free from hypocritical Christian morality.

FIGURE 13.11 Aleister Crowley 1902 K2. English occultist, poet, and novelist Aleister Crowley bathing in a spring on the lower Baltoro Glacier during his 1902 expedition to climb K2 in the Himalayas.

Jediism

Jediism has its roots in the 1977 *Star Wars* movie, sequels, and prequels (the latter, now that Mickey Mouse owns Darth Vader). The loose Internet groups define the "Force" as a spiritual energy that connects all living things. This is their answer to "You know it's just a movie, right?" They argue that George Lucas, *Star Wars's* creator, was addressing a basic truth in his fictional films.

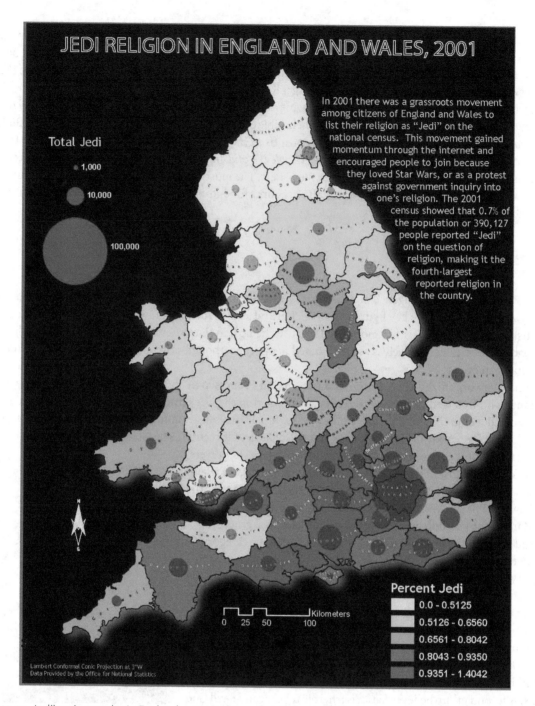

FIGURE 13.12 Jediism is popular in England, seen in this census taken in 2001.

Jediism is an Internet religion, with different online temples offering courses in how to become a Jedi knight and how to manipulate the force. One video has a "knight" summoning the wind to blow leaves.

There are both the light and dark side of the Force Jedis. One group refers to itself as a noble order of protectors, guardians of peace and justice. They use the Force to protect society. Then there are Dark Jedi, or Sith. The Sith Code perceives the Force from a more individualistic perspective, emphasizing personal passion, power, and victory rather than peace. The Force is used to advance in school, business, or social situations.

The Jedi Vow, which describes the Jedi path as a way to "illumination, to inner peace, and to calmness of mind," is based on "allegiance and devotion to the Living Force." But the vow often takes the form of the Prayer of St. Francis, with or without attribution.

Wicca and Neopaganism

Wicca and neopaganism are "new religions" in that they have no historical connection to nature, the folk religions of the Middle Ages, or the ancient Greek, Roman, or Norse religions. There were no self-professed witches burned in the Middle Ages, unless they were tortured into saying they were witches. There were no witches hung in Salem, Massachusetts.

Wicca, also known as witchcraft, and neopaganism have their origins in the Hermetic Order of the Golden Dawn which was established in 1888 in London. This order dedicated itself to the philosophical, spiritual, and psychic evolution of humanity. It billed itself as a repository of occult science and magic.[9]

Gerald B. Gardner (1884–1964), amateur anthropologist, folklorist, British customs officer, and former nudist, revived interest in witchcraft. He published a novel, *Magic's Aid,* in 1949 under an assumed name. After England's witchcraft acts were repealed in 1951, he published the nonfiction books *Witchcraft Today* (1954) and *The Meaning of Witchcraft* (1959). Members of the "Craft" came out in the open. Included in his books were spells and rules of conduct.[10]

FIGURE 13.13 This Wiccan altar cloth has a circle that protects a spell until it is released. Two athame, which transmit magic, are on the cloth.

Wicca came to the United States in the 1960s via Raymond and Rosemary Buckland. They brought the Gardnerian tradition and published *Witchcraft from the Inside* (1971). The Gardnerian tradition stressed Wicca was a religion that required strict adherence to Gardner's beliefs and regulations. A more open approach to witchcraft was taken by Raymond Buckland in his 1974 book *The Tree,* which followed the breakdown of his marriage. He said witchcraft should be open to anyone, despite their beliefs.[11]

Wicca today defines itself as a nature-based religion. Its members, mainly women, consider themselves goddesses of nature. There is usually no God, heaven, or hell in Wicca theology. Membership can be organized in covens, but often witches are sole practitioners.

One of the main rituals is the "Drawing Down of the Moon." Participants, nude, summon the powers of nature while standing in a circle around a fire at night. Members absorb the powers of nature during a ceremony.

Neopaganism first came in organized form to the United States in the Church of Aphrodite in 1938 in Long Island, New York. A Russian refugee from the Romanov court deified Anastasia, which later led to a goddesses-type religion.[12]

The Ancient Order of Druids was established in England as a distinctive type of Freemasonry. Neopagans began joining it in the 1960s and 1970s and started worshipping at Stonehenge in the way they thought the ancient Druids had, although nothing is known about the latter's worship.[13]

Neopagans today are an eclectic group. They mix what they believe are tenets from ancient Norse, Roman, Greek, and Native American religions and even include those of Christianity. They have no central creed, and attempts at organizing them have ended in failure because they are very individualistic.

Santeria and Voodoo

These two religions are syncretized religions, meaning they are the sum of a combination of two religions: Catholicism and African Yoruba religions. The Yoruba of West Africa were brought to the New World as slaves. They brought with them their gods, called Orishas.

Because their slave owners were predominately Catholic, the Yoruba were strongly encouraged to pray to the Catholic saints. So the slaves combined the Orishas with the saints, and this is why Santeria is called "the Way of the Saints." Santeria is tightly tied to Catholicism; candidates for Santeria priesthood must be baptized Catholics.

FIGURE 13.14 Dancers dressed as Chango, the thunder god, and other deities celebrate Santería in Havana, Cuba.

A combination of French Catholicism and Yoruba religion results in Voodoo, also known as Vodun. Both use magic and influencing the gods and/or spirits to do one's will.

SUMMARY

New religions develop for various reasons—whether in response to older ones or a perceived end of the world—but they are prevalent. They still make up a very small percentage of the religions of the world in terms of membership. They can be cultural, alien, or nature based. And they attract a small, and often committed, section of the population.

FOR FURTHER READING

Buckland's Complete Book of Witchcraft, Raymond Buckland, Llewellyn Publications, 2002

Dianetics: the Modern Science of Mental Health, L. Ron Hubbard, Bridge Publications, 2007

Exposition of the Divine Principle, Sun Myung Moon, HSA-UWC, 2014

Intelligent Design: Message from the Designers, Rael, Nova Distribution, 2006

Jah Rastafari Prayers: Rasta Prayers & Healing Scriptures, Empress Yuajah Ms, CreateSpace Independent Publishing Platform, 2016

Jehovah's Witnesses: Proclaimers of God's Kingdom, Watchtower Bible and Tract Society of New York, 1993

Scientology, Bridge Publications, 1998

The Meaning of Witchcraft, Gerald Gardner, Weiser Books, 2004

New World Translation of the Holy Scriptures, Watch Tower Bible and Tract Society of Pennsylvania, 2013

The Satanic Bible, Anton Szandor LaVey, Avon, 1969

Witchcraft Today, Gerald Gardner, Citadel, 2004

ENDNOTES

1   G. Gardner, *Witchcraft Today* (New York: Citadel Press, 2004).

2   Rael Press, "Suspended from Facebook for posted photo of a vegetable, spiritual leader Rael calls for protests against Facebook policy of 'Western Puritanism,'" 2017, http://www.raelpress.org/news.php?item.465.1.

3   "Flaming Chalice," Unitarian Universalist website, 2017, https://www.uua.org/beliefs/who-we-are/chalice.

4   *Theology and Practice of Contemporary Religion: Scientology* (Los Angeles: Bridge, 1988).

5   Ibid, 121.

6   Ibid, 159.

7   "Watch Tower," *Jehovah's Witnesses: Proclaimers of God's Kingdom* (New York: Watchtower Bible and Tract Society of New York, 1993).

8   Ibid, 132.

9   J. G. Melton, *Encyclopedia of American Religions,* 6th ed. (Detroit, MI: Gale Research, 1999).

10 M. Adler, *Drawing Down the Moon* (New York: Penguin/Arkana, 1986).

11 Ibid, 92.

12 Ibid, 233–234.

13 G. Harvey, *Contemporary Paganism* (New York: New York University Press, 1997), 18–19.

CREDITS

- Figure 13.1: Copyright © Kmarinas86 (CC BY-SA 3.0) at https://commons.wikimedia.org/wiki/File:Adam,_Eve,_and_Elohim_(Ra%C3%ABlism).png.

- Figure 13.2: Copyright © Everyguy (CC BY-SA 3.0) at https://commons.wikimedia.org/wiki/File:Rev._Sun_Myung_Moon_speaks,_Las_Vegas,_NV,_USA_on_April_4,_2010.png.

- Figure 13.3: Source: https://commons.wikimedia.org/wiki/File:CropSelassie.jpg.

- Figure 13.4: Source: https://commons.wikimedia.org/wiki/File:Peyote_drummer_by_ES_Curtis.jpg.

- Figure 13.6: Source: https://commons.wikimedia.org/wiki/File:L._Ron_Hubbard_in_1950.jpg.

- Figure 13.9: Source: https://commons.wikimedia.org/wiki/File:Russell_Charles_Taze_1911.jpg.

- Figure 13.11: Source: https://commons.wikimedia.org/wiki/File:Aleister_Crowley_1902_K2.jpg.

- Figure 13.12: Copyright © DeVo787 (CC BY-SA 3.0) at https://commons.wikimedia.org/wiki/File:Jedi_census_phenomenon_2001.pdf.

- Figure 13.14: Copyright © Bernardo Capellini (CC BY-SA 4.0) at https://commons.wikimedia.org/wiki/File:Santeria_Centro_Habana.JPG.